HARM
Reduction

HARM
Reduction

National
and
International
Perspectives

James A. Inciardi • Lana D. Harrison Editors

Sage Publications, Inc.
International Educational and Professional Publisher
Thousand Oaks ■ London ■ New Delhi

For information:

Sage Publications, Inc.
2455 Teller Road
Thousand Oaks, California 91320
E-mail: order@sagepub.com

Sage Publications Ltd.
6 Bonhill Street
London EC2A 4PU
United Kingdom

Sage Publications India Pvt. Ltd.
M-32 Market
Greater Kailash I
New Delhi 110 048 India

Printed in the United States of America

Library of Congress Cataloging-in-Publication Data

Main entry under title:

　　Harm reduction: National and international perspectives / edited
by James A. Inciardi and Lana D. Harrison.
　　　　p.　cm.
　　ISBN 0-7619-0687-8
　　ISBN 0-7619-0688-6
　　1. Drug abuse—Prevention.　2. AIDS (Disease)—Prevention.
I.　Inciardi, James A.　II.　Harrison, Lana D.
　　HV5801 .H335　1999
　　262.29'17—dc21　　　　　　　　　　　　　98-58136

This book is printed on acid-free paper.

00　01　02　03　04　05　06　7　6　5　4　3　2　1

Acquiring Editor:	C. Terry Hendrix/Kassie Gavrilis
Editorial Assistant:	MaryAnn Vail
Production Editor:	Astrid Virding
Editorial Assistant:	Patricia Zeman
Typesetter:	Lynn Miyata
Indexer:	Rick Hurd
Cover Designer:	Michelle Lee

Contents

Introduction: The Concept of Harm Reduction

James A. Inciardi and Lana D. Harrison

During the past decade, municipal, state and national governments in Europe and Australia have responded to local drug problems with a variety of initiatives that merit close examination in the United States. Based on the evolving notion of "harm reduction," these initiatives focus on reducing the adverse consequences of both psychoactive drug use and drug control policies without eliminating drug use.

—Nadelmann et al. (1997, p. 22)

There is no clear consensus on the meaning of the term *harm reduction*, although at its hub is a focus on reducing the adverse consequences of psychoactive drug use. In fact, it would appear that with each new article or presentation on the topic, a new conceptualization is offered. At one end of the continuum is the view of Dr. Arnold S. Trebach, a professor of law at American University and the founder and former director of the Drug Policy Foundation. Dr. Trebach argues that harm reduction accepts the reality of both the desire for drugs by millions of people and the related fact that many of these individuals may be harmed by their use of drugs. Accordingly, he suggests, people should be allowed to make choices—to use drugs in either relatively harmless ways or in very destructive ways, or to use no drugs at all. Regardless of their choice, they must not be treated as enemies of the state, and if they encounter trouble as a result of their drug use, help should be available to them (Trebach & Inciardi, 1993, p. 77).

Within this context, harm reduction covers a wide variety of programs and policies, including the following:

1. *Advocacy for changes in drug policies*—legalization, decriminalization, ending the drug prohibition, changes in drug paraphernalia laws, reduction of penalties for drug-related crimes, and treatment alternatives to incarceration

2. *HIV/AIDS-related interventions*—needle/syringe exchange programs, HIV prevention/intervention programs, bleach distribution, referrals for HIV testing and HIV medical care, and referrals for HIV/AIDS-related psychosocial care and case management

3. *Broader drug treatment options*—methadone maintenance by primary care physicians, changes in methadone regulations, heroin substitution programs, and new experimental treatments

4. *Drug abuse management for those who wish to continue using drugs*—counseling and clinical case management programs that promote safer and more responsible drug use

5. *Ancillary interventions*—housing and other entitlements, healing centers, and support and advocacy groups

Dr. Robert L. DuPont, a faculty member at Georgetown University School of Medicine and a former director of the National Institute on Drug Abuse, offers a substantially contrasting perspective. He sees harm reduction as an alternative to both drug prohibition and drug legalization. Harm reduction, in Dr. DuPont's view, seeks to preserve prohibition while softening some of its harsh consequences (DuPont, 1996). As such, DuPont sees harm reduction as a compromise position with the aim of reducing aspects of drug-related harm.

On the whole, there are many who would disagree with both of these positions. Furthermore, there is a problem with achieving any level of consensus because harm reduction is neither a policy nor a program. Harm reduction is a *goal* for policies and programs; it is a willingness to trade potential increases in drug use for potential decreases in drug-related harm (Reuter & MacCoun, 1996). Stated differently, the essential feature of harm reduction is the attempt to ameliorate the adverse health, social, or economic consequences associated with the use of mood-altering substances without necessarily requiring a reduction in the consumption of these substances.

THE EMERGENCE OF HARM REDUCTION

The harm reduction movement has its roots in the drug policies of the Netherlands, which take a public health or sociomedical approach to drug use and its consequences. For example, the Dutch instituted the first needle exchange program in 1984 in an attempt to stem the rising number of hepatitis cases related to injection drug use (van Haastrecht, 1997). Because the Dutch viewed hepatitis as the greater evil, programs were established to provide new needles and syringes to injectors. And, because these syringe exchange programs were in place not too long after the beginning of the spread of HIV/AIDS among injection drug users in Western Europe, it is believed that the incidence and prevalence of HIV infection never reached the epidemic levels among drug users in the Netherlands that became apparent elsewhere (van Haastrecht, 1997).

Several other European nations, including the United Kingdom and Switzerland, adopted harm reduction policies in response to the AIDS epidemic. Their position was that AIDS represented a greater threat to public health than did drug use, and that AIDS prevention should take precedence over antidrug efforts. Within this same perspective, Australia implemented its needle exchange policies in April 1985. Although the street drug cultures in Australia and the United States are not fully comparable, Australia has a 5% HIV infection rate among injection drug users as compared to 14% in the United States. Furthermore, it has been argued that this difference is due to the limited number of needle exchange programs in the United States (Wodak & Lurie, 1997). In fact, one recent estimate suggests that between 4,000 and 10,000 HIV infections could have been prevented in the United States had needle exchange programs followed the same pattern of growth as in Australia (Lurie & Drucker, 1997).

Currently, the U.S. approach to drug abuse and drug control includes a variety of avenues for reducing both the *supply of* and the *demand for* illegal drugs. "Supply reduction" includes interdiction activities designed to keep illegal drugs from entering the United States, legislation and enforcement for the sake of keeping drugs off the streets and away from consumers, and foreign assistance programs designed to support U.S. antidrug policies abroad. "Demand reduction" includes a variety of treatment alternatives for drug users, education and prevention for both youths and adults, and research to determine how to best develop and implement plans for treatment, education, and prevention. For the most part, these supply-and-demand reduction strategies are grounded in the classic deterrence model: through legislation and criminal penalties, individuals will be discouraged from using drugs. By setting an example of drug users, current and potential users will be dissuaded from using illicit drugs. Furthermore, by punishing traffickers, the government can force potential dealers to seek out other economic pursuits. Drug prohibition is also meant to shape norms about the appropriateness of illicit drug use.

Although supply reduction is the dominant feature of American drug policy, some elements of harm reduction are also apparent. For example, providing methadone to heroin users who are either unwilling or unable to abstain from narcotics use is a clear example of harm reduction. Introduced in the United States during the 1960s, methadone is a relatively long-lasting opioid that reduces some of the highs and lows associated with heroin use. A vast body of research demonstrates methadone's efficacy in reducing drug-related morbidity, mortality, and criminality, and in improving the quality of life for those dependent on heroin (Ball, Rosen, Flueck, & Nurco, 1981; Gerstein & Harwood, 1990; Nurco, Hanlon, Kinlock, & Duszynski, 1988; Speckart & Anglin, 1985). Furthermore, medical research has demonstrated that methadone has few negative health consequences (Kreek, 1983). However, because methadone maintenance treatment has not always been popular or well received by either the public or policymakers, there have been a number of consequences for those in the greatest need for the programs. For example, inadequate dosing is widespread, and there are far too few treatment slots. In much of Europe and Australia, methadone treatment was initially even more controversial than in the United States. However, in those countries that have embraced methadone maintenance, physicians have far more flexibility in prescribing methadone, and patients generally have greater access to the drug. In Belgium, Germany, and Australia, the principal means of distribution is from general practitioners, with local pharmacies filling prescriptions.

Drug abuse treatment and drug prevention are harm reduction strategies, and both have become more prominent in American drug policy. Nevertheless, the great majority of drug control funds are earmarked for supply reduction activities, with the balance targeting demand reduction efforts. As such, much of the drug control resources are spent on the apprehension and incarceration of drug users, dealers, and traffickers (Reuter, 1992). The result has been high rates of arrest and incarceration of drug users—neither of which has significantly affected America's drug problem (Butterfield, 1998).

In contrast to the more punitive drug strategies seen in the United States, harm reduction is a pragmatic policy aimed at minimizing the damage that drug users do to themselves, others, and society at large (Buning, Coutinho, van Brussel, & van Zadelhoff, 1986). Harm reduction approaches reject the notion of a "drug-free" society as unachievable, recognizing that drug use has been a part of human societies since their very beginning. Although the official U.S. policy tends to equate harm reduction with legalization, most advocates of harm reduction do not support the idea of legalizing drugs, expressing concern that it would substantially increase drug use. Yet they recognize that prohibition is not sufficient to stop drug use because it increases crime and marginalizes drug users. Harm reduction interventions focus on integrating or reintegrating drug users into the community, taking care not to further isolate, demonize, or ostracize them. Priority is placed on maximizing the number of drug users in contact with drug treatment, outreach, and other public health services. Drug policies are evaluated in terms of their potential effects on minimizing the harm of drugs to the user and society at large. As such, "the challenge is thus making prohibition work better, but with a focus on reducing the negative consequences of both drug use and prohibitionist policies" (Nadelmann, 1997, p. 114).

Harm reduction asks questions like the following:

- How can we reduce the likelihood that drug users will engage in criminal and other undesirable activities?

- How can we reduce overdoses, HIV/AIDS, and the hepatitis B and C infections associated with the use of some drugs?

- How can we increase the chances that drug users will act responsibly toward others?

- How can we increase the likelihood of rehabilitation?

- More generally, how do we ensure that drug control policies do not cause more harm to drug users and society than drug use itself?

PERSPECTIVES ON HARM REDUCTION

The opening chapter in this book, "Harm Reduction: History, Definition, and Practice," by Diane Riley and Pat O'Hare, provides an overview of the history and development of harm reduction worldwide. The authors point out that harm reduction policy has increased in popularity, largely in response to the AIDS epidemic among injection drug users. Because drugs can negatively affect the health, social, and economic status of the user, harm reduction seeks to minimize the consequences of drug use at the individual, community, and societal levels. Riley and O'Hare identify a wide range of harm reduction policies and programs, including needle exchange; methadone maintenance; education and outreach to reduce risks associated with drug use; "tolerance areas," where drug users can obtain clean needles, condoms, and medical attention; and law enforcement policies that publicly support harm reduction methods. The authors suggest that although support for harm reduction policies is on the increase, there are still numerous barriers to their implementation, especially in the United States, where abstinence is often seen as the only acceptable outcome of drug abuse.

Ernest Drucker's "From Morphine to Methadone: Maintenance Drugs in the Treatment of Opiate Addiction" provides an analysis of the history and implications of methadone maintenance programming. He points out that during the 19th century, opiates (including morphine and heroin) gained popularity as medicinal remedies. As a result, some people experienced prolonged anxiety, restlessness, sleep disturbance, and other withdrawal symptoms when they discontinued use. The concept of addiction as a disease grew from this phenomenon, and the search for effective medical treatments led to the use of narcotics (including morphine, heroin, and methadone) to loosen the bonds of addiction. Some physicians in the United States and Great Britain recognized the value of this approach and instituted narcotic maintenance treatment early in the century. In the United States, drug maintenance programs generally have been frowned upon by the medical and legal communities, so methadone—a synthetic opioid that can be taken orally with effects generally lasting 24 to 36 hours for a single dose—was first tried on the worst cases. Its efficacy was demonstrated in repeated clinical trials, although hostile attitudes toward maintenance approaches have not been abandoned, and many programs attempt to detoxify clients or provide doses too low to be of substantial benefit. However, in light of the AIDS epidemic among injection drug users, methadone maintenance has gained more acceptability.

"The Coming of Age of Needle Exchange," by Sandra D. Lane, Peter Lurie, Benjamin Bowser, Jim Kahn, and Donna Chen, documents the history of needle exchange programs. Although needle exchange programs have become one of the more controversial public health programs of our time, advocates see them as improving the health of drug injectors, whereas opponents believe that they encourage drug use. Many of the early needle exchange programs were operated illegally as explicit acts of civil disobedience. By the 1990s, however, needle exchange programs were active in some two dozen countries in North America, Europe, and Asia.

Lana D. Harrison's "The Medicalization of Marijuana" provides a historical analysis of marijuana as medicine, and it also discusses the current controversy surrounding medical marijuana in the United States. Marijuana has a long history as a medicinal remedy. Recent research has shown cannabis to relieve symptoms connected with glaucoma, HIV wasting syndrome, and nausea and vomiting associated with cancer chemotherapy. The voter support for propositions in California and Arizona in November, 1996, allowing physicians to prescribe marijuana for medical purposes has generated much criticism from the U.S. government. Such federal agencies as the Drug Enforcement Agency and the Food and Drug Administration claim that more research is needed on the efficacy of marijuana's medicinal properties and side effects, as well as on marijuana's role as a "gateway" drug. Although more research has been commissioned by the federal government, 25 states currently have some form of medical marijuana laws.

In "Pregnancy, Drugs, and Harm Reduction," Marsha Rosenbaum and Katherine Irwin address a number of issues in the area of drug abuse among women. They point out that the increasing problem of substance abuse among women has been exacerbated, if not caused, by two national trends. First, poverty, homelessness, and substandard education and health care have increased since 1980, and as members of America's ever-growing "underclass," drug users' lives have become more chaotic, risky, dangerous, and violent. Second, for addicts without financial resources, access to drug treatment has become increasingly problematic due to a decline in federal funding of programs. Within this context, they describe the activities in which drug-using women in general, and pregnant drug users in particular, engage to reduce drug-related harm.

The chapter titled "Coffee Shops, Low-Threshold Methadone, and Needle Exchange," by Dirk J. Korf and Ernst C. Buning, provides an overview of Dutch drug policy. Since 1976, Dutch policy has been a combination of legal and sociomedical control, with the aim of striking a balance between supply reduction by statutory intervention, and the reduction of demand and health hazards through a public health approach. Legal control has resulted in intensified criminalization of the drug trade. At the same time, however, there has been the decriminalization of hashish and marijuana and the toleration of small-scale vending of cannabis in coffee shops. Dutch drug policy also emphasizes sociomedical controls, which have inspired such interventions as low-threshold methadone programs, outreach, drug-free treatment centers, and syringe exchange programs. Despite criticism from prohibitionists, the predominant pattern of cannabis use in the Netherlands today is experimental and recreational, in contrast to alcohol and tobacco, which are used more habitually. Furthermore, the coffee shop phenomenon has helped to create and maintain a separation of the cannabis and heroin markets, with a consequent stabilization of heroin use in the Netherlands.

In "The Harm Reduction Movement in Brazil: Issues and Experiences," Hilary L. Surratt and Paulo R. Telles document the evolution of harm reduction strategies for drug users in Brazil. Harm reduction policies have emerged in Brazil only recently, and they focus almost exclusively on quelling the HIV/AIDS epidemic among injection drug users. Central to the movement is changing the legal status of needle/syringe exchange programs, which are perhaps *the* key features of harm reduction in Brazil. Two sites established small needle/syringe exchange programs in 1995, whereas others, such as Rio de Janeiro, became operational only in mid-1997. Public and police opposition to such programs remains high, leaving many injection drug users without access to such programs. Surratt and Telles also point out that there continues to be tremendous unmet need for services among *noninjection* drug users, who are also at risk for HIV/AIDS. To address this need, an initiative targeting segments of the Rio de Janeiro population at high risk for HIV/AIDS acquisition and transmission was implemented in 1993. The community-based HIV/AIDS prevention/intervention program for cocaine injectors and snorters provided more than 1,600 clients with risk reduction information, hygiene materials, voluntary HIV testing, and service referrals. For nearly 70% of the clients, this project provided the first AIDS risk reduction information and materials that they had *ever* received.

Patricia G. Erickson's "The Harm Minimization Option for Cannabis: History and Prospects in Canadian Drug Policy" provides a historical overview of Canadian drug policy with a focus on recent harm reduction developments.

Historically, drug policy in Canada and the United States has been grounded in punishing users through criminal sanctions. However, in 1987, Canada appeared to be taking a more public health-directed approach to harm minimization by declaring a new National Drug Strategy, and in 1992, it adopted harm reduction as the goal of that drug strategy. However, an analysis of the hearings debating Canada's new policy revealed the intent to continue punishing cannabis users within the legal system, thus reinforcing and upholding the traditional criminal justice approach.

Toni Makkai's chapter, "Harm Reduction in Australia: Politics, Policy, and Public Opinion," provides an analysis of recent drug policy developments in Australia. Over the past 10 to 15 years, Australian drug policy has focused more on public health than on the legal aspects of drug use. The National Campaign Against Drug Abuse (later renamed the National Drug Strategy) was formed in 1985 as an attempt to minimize the harmful effects of both licit and illicit drugs. Major policy initiatives have occurred with regard to alcohol and tobacco, such as taxation, lowering of the blood alcohol content used to determine impairment/drunkenness, banning smoking in many public areas, and eliminating much of the advertisements promoting these products. Additionally, the HIV risk associated with injection drug use was instrumental in establishing methadone and needle exchange programs. However, despite dedication to harm minimization in the past, a newly elected Australian conservative federal government threatens the future of this approach in dealing with illicit drug use.

In his chapter, titled "The Harm Reduction Roles of the American Criminal Justice System," James A. Inciardi takes the position that like it or not, America's punitive approaches to drug control are here to stay—at least for a while. Given that, and because so many drug users come to the attention of the criminal justice system, a logical approach is to make the American criminal justice system more humane. Inciardi begins his chapter with a discussion of how the punitive policies emerged and why drugs/crime tend to be so linked to policy alternatives. He then suggests how criminal justice-based treatment approaches can play a harm reduction role.

POSTSCRIPT

Although the harm reduction movement is having a positive impact on the lives of drug users in many parts of the world, it may face some difficult times in the years ahead. Drug policies in the United States and throughout most of the world are of a punitive nature, and most will likely remain so for some time to come, especially in the United States. This seems to be the case for several reasons.

First, a vast body of research demonstrates the relationship between drug use and criminal behavior (Hunt, Lipton, & Spunt, 1984; Inciardi, 1986; Johnson, Elmoghazy, & Dunlap, 1990; Nurco et al., 1988; Speckart & Anglin, 1985; Wish

& Johnson, 1986). Alcohol is associated with criminal behavior as both a situation-specific crime (i.e., drunkenness) and a concomitant, because large numbers of incarcerated prisoners display high levels of alcohol problems (Harrison, 1992a). Prisoners also display high levels of problems with illicit drugs. Research has consistently shown that patterns of frequent and intense heroin use are accompanied by correspondingly higher rates of criminal activity (Nurco et al., 1988). The same pattern appears to be evident with heavy crack users as well (Johnson et al., 1990; Inciardi & Pottieger, 1991). Research suggests, however, that even among criminally active drug abusers, the major criminal activity is generally drug sales. Only a small number are actively engaged in non-drug crimes (i.e., robbery, burglary, shoplifting, other larcenies, prostitution, etc.), committing crimes on a daily or near-daily basis (Nurco, Hanlon, Balter, Kinlock, & Slaght, 1991; Johnson et al., 1990).

Some illegal drugs, especially heroin, are intertwined with patterns of relative poverty and urban inequality. For the class of users that has few skills and few opportunities for advancement in middle-class society, frequent licit and illicit drug use may become part of a lifestyle that includes participation in a number of deviant activities. The lifestyle of a criminal addict may be one of the few alternatives for a successful and rewarding lifestyle open to people suffering from socioeconomic deprivation, because the addict/crime scene offers meaning, excitement, pleasure, financial reward, and peer recognition (Harrison, 1992b).

Research has aptly demonstrated that for many of these users, their drug use does not necessarily initiate their criminal careers, although it does tend to intensify and perpetuate them. Thus, for as long as drug users continue to commit crimes—regardless of their reasons for doing so—policies are likely to remain punitive.

Second, many drugs will continue to pose a public health problem in terms of their morbidity and mortality—and this applies to licit as well as illicit drugs. Although use of licit drugs is relatively common, illicit drug use is, statistically, a rare behavior in most societies. The most common pattern of use, even among users, is experimental—or the experience of having tried the drug, but no longer using. Community studies of cocaine users, which were not focused on individuals drawn from the treatment and criminal justice systems, shows that the normal pattern of use is sustained light use. The next most frequent pattern was an increase in use subsequent to initiation, followed by a return to levels of use similar to those experienced in the early phases of use. Only a small proportion of cocaine users develop frequent and intense patterns of use that do not decline over time (cf. Harrison, 1994). Many of those who escalated to daily use managed to reestablish controlled recreational use patterns. Rather than cocaine overpowering user concerns with family, health, and career, the high value that most users placed upon family, health, and career achievement mitigated against abuse and addiction. Most also employed control strategies like limiting the times and spheres in which they allowed themselves to use cocaine (Reinarman, Murphy, & Waldorf, 1994). Therefore, informal social control and group norms mediate the force of pharmacological and psychological factors that can lead to addiction.

The problem, however, is that many of the elements of informal social control that are operant in the lives of more middle-class users are absent in the lives of underclass users. As previously mentioned, illegal drugs such as heroin and crack cocaine are intertwined with patterns of relative poverty and urban inequality. Perhaps one of the most important phenomena keeping users from becoming chronically dependent is involvement in a social network and competing activities and interests. Less privileged people with fewer options are more vulnerable to deviant adaptations because of their lack of access to more conventional ones. To optimize success, a harm reduction policy needs to be embedded within an overall welfare policy that is not in place in countries with the biggest problem, such as the United States, or in Europe, Italy, and Spain.

Rather than addicts using a fixed amount of drugs per day, research shows that they titrate their use in general, and their use of costly drugs largely in accordance with their available economic resources (Grapendaal, Leuw, & Nelen, 1992; Johnson, 1987). It appears that a strong social welfare system represses criminal involvement among users (Grapendaal et al., 1992; Reuband, 1992). But as long as drug use remains a public health problem, and particularly in those countries without a strong welfare system to help soften the linkages between use of expensive illicit drugs and crime, policies are likely to remain punitive.

Third, there is politics or, perhaps, lack of an informed citizenry. This may be somewhat of a global problem, but it is certainly true in the United States, where the majority of individuals are either under- or miseducated about drugs, including alcohol and tobacco. The costs of alcohol and tobacco use and abuse are much greater than the costs of all illicit drugs combined in the United States (McGinnis & Foege, 1993), yet the citizenry consistently rates illicit drugs and crime as the most important problems facing the nation. This is because views about drugs are largely informed by media presentations, and the U.S. media pay disproportionate attention to the problems of illicit drug use and abuse. Certainly, not all media reporting is bad or in error, but the media present an unbalanced view of drugs. The media appear to be most interested in dealing with stories that are designed to grab the attention of their audience with reports of vice or avarice. And media are the major means of information not only for the general populace, but for policymakers as well (NIDA, 1993). Therefore, because drug users and drug dealers have been demonized, punitive policies are attractive to policymakers and the masses. In the United States, presidents, members of Congress, governors, mayors, and legislators can garner far more political fodder from the numbers of arrests and convictions that their policies yielded than from the number of drug treatment beds that were put on line or the number of needles that were exchanged. There is greater affinity for harm reduction policies in countries such as Australia, which, as part of its National Drug Strategy, has concentrated efforts on educating the public about all drugs—including alcohol and tobacco—which helps to put the illicit drug problem in perspective.

Fourth, there is the harm reduction movement itself. As noted in the beginning of this chapter, there is tremendous diversity with respect to the definitions of harm reduction. Therefore, supporters can hold widely divergent opinions as to appropriate strategies, which has tended to splinter the movement rather than unify it. Although this is to be expected with any attempt to bring about major social changes, a high priority must be placed on building common principles and unity rather than distracting from the major foci of the movement. But as in any social movement, the harm reduction crusade has its fair share of extremists and zealots, who advocate an all-or-nothing approach and denigrate those who are not so committed. Such a position tends to limit the influence and scope of advocacy and prevent harm reduction from gaining broad acceptance.

As a final note, it is important to note that those countries that have embraced more openly the harm reduction approach to setting drug policy have often included the legal drugs of alcohol and tobacco as well. In the opening of the 1994 Commission on Narcotic Drugs, the Director General of the United Nations's Drug Control Program (UNDCP), Giorgio Giacomelli, noted that it was "increasingly difficult to justify the continued distinction among substances solely according to their legal status and social acceptability." At the same meetings, the Director of the World Health Organization (WHO) Programme on Substance Abuse said that

current drug strategies are, to some extent, driven by a few industrialized countries. On the one hand, they are making strenuous efforts to exclude from their shores every conceivable kind of illegal substance. But on the other hand, these countries are also vigorously pushing *their own* substances, such as alcohol, tobacco, and pharmaceuticals onto the very same countries from which they are doing their best to exclude illegal drugs. (Emblad, 1994)

REFERENCES

Ball, J. C., Rosen, L., Flueck, J. A., & Nurco, D. N. (1981). The criminality of heroin addicts when addicted and when off opiates. In J. A. Inciardi (Ed.), *The drug crime connection*. Beverly Hills, CA: Sage.

Buning, E. C., Coutinho, R. W., van Brussel, G. H. A., & van Zadelhoff, A. W. (1986). Preventing AIDS in drug addicts in Amsterdam. *Lancet, ii*(8521), 1435, letter.

Butterfield, F. (1998, January 19). As crime rate falls, number of inmates rises. *New York Times.*

DuPont, R. L. (1996). Harm reduction and decriminalization in the United States: A personal perspective. *Substance Use and Misuse, 31,* 1929-1945.

Emblad, H. (1994, April 13-22). Statement by Hans Emblad, Director, WHO Programme on Substance Abuse. Geneva: World Health Organization.

Gerstein, D. R., & Harwood, J. H. (Eds.). (1990). *Treating drug problems.* Washington, DC: National Academy Press.

Giacomelli, G. (1994, April 13). Statement by Executive Director of the United Nations International Drug Control Programme at the Thirty-Seventh Session of the Commission on Narcotic Drugs, Vienna.

Grapendaal, M., Leuw, E., & Nelen, H. (1992). Drugs and crime in an accommodating social context: The situation in Amsterdam. *Contemporary Drug Problems, 19,* 303-326.

Harrison, L. D. (1992a). The drug crime-nexus in the USA. *Contemporary Drug Problems, 19,* 203-224.

Harrison, L. D. (1992b). International perspectives on the interface of drug use and criminal behavior: An editor's introduction. *Contemporary Drug Problems, 19,* 181-202.

Harrison, L. D. (1994). Cocaine using careers in perspective. *Addiction Research, 2*(1), 1-20.

Hunt, D. E., Lipton, D. S., & Spunt, B. (1984). Patterns of criminal activity among methadone clients and current narcotics users not in treatment. *Journal of Drug Issues, 14,* 687-701.

Inciardi, J. A. (1986). *The war on drugs: Heroin, cocaine, crime and social policy.* Palo Alto, CA: Mayfield.

Inciardi, J. A., & Pottieger, A. E. (1991). Kids, crack and crime. *Journal of Drug Issues, 21,* 257-270.

Johnson, B. D. (1987). *The economic behavior of street opiate addicts.* Final report to the National Institute on Drug Abuse. Rockville, MD: NIDA.

Johnson, B. C., Elmoghazy, E., & Dunlap, E. (1990). *Crack abusers and noncrack drug abusers: A comparison of drug use, drug sales, and nondrug criminality.* Paper presented at the annual meeting of the American Society of Criminology.

Kreek, M. J. (1983). Health consequences associated with the use of methadone. In J. R. Cooper (Ed.), *Research on the treatment of narcotic addiction: State of the art.* Rockville, MD: NIDA.

Lurie, P., & Drucker, E. (1997). An opportunity lost: HIV infections associated with lack of a national needle-exchange programme in the USA. *The Lancet, 349,* 604-608.

McGinnis, J., & Foege, W. (1993). Actual cause of death in the United States. *Journal of the American Medical Association, 270,* 2207-2212.

Nadelmann, E. A., Cohen, P., Drucker, E., Locher, U., Stimson, G., & Wodak, A. (1994). *The harm reduction approach to drug control: International progress.* Unpublished manuscript.

Nadelmann, E., McNeely, J., & Drucker, E. (1997). International perspectives. In J. H. Lowinson, P. Ruis, R. B. Millman, & J. Langrod (Eds.), *Substance abuse: A comprehensive textbook* (3rd Ed., pp. 22-39). Baltimore: Williams and Wilkins.

National Institute on Drug Abuse (NIDA). (1993). *Views of area opinion leaders about drug abuse in the Washington, DC, metropolitan area.* Rockville, MD: Author.

Nurco, D. N., Hanlon, T. E., Balter, M. B., Kinlock, T. W., & Slaght, E. (1991). A classification of narcotic addicts based on type, amount, and severity of crime. *Journal of Drug Issues, 21,* 429-448.

Nurco, D. N., Hanlon, T. E., Kinlock, T. W., & Duszynski, K. R. (1988). Differential criminal patterns of narcotic addicts over an addiction career. *Criminology, 26,* 407-423.

Reinarman, C., Murphy, S., & Waldorf, D. (1994). Pharmacology is not destiny: The contingent character of cocaine abuse and addiction. *Addiction Research, 2*(1), 21-36.

Reuband, K. H. (1992). Drug addiction and crime in West Germany: A review of the empirical evidence. *Contemporary Drug Problems, 19,* 327-350.

Reuter, P. (1992). Hawks ascendant: The punitive trend of drug policy. *Daedalus, 121*(3), 15-52.

Reuter, P., & MacCoun, R. J. (1996). Harm reduction and social policy. *Drug and Alcohol Review, 15,* 225-230.

Speckart, G., & Anglin, M. D. (1985). Narcotics and crime: An analysis of existing evidence for a causal relationship. *Behavioral Sciences and the Law, 3,* 259-282.

Trebach, A. S., & Inciardi, J. A. (1993). *Legalize it? Debating American drug policy.* Washington, DC: American University Press.

van Haastrecht, H. (1997). HIV infection and drug use in the Netherlands: The course of the epidemic. *Journal of Drug Issues, 27,* 57-72.

Wish, E. D., & Johnson, B. D. (1986). The impact of substance abuse on criminal careers. In A. Blumstein, J. Cohen, J. A. Roth, & C. A. Visher (Eds.), *Criminal careers and "career criminals": Volume 2.* Washington, DC: National Academy Press.

Wodak, A., & Lurie, P. (1997). A tale of two countries: Attempts to control HIV among injecting drug users in Australia and the United States. *Journal of Drug Issues, 27,* 117-134.

Harm Reduction: History, Definition, and Practice

Diane Riley
Pat O'Hare

First, do no harm.
    —Hippocrates

THE NATURE AND ORIGINS
OF HARM REDUCTION

Harm reduction is a relatively new social policy with respect to drugs that has gained popularity in recent years—especially in Australia, Britain, and the Netherlands—as a response to the spread of Acquired Immune Deficiency Syndrome (AIDS) among injection drug users. This chapter provides an overview of the origins, background, and nature of harm reduction and some detailed examples of harm reduction as it is being practiced around the world.

Although harm reduction can be used as a framework for all drugs, including alcohol, it has primarily been applied to injection drug use (IDU) because of the pressing nature of the harm associated with this activity. The main focus of this chapter is the reduction of injection drug-related harm, although brief mention is made of alcohol and other noninjection drugs. Barriers to the adoption of harm reduction, as well as its limitations, are also discussed.

AUTHORS' NOTE: Parts of this chapter are based on a paper prepared for the Canadian Centre on Substance Abuse National Working Group on Drug Policy by Riley et al. (1999).

Harm reduction has as its first priority a decrease in the negative consequences of drug use. This approach can be contrasted with abstentionism, the dominant policy in North America, which emphasizes a decrease in the prevalence of drug use. According to a harm reduction approach, a strategy that is aimed exclusively at decreasing the prevalence of drug use may only increase various drug-related harms, and so the two approaches have different emphases. Harm reduction tries to reduce problems associated with drug use and recognizes that abstinence may be neither a realistic nor a desirable goal for some, especially in the short term. This is not to say that harm reduction and abstinence are mutually exclusive but only that abstinence is not the only acceptable or important goal. Harm reduction involves setting up a hierarchy of goals, with the more immediate and realistic ones to be achieved in steps on the way to risk-free use or, if appropriate, abstinence; consequently, it is an approach that is characterized by pragmatism.

Harm reduction has received impetus over the past decade because of the spread of AIDS: Drug use is one of the risk behaviors most frequently associated with human immunodeficiency virus (HIV, or the virus thought to be necessary for AIDS). In some areas, IDU has become the main route of drug administration, and globally, it is now one of the primary risk factors for HIV infection. For example, in the United States, more than 20% of reported AIDS cases are directly associated with a history of injecting, and more than 30% of new HIV infections are in injection drug users. In some areas of Europe, injection of drugs accounts for as many as 60% of AIDS cases. What is more significant still is the rate at which HIV can spread among injection drug users. In cities such as Barcelona, Edinburgh, Milan, and New York, between 50% and 60% of drug users have become infected. In Thailand, where less than 1% of users were infected in January 1988, more than 40% were positive by September of that year, with a monthly incidence rate of 4% (Rana, 1996). Less than a decade later in the northeastern province of Chiang Rai, one in six male military recruits and one in eight pregnant women were infected with HIV (Rana, 1996).

In all countries, HIV infection is not just a concern for the drug users themselves but also for their sexual partners. A number of studies in the United States and the United Kingdom have shown that between 60% and 100% of heterosexually acquired HIV is related to IDU, and that at least 40% of IDUs are in relationships with nonusers (Drucker, 1986; Rhodes, Myers, Bueno, Millson, & Hunter, 1998). Because of sexual spreading from injection drug-using partners, and because approximately one third of IDUs are female, vertical spreading to newborn children occurs. The possibility of transmission to the noninjecting community is increased by the fact that prostitution is sometimes used as a means of obtaining money for drugs, and many prostitutes are regular or occasional injectors. In addition, IDUs are a potential source of perinatal transmission: More than 50% of all pediatric AIDS cases in the United States are associated with injection drug use by one or both parents.

AIDS has thus been a catalyst for the rise in popularity of harm reduction. Before the AIDS pandemic, drug use was associated with a relatively low mortality rate because of periods of abstinence and natural recovery (Brettle, 1991; Wille, 1983). During the 1980s, there was a rapid increase in both AIDS- and non-AIDS-related deaths in drug users (Stroneburner et al., 1989). Brettle (1991) has suggested that "this increase in mortality for drug users is the driving force behind harm reduction and the reason we can no longer rely on spontaneous recovery for drug users" (p. 125). This is no doubt a correct assessment of the primary force behind harm reduction, but it is by no means a full account of it. In North America in particular, harm reduction attracted attention because of the effects of drug prohibition other than the spread of AIDS alone. The violent crime, gang warfare, prison overcrowding, and police corruption associated with prohibition have reached a level such that policymakers, practitioners, and members of the public alike are seeking alternatives to prohibitionist drug policy.

It has been claimed that attempts to legislate and enforce abstinence are counterproductive, and that there are harms due to these measures that are far worse than the effects of the drugs themselves (Erickson, 1992; Nadelmann, 1993; O'Hare, 1992; Riley & Oscapella, 1997). The harm reduction approach attempts to identify, measure, and minimize the adverse consequences of drug use at a number of levels, not just that of society as a whole. In a harm reduction framework, the term *risk* is used to describe the probability of drug-taking behavior resulting in any of a number of consequences (Newcombe, 1992). The terms *harm* and *benefit* are used to describe whether a particular consequence is viewed as positive or negative. In most cases, drug-taking behaviors result in several kinds of effects: beneficial, neutral, and harmful. The consequences of drug use can be conceptualized as being of three main types: health (physical and psychological), social, and economic. These consequences can be said to occur at three levels: individual; community (family, friends, colleagues, etc.); and societal (the structures and functions of society) (see Figure 1.1). They can also be broken down with respect to the time of their occurrence, into short-term and long-term effects. It is clear, given the wide range of moral and political views on the subject, that some consequences of drug use will remain highly controversial, and that assigning a positive or negative value will be purely subjective. Nevertheless, the harm reduction framework can be used as a means of better objectifying the evaluation process with respect to both drug programs and policies by allowing for the identification of harms that are to be dealt with.

The roots of harm reduction are in the United Kingdom, the Netherlands, and North America (Riley, 1993, 1994). Merseyside became a center for harm reduction policy because, like many other areas of the United Kingdom, it witnessed an epidemic spread of drug use, particularly heroin, in the early 1980s. Three important factors led to the establishment of the Mersey model of harm reduction. The first was the policy of the local drug dependency clinic, which was based on the old British system. Merseyside's major city, Liverpool, did not

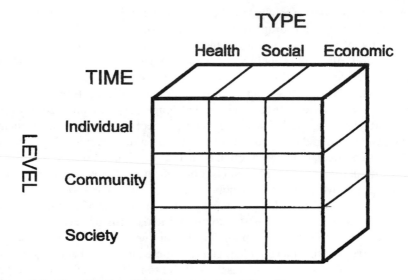

Figure 1.1. Classification of the Consequences of Drug Use
NOTE: Based on a figure by Newcombe (1992).

have its own drug dependency clinic until the mid-1980s. Prior to this, out-patient drug treatment was limited to a few psychiatrists who, in contrast to doctors in most other parts of the country, did not completely abandon the old British system. The British system emerged as a response to the recommendations of the Rolleston Committee, a group of leading physicians, on treatment of drug abusers in England during the 1920s. One of the most significant conclusions of the committee was that in certain cases, maintenance on drugs may be necessary for the patient to lead a useful life. To this day, injectable opiates have continued to be prescribed on a take-home basis in Merseyside.

A second factor in the emergence of the Mersey model was that in 1986, the Mersey Regional Drug Training and Information Centre began one of the first syringe exchange schemes in the United Kingdom, with the aim of increasing the availability of sterile injecting equipment to drug users in the area. The third factor was the cooperation of the local police, who agreed not to place drug services under observation and began to refer to drug services those drug users who had been arrested, a policy known as "cautioning."

In Merseyside, the harm reduction services include needle exchange; counseling; prescription of drugs, including heroin; and employment and housing services. One of the reasons that the Merseyside approach has proven so effective is that many levels of service and a wide variety of agencies are involved.

The services for the drug user are integrated so that they can obtain help more readily when they need it. Together, Mersey Authority and the Merseyside Police have devised a comprehensive and effective harm reduction strategy, which came to be known as the "Mersey Model" of harm reduction (O'Hare, 1992).

All of the available evidence on HIV infection among IDUs in Merseyside suggests that the Mersey HIV prevention strategy for IDUs is very effective (see Stimson, 1997, for a review of approaches to HIV among drug users in the United Kingdom). Contacts with drug users have increased steadily over the past 5 years, and anecdotal evidence suggests that the number of drug-related health problems seen by services has dropped. Self-reported sharing of injecting equipment has declined, indicating positive behavioral change. By the end of 1994, only 29 drug injectors were known to be HIV positive and resident in the region. Official statistics indicate a decrease in drug-related acquisitive crime in many parts of the region, whereas the national rate is increasing (HIT, 1996). It is thought that the low prevalence of crime and HIV infection can be related to the various policies for dealing with drug use in the area.

In the early 1980s, Amsterdam recognized that drug use is a complex, recurring behavior, and that reduction of harm means providing medical and social care while waiting for natural recovery in order to avoid some of the more harmful consequences of injection drug use (Buning, 1990). Needle exchange began in 1984 after the Junkie Union advocated and then initiated the first exchange in order to prevent the spread of hepatitis B among users (Buning et al., 1986; Buning, van Brussel, & van Santen, 1988). Amsterdam has taken a pragmatic and nonmoralistic attitude toward drugs, and this has resulted in a multifaceted system that offers a variety of harm reduction programs. Police in the Netherlands focus attention and resources on drug traffickers, not users.

Although North America is not usually thought of in connection with harm reduction, Canada and the United States have been home to a very significant harm reduction strategy. One of the earliest forms of harm reduction for IDUs were methadone maintenance programs that began in Canada in the late 1950s and in the United States in the early 1960s. Methadone maintenance was seen as harm reduction for society, usually in terms of the reduction of crime or the reentry of drug users to the workforce (Brettle, 1991); improvement of the individual's physical health or protection of their human rights was not a priority. The spread of AIDS in opiate users has changed the entry and evaluation criteria for methadone programs, and it has also highlighted the need to modify these programs in order to reduce individual as well as societal harms (Jurgens & Riley, 1997; Newman, 1987; Springer, 1990).

A number of countries and organizations have now adopted harm reduction as both policy and practice. For example, the British Advisory Council on the

Misuse of Drugs (1988) responded to the spread of HIV in IDUs by revising its policy on drug use to one of harm reduction: "We have no hesitation in concluding that the spread of HIV is a greater danger to individual and public health than drug misuse. Accordingly, services which aim to minimize HIV risk behaviour by all available means should take precedence in developmental plans" (para. 2.1). The World Health Organization (1986) has expressed a similar opinion, stating that policies aimed at reduction of drug use must not be allowed to compromise measures against the spread of AIDS.

The Nature of Harm Reduction

Features of Harm Reduction

The essence of harm reduction is embodied in the following statement: "If a person is not willing to give up his or her drug use, we should assist them in reducing harm to himself or herself and others" (Buning, 1993, p. 1). The main characteristics or principles of harm reduction are as follows:

Pragmatism. Harm reduction accepts that some use of mind-altering substances is inevitable, and that some level of drug use is normal in a society. It acknowledges that, although carrying risks, drug use also provides the user with benefits that must be taken into account if drug-using behavior is to be understood. From a community perspective, containment and amelioration of drug-related harms may be a more pragmatic or feasible option than efforts to eliminate drug use entirely.

Humanistic values. The drug user's decision to use drugs is accepted as fact, as his or her choice; no moralistic judgment is made to either condemn or support the use of drugs, regardless of level of use or mode of intake. The dignity and rights of the drug user are respected.

Focus on harms. The fact or extent of a person's drug use per se is of secondary importance to the risk of harms consequent to use. The harms addressed can be related to health, social, economic, or a multitude of other factors, affecting the individual, the community, and society as a whole. Therefore, the first priority is to decrease the negative consequences of drug use to the user and to others, as opposed to focusing on decreasing the drug use itself. Harm reduction neither excludes nor presumes the long-term treatment goal of abstinence. In some cases, reduction of level of use may be one of the most effective forms of harm reduction. In others, alteration to the mode of use may be more effective.

Balancing costs and benefits. Some pragmatic process of identifying, measuring, and assessing the relative importance of drug-related problems, their associated harms, and costs/benefits of intervention is carried out in order to focus resources on priority issues. The framework of analysis extends beyond the immediate interests of users to include broader community and societal interests. Because of this "rational" approach, harm reduction approaches theoretically lend themselves to systematic evaluation to measure their impact on the reduction of harms in both the short and the long term, thereby determining whether their cost is warranted compared to some other, or no, intervention. In practice, however, such evaluations are complicated because of the number of variables to be examined in both the short and long term.

Hierarchy of goals. Most harm reduction programs have a hierarchy of goals, with the immediate focus on proactively engaging individuals, target groups, and communities to address their most pressing needs. Achieving the most immediate and realistic goals is usually viewed as the first step toward risk-free use, or, if appropriate, abstinence (e.g., see the guidelines from the Advisory Council on the Misuse of Drugs).

Definition

At present, there is no agreement in the addictions literature or among practitioners as to the definition of harm reduction. One working definition is the following: "an attempt to ameliorate the adverse health, social or economic consequences of mood-altering substances without necessarily requiring a reduction in the consumption of these substances" (Heather, Wodak, Nadelmann, & O'Hare, 1993, p. vi).

In the literature, the term *harm reduction* is often used interchangeably with the lesser-used term *harm minimization.* Two additional terms that are frequently used synonymously with harm reduction are *risk reduction* and *risk minimization.* Other terms occasionally used in conjunction with harm reduction are *responsible drug use, problem prevention, secondary prevention,* and *risk management.*

The definition of harm reduction has become an issue because of the broad nature of the term, its multiple meanings, and the conceptual fuzziness of the area in general. This has led to confusion among both harm reduction practitioners and its critics. For example, imprisonment of drug users for simple possession is, at present, construed by some to be a form of harm reduction. Practitioners dedicated to abstinence may also think of themselves as reducing the harms of substance abuse.

Harm reduction can be viewed as both a goal—the reduction of the number of harms associated with drug use—and a strategy—a specific approach that focuses on the negative consequences of drug use rather than on level of use. In both cases, one of the key definitional points is that the person's use of drugs is accepted as fact. Harm reduction approaches, then, are those that aim to reduce the negative consequences of drug use for the individual, the community, and society while allowing that a person may choose to continue to use drugs. This does not mean that harm reduction approaches preclude abstinence, only that there is acceptance of the fact that there are many possible approaches or strategies that can be taken to address drug-related problems, harm reduction and abstention being two of these. A harm reduction approach to a person's drug use in the short term does not rule out abstinence in the longer term, and vice versa.

Amid these diverse applications and levels of generality, the unique meaning and value of harm reduction as a concept and programming approach can easily be lost. This argues for a more restrictive definition of harm reduction, such as the following: "A policy or program directed toward decreasing adverse health, social, and economic consequences of drug use while the user continues to use drugs."

Understanding "Harms"

On the surface, it is easy enough to understand and endorse the primary goal of reducing the harms associated with drug use. Beyond that, however, it can be very difficult to get a clear picture of what exactly constitutes a harm, and to whom. The literature describes a broad range of harms. Most are attributed directly to drugs and behaviors related to their use; other harms are seen as resulting from the policies and programs in place to deter drug use. Thus, questions such as: What constitutes a harm as opposed to a benefit? To whom? What harms should be given priority, and when? can become very difficult to answer in practice.

Another area of debate concerns whether or not dependence constitutes a harm in and of itself. Consistent with the principles of harm reduction, many of its proponents do not view dependence as the priority; rather, they aim at reducing the clearly harmful consequences associated with drug use without requiring elimination of use itself. Practitioners of solely abstinence-oriented programs often view this as an unacceptable aspect of harm reduction.

Harm reduction takes a rational approach to drugs and requires a framework for identifying and assessing the relative effects of various kinds of drug use. This, in turn, rests on some classification of effects; some methodology for counting and costing the negative and positive outcomes of drug use; and a database from which to make comparative assessments of drug-related consequences for different types of drugs, target groups, and settings. In the majority of countries, the elements of such a framework exist in fragmented form only. In the absence of objective data, much of the planning and delivery of harm reduction programs to date has been based on observation of risks and perceived priority of interventions.

Relationship to Other Approaches

Despite the current prominence of harm reduction, the notion of reducing harms associated with drug use has a long history. It has been a feature of British drug policy in particular for many decades, periodically surfacing and then fading (Berridge, 1993). This idea is firmly rooted in public health practice to secondary prevention with high-risk groups. Thus, harm reduction is neither a new nor an alternative approach so much as it is an extension and focusing of existing and accepted approaches.

Many harm reduction-based programs, such as needle exchanges, are of recent origin. Others, however, have a long and proven history; methadone programs, for example, date back to the 1960s and have demonstrated their effectiveness in assisting drug users to stabilize and normalize their lifestyles and in providing many with a bridge to abstinence from narcotic use. Helping people avoid harms has also been an established part of the alcohol field for many years; examples include promotion of responsible drinking, controlled drinking interventions, avoidance of drinking and driving, and low-alcohol-content beverages.

The recent increase in popularity of harm reduction is linked primarily to an increase in the influence of public health-based approaches to drug use and AIDS. Harm reduction is closely linked to a public health perspective through the sharing of common concepts and tools. In particular, harm reduction falls neatly in the conceptual framework of health promotion, with the minimization of risks and harms forming one part of the broader continuum of strategies to promote health and avoid disease. Both approaches emphasize the importance of respecting individuals and empowering them to increase opportunities to maximize their health, whatever the circumstances. As such, harm reduction, like health promotion, fits well with approaches that emphasize the importance of understanding the broad determinants of health and ensuring cost-effective approaches to the well-being of the entire population.

With respect to legal approaches, harm reduction in and of itself does not favor any one regulatory system over another. Rather, the issue is seen as an empirical one to be addressed through determining how best to regulate drugs in order to achieve a balance in minimizing harms to the individual, the community, and society as a whole. Nevertheless, advocates of harm reduction have been criticized severely for this view, with some opponents in North America, in particular, arguing that harm reduction is tantamount to advocacy for drug legalization. Although they do not necessarily favor legalization, many harm reductionists do believe that policies of drug prohibition have served only to exacerbate drug-related harm (Hawks, 1993; Jurgens & Riley, 1997; Kirby, 1996; Lurie & Drucker, 1997; Nadelmann, 1993; Riley & Oscapella, 1997).

THE PRACTICE OF HARM REDUCTION

Harm Reduction Programs and Policies

Syringe Exchange and Availability

Needle and syringe exchange programs are, to many people, the epitome of the harm reduction approach. They were first established in a few European countries in the mid-1980s and, by the end of the decade, were operating in numerous cities around the world. The rationale behind syringe exchanges is that many people who are currently injecting are unable or unwilling to stop, and intervention strategies must help reduce their risk of HIV infection and transmission to others. Provision of sterile needles and syringes is a simple, inexpensive way to reduce the risk of spreading HIV infection. It is also a way of providing contact with drug users through outreach services. The strategy is based on a knowledge and means approach to behavioral change: People are provided with information about the changes that are needed and also with the means to bring about this change (sterile needles, syringes, other "works," and condoms).

Some exchange programs provide outreach services in the form of mobile vans or street workers to deliver services to drug scenes or to users' homes. Automated syringe exchange machines are now being used in many European and Australian cities. These vending machines release a clean syringe when a used one is deposited. Such machines are fairly inexpensive and accessible on a 24-hour basis. The machines, however, decrease the important personal contact between drug users and health care workers. In Amsterdam, which has the world's oldest syringe exchange (1984), and where there is a broad range of outreach services to hard-core drug users, even some police stations will provide clean syringes on an exchange basis to people detained or arrested.

In areas where syringes cannot be made available, bleach kits (containing bleach and instructions for cleaning equipment) can be distributed. Although bleach is not totally effective in eliminating HIV and does not kill the pathogen that causes hepatitis (CDC, 1993), such kits help to reduce the likelihood of infection being passed through sharing of dirty equipment.

There is now clear direct and indirect evidence that attendance at syringe exchanges and increased syringe availability are associated with a decrease in risk (e.g., decreased sharing) as well as a decrease in harm (e.g., lower levels of

HIV infection, increased access to medical care) (Hart, Carvell, Woodward et al., 1989; Jurgens, 1996; Lurie & Reingold, 1993; Rana, 1996; Robertson, 1990; Stimson, 1989, 1997; Stimson et al., 1988; van den Hoek, van Haastrecht, & Coutinho, 1989; Wodak, 1990, 1996).

Despite fears and propaganda to the contrary, needle exchanges are not associated with an increase in the number of injectors or a decrease in the average age of injectors. Thus, needle exchange has been shown to be a highly cost-effective means of reducing injection-related harms. In Australia, for example, early intervention with needle exchange programs and rapid tenfold expansion of methadone treatment kept the HIV rate among injection drug users below 2% after 1988 (Wodak, 1990, 1996).

The situation is markedly different in the United States, which has remained, for the most part, resistant to the adoption of harm reduction strategies. In 1996, Peter Lurie and Ernest Drucker used modeling techniques to estimate the number of HIV infections associated with the U.S. government's opposition to needle exchange programs. They estimated that between 4,000 and 10,000 IDUs in the United States would not now be infected with HIV had they had access to clean needles. Using the estimate of US$119,000 for the lifetime cost of treating an HIV infection, the authors conclude that these infections have cost the U.S. health care system some US$250 to US$500 million. The model does not include the indirect costs of HIV infection and uses conservative estimates. The median annual budget of a needle exchange in North America is US$168,650. The average cost per syringe distributed is just US$1.35 (Lurie & Drucker, 1997). Two national AIDS commissions, the National Academy of Science's Institute of Medicine, and leading government experts have called repeatedly for repeal of the ban on needle exchange funding, but federal health authorities still maintain that harm reduction programs give the wrong message. The U.S. government, fearing that a move toward harm reduction will be viewed as a softening of its stance on illicit drugs, remains committed to prohibition and all of the many harms, including death, that attend it.

An important new development is the operation of needle exchange programs in an increasing number of prisons, primarily in Switzerland (Jurgens, 1996; Jurgens & Riley, 1997). Syringe exchange helps to prevent the spread of HIV and hepatitis in prisons and to fulfill legal and ethical obligations toward inmates, staff, and the public. Following their success in several prisons in Switzerland, programs to provide sterile needles have started in Spain and Germany (Jurgens, 1996). The Swiss found that the health status of prisoners improved, no new cases of infection with HIV or hepatitis occurred, a decrease in needle sharing was observed, there was no increase in drug consumption, and needles were not used as weapons. Several other countries, including Australia and Canada, are currently studying the feasibility of providing syringe exchange in their correctional facilities.

Methadone Programs

Although methadone programs began in Canada and the United States, many of these programs have been criticized for their failure to provide the flexibility and range of services necessary for a cost-effective, harm-reducing program (Riley, 1993, 1995; Springer, 1990). Methods of providing methadone in the United Kingdom, the Netherlands, and Australia offer some examples of the range of possibilities necessary for effective harm reduction.

In the Netherlands, methadone is used in three different ways—to contact, stabilize, and detoxify/treat heroin users. By providing methadone without too many impediments—"low-threshold programs"—contact can be made with large sections of the heroin-using population. For example, there is a methadone bus program in which buses are used to distribute methadone throughout the drug-using community (no take-home dosages are provided). The primary disadvantages of the Dutch programs appear to be that they, like the U.S. programs, do not maintain all clients on levels of methadone that are high enough to prevent use of heroin, and they do not provide anything other than oral methadone.

Measures introduced to combat the spread of AIDS in Australia included the marked expansion of methadone programs. The criteria for admission to these programs were also made less stringent, and many more spaces were allowed for maintenance of clients with little motivation to change drug-using behavior. These changes to drug programs have been supported by a change in national and state policy toward drug abuse such that the highest priority has been given to the containment of HIV.

In the United Kingdom, parts of continental Europe, and Australia, methadone is available from clinics as well as general practitioners, who provide health care and counseling. In a number of European cities, more than 25% of all general practitioners prescribe methadone. Users pick up their prescription from pharmacies. Amsterdam, Barcelona, Frankfurt, and other cities distribute methadone through methadone buses or mobile clinics. Opiate-substitute programs in Canada are, at present, very limited both in terms of size and in terms of the options available to users (Riley, 1996).

There have been numerous studies on the effectiveness of methadone, and the vast majority of these have shown that methadone reduces morbidity and mortality, reduces the users' involvement in crime, curbs the spread of HIV, and helps drug users to gain control of their lives (Ball & Ross, 1991; Dole, 1989; Fazey, 1992; Gossop, 1978; Newman, 1976, 1987; Rana, 1996; Wodak, 1990, 1996; WHO, 1989, 1990). In all countries, one of the key factors underlying the success of methadone as a harm reduction measure is that it brings the user back into the community rather than treating him or her like an outsider or a criminal.

This not only allows for rehabilitation of the user but it also means that the drugs and crime cycle can be broken. The experience of other countries shows that methadone programs work best if they are numerous, accessible, flexible, and liberal. Such expansion should take into account the need for methadone programs in prisons as well as the advantages of offering methadone treatment as an alternative to imprisonment and other forms of criminalization.

In prison itself, methadone programs are usually not available, creating problems and health risks for prisoners who were on methadone on the outside. A small but increasing number of prison systems worldwide are offering methadone maintenance to inmates, and a study undertaken in Australia suggests that the reduction of injecting and syringe sharing demonstrated in methadone programs in community settings also occurs in prisons (see Jurgens, 1996, for a review). A recent court case in British Columbia, Canada, may mean that methadone will be made available to some prisoners in that province. Currently, because many drug users end up spending time in prisons, it is important to ensure wider availability of methadone in prisons, and to explore the advantages of offering methadone treatment as an alternative to imprisonment.

Prescribing of Drugs Other Than Methadone

In a tradition dating back to the 1920s, physicians in the United Kingdom prescribe drugs to users. In many regions, these services are provided through drug dependency clinics or community drug teams. These services offer flexible prescribing regimes ranging from short-term detoxification to long-term maintenance. The majority of clients receive oral methadone, but some receive injectable methadone; others receive injectable heroin; and a small number receive amphetamines, cocaine, or other drugs. These drugs are dispensed through local pharmacists (HIT, 1996; O'Hare, 1992; Riley, 1993, 1994).

In some parts of the United Kingdom, users can also be prescribed smokable drugs in the form of reefers. Drug users who are able to give up injecting often find that they are not able to switch immediately to oral prescriptions that do not provide the "rush" that an injected drug does (Palombella, 1990; Riley, 1993). Smokable drugs do provide a rush, although less powerful. In the Mersey region, where prescribing and other harm reduction programs are well established, anecdotal evidence suggests that drug-related health problems seen by services and acquisitive crime have decreased as a result of these services. There is a relatively high prevalence of heroin use, with there being an estimated 15,000 regular heroin users, of whom at least 50% inject. In 1994, the Mersey region had the second highest rate of notified addicts (4,088) of any regional health authority in the UK. The level of HIV infection among drug injectors in the Mersey region is very low (HIT, 1996).

Switzerland is carrying out a national experiment with prescribing of heroin and other drugs to users. The experiment is being conducted to determine whether prescribing of heroin and other drugs legally to users will reduce the users' criminal activity and their risk of contracting and spreading AIDS and other infections. The Swiss studied the British prescribing programs before setting out on the largest and most scientific study of heroin maintenance ever attempted. The program started in January 1994 with sites in eight cities. In each city, the program offers accommodation, employment assistance, treatment for disease and psychological problems, clean syringes, and counseling. Users are in regular contact with health workers and links to drug-free treatment. Some programs started off by giving some users heroin and others morphine or injectable methadone. It was soon found, however, that most users preferred heroin, which is provided up to three times a day for a small daily fee. Two programs allow clients to take a few heroin reefers home each night. Preliminary reports on the program suggest that heroin maintenance is efficacious (there were insufficient data to draw conclusions about cocaine). The programs have not resulted in a black market of diverted heroin, and the health of the addicts in the programs has clearly improved. The authorities have concluded from these preliminary data that heroin causes very few, if any, problems when it is used in a controlled manner and is administered under hygienic conditions. Based on these findings, the Swiss government expanded the program to more than 1,000 users in 1995 (approximately 800 slots for heroin, 100 each for morphine and injectable methadone) (Haemig, 1997). As part of this program, eight inmates in one prison in Switzerland are being maintained on heroin, so far with good results.

Holland began a heroin maintenance experiment in 1997, and several German cities would also like to begin programs. The Australian Capital Territory is also preparing to institute a heroin maintenance program.

Education and Outreach Programs

Educational materials about drugs that have a harm reduction focus are readily available in a number of countries, including the United Kingdom, Holland, and Australia, but they remain extremely controversial and are often unavailable in most other countries. Although not promoting drug use, such materials tell the user how to reduce the risks associated with using drugs, teaching such things as safer injecting practices. In some countries, such as the United Kingdom, these techniques are taught by nurses at clinics.

In many countries, outreach workers are used to contact people such as drug injectors and prostitutes at risk of becoming infected with HIV. These workers distribute educational material, syringes, condoms, and bleach kits, and they help users contact other services.

Law Enforcement Policies

Merseyside police in the northwest of England have devised a harm reduction approach known as "responsible demand enforcement" (Merseyside Police Force, 1990; Riley, 1993, 1994). They developed a cooperative harm reduction strategy with the regional health authority to improve the prevention and treatment of drug problems, particularly with respect to the spread of HIV infection among IDUs. The police are represented on Health Authority Drug Advisory Committees and employ health authority officers on police training courses involving the drugs/HIV issue. They have also supported the health authority by agreeing not to conduct surveillance on them, referring arrested drug offenders to services, not prosecuting for possession of syringes that are to be exchanged, and publicly supporting syringe exchange. One of the most important features of the Merseyside police strategy has been its emphasis on using resources to deal with drug traffickers while operating a cautioning policy toward drug users. Cautioning, which has now been adopted to some extent by all police authorities in Great Britain, has been recommended by the Attorney General of the United Kingdom as an appropriate option for some classes of offense, such as drug possession. Cautioning involves taking an offender to a police station, confiscating the drug, recording the incident, and formally warning the offender that any further unlawful possession of drugs will result in prosecution in court. The offender must also meet certain conditions, such as not having a previous drug conviction and not having an extensive criminal record. The offender is also given information about treatment services in the area, including syringe exchanges. The first time an offender is cautioned, he or she is not given a criminal record. On the second and third occasions, the offender is sent to court, where he or she is fined for possession of small quantities and sentenced for possession of large amounts. If an addict becomes registered through getting in touch with service agencies, then he or she is legally entitled to carry drugs prescribed to them for personal use. The overall effect of this policy is to steer users away from crime and possible imprisonment. In recent years, the approach has been extended to ecstasy, amphetamine, and cocaine, as well as heroin. In Merseyside, approximately 50% of drug possession incidents are dealt with by cautioning; in the rest of the United Kingdom, this figure is 25% (Dorn, personal communication, 1996).

In the Netherlands, police have long been supportive of harm reduction programs, including de facto decriminalization of marijuana and tolerance zones; enforcement efforts are concentrated on large-scale traffickers and on ensuring a safe and peaceful environment. As previously noted, some police stations in Amsterdam will provide clean syringes on an exchange basis. In Hamburg, Germany, a recent policy shift to harm reduction has been reflected in cooperation between police, health officials, and drug users' groups working together to help drug users access social services.

Tolerance Areas

One innovative harm reduction approach being practiced in several European cities involves toleration by authorities of facilities known as "injection rooms," "health rooms," "contact centers," or similar terms. These are facilities where drug users can get together and obtain clean injection equipment, condoms, advice, medical attention, and so forth. The majority of these places allow users to remain anonymous. Some include space where drug users, including injectors, can take drugs in a comparatively safe environment. This is regarded as better than the open injection of illicit drugs in public places or consumption of drugs in "shooting galleries" that are usually unhygienic and controlled by drug dealers.

In Switzerland, the first drug rooms were established by private organizations in Bern and Basel in the late 1980s. By the end of 1993, there were eight such facilities, most operated by city officials. Several other cities in the German-speaking parts of Switzerland opened drug rooms in 1994. An evaluation of three of these facilities after their first year of operation showed that they had been effective in reducing the transmission of HIV and the risk of drug overdose (Nadelmann, 1995). Drug rooms are also provided by programs in Germany and Australia.

In the Netherlands, Rotterdam has also informally adopted a policy known as the "apartment dealer" arrangement. Following this policy, police and prosecutors refrain from arresting and prosecuting dealers who are living in apartments providing they do not cause problems for their neighbors. This approach is part of a "safe neighborhood" plan in which residents and police work together to keep neighborhoods clean, safe, and free of nuisances.

Not all tolerance zones have been successful. The first Swiss attempt at an open drug scene, "Needle Park" in Zurich, grew unmanageable and was closed in 1992. A second attempt also became uncontrollable and was closed in March 1995.

In Germany, open drug scenes emerged in Frankfurt during the 1970s and settled in two adjacent parks in the 1980s when police officials decided that their earlier attempts to suppress them had failed. Local authorities in Frankfurt established three crisis centers next to the drug scenes, provided a mobile ambulance to provide needle exchange services and medical help, offered first aid courses to users, and provided a separate bus for prostitutes. The police maintained their policy of apprehending dealers but initiated a new policy of tolerating an open scene within a clearly defined area of one of the parks. These activities were carried out along with efforts to draw users away from the drug scene by providing accommodations and treatment centers outside the city center. These efforts proved successful, and in 1992, the park drug scene was shut down. The policy has led to a significant reduction in the number of homeless drug users, drug-related crimes, and drug-related deaths in the city (Schneider, 1993, 1996).

Toleration and regulation of open drug scenes and apartment dealers are forms of informal control similar to those used to regulate illegal prostitution. These controls are also compatible with the philosophy of community policing. In addition, local residents are chiefly concerned about the safety and peacefulness of their neighborhoods, not with drug use itself. Public health and social service workers find that it is easier to provide services when drug scenes are readily accessible and relatively static.

Alcohol Programs

Moderate drinking programs. One means of reducing the harms associated with alcohol is to teach people to consume alcohol in a moderate or sensible manner. A number of programs have been designed for problem drinkers. These programs are targeted toward people for whom drinking seriously interferes with life in such ways as disrupting close relationships, causing health concerns, and impairing driving.

Standard drink labels. One means of reducing drug-related harm is to provide consumers with factual information about what they are consuming so that they may better regulate their consumption. Standard-serving information involves stating the amount of ethyl alcohol in the container in relation to the amount of alcohol in a normal or standard serving. Normally, the size of the serving is chosen to correspond to the amounts of alcohol typically found in standard servings of regular-strength beer, wine, and spirits—which are often approximately equal. It has been suggested that providing standard-serving information would better enable drinkers and servers to avoid intoxication, enable drivers to be sure that they are below the legal blood alcohol level for driving, and assist anyone who wished to drink at levels defined as "low risk" by health experts. Standard-serving information in terms of grams of alcohol has been introduced in Australia. Standard unit information has already been introduced on a voluntary basis by Australian wine producers and a chain of grocery stores in the United Kingdom.

Server intervention programs. One way to reduce the harms associated with immoderate alcohol consumption is to train servers to recognize impairment and intervene to limit it in their patrons. Studies show that trained servers are less likely to serve someone who is underage or intoxicated. The success of server training has been due to the support of the hospitality industry and the focus on the drinking environment. To date, efforts to reduce impaired driving have focused on deterrence via criminal sanctions or educational measures aimed at individual drivers. Civil liability and server training, on the other hand, are directed at situations that give rise to impaired driving.

Nicotine Policies and Programs

Harm reduction approaches to nicotine products focus on reducing the harms to the user as well as to the inhaler of secondhand smoke. They include a wide range of approaches, from policies controlling smoking in public places to delivery of nicotine through gum, patches, inhalers, and smokeless cigarettes.

Workplace policies. Workplaces in many countries have now adopted policies restricting smoking either to designated areas within the building or to the outside. These policies have been associated with a decrease in smoking in the adult population. Because several other interventions have occurred in this time period (e.g., increased taxes, aggressive education campaigns), it is difficult to determine the role that workplace policies have played in changing smoking patterns. However, these policies are clearly related to decreasing numbers of complaints pertaining to the effects of secondhand smoke.

Smoking in public places. Like workplace policies, policies restricting smoking in public places such as restaurants and shopping plazas have been accompanied by decreased levels of smoking in the adult population. For the same reasons, it is difficult to determine the extent to which these changes are a response to the specific intervention or part of an overall pattern. The clearest effects of public policies are on decreasing exposure to secondhand smoke.

Nicotine gum. Chewing gum containing low levels of nicotine has become a popular means of reducing the harms of tobacco (by elimination of smoking) while avoiding some of the withdrawal symptoms associated with cessation of cigarette use.

Nicotine patch. Nicotine patches are adhesive pads that stick to the skin and release small amounts of nicotine into the bloodstream. They are intended to reduce the withdrawal symptoms that accompany smoking cessation. Research has demonstrated that users are most successful at quitting smoking and staying off cigarettes when the patch is accompanied by some form of counseling or behavior modification. The nicotine patch addresses the physical addiction to nicotine but does not deal with the psychological and behavioral aspects of smoking. Nevertheless, it is an important tool in assisting users to reduce and even eliminate smoking, thereby reducing nicotine-related harm substantially.

Nicotine inhalers. Still in the developmental stage, this delivery system offers the benefits of a clean delivery system but the problems of ensuring delivery of safe doses remain.

Smokeless cigarettes. A tar-free cigarette was developed by at least one tobacco manufacturer in the 1960s. The product was not released onto the market, however, because the company's lawyers advised that this would alert the public to the harms caused by regular cigarettes, thereby implicating the company with respect to any future legal suits. Interest in the production of smokeless cigarettes has been renewed by the acceptance of the relationship between tar and lung cancer by the public and the courts.

Marijuana Policies

Several countries or parts thereof, including the Netherlands, South Australia, and Germany, have introduced de facto decriminalization of small amounts of cannabis as a harm reduction strategy. The main reasons put forward for marijuana law reform to decriminalize personal use and cultivation include the following:

- Laws requiring court appearances are very expensive in terms of both money and human resources, and they place extremely heavy demands on the court system. Decriminalization for personal use frees up resources that can be directed toward detecting large-scale drug traffickers and money launderers.

- A criminal conviction for using or cultivating small amounts of marijuana in private is a consequence that is out of proportion to the seriousness of the offense; it leaves large numbers of people with criminal records who might otherwise never have a record but who will be affected for life by the stigma.

- By relying on criminal prosecution procedures to deal with small-scale marijuana offenses, the law may be contributing to the belief among many young people who have experimented with marijuana that the dangers of other illicit drugs have been overstated.

- The decriminalization of marijuana use will maintain a separation of drug markets so that small-scale users will have no need to come into contact with wholesale drug dealers.

- Existing marijuana laws cause more harm to the users than the drugs themselves through erosion of civil liberties, fines, and imprisonment.

- The existing laws allow corruption in law enforcement agencies.

- A prohibitionist approach leads to an increase in the use and price of the prohibited substance and creates a market that is devoid of controls, quality, standards, and accurate information.

In each of the cases where marijuana law reform has occurred, the final decision was based on the fact that the costs associated with the existing system were seen to be too high by many segments of society, and too many people were seen as being adversely affected by the existing laws. In all of the cases where de facto decriminalization of marijuana has occurred, reduced financial and social costs were achieved without an increase in the risks to the community associated with drug use in general. Other, longer-term benefits have stemmed from the separation of high- and low-risk drug markets.

BARRIERS TO HARM REDUCTION

There are numerous barriers to both the policy and practice of harm reduction in many countries. One of the main barriers to the adoption of nonprohibitionist policies is idealism. Adopting harm reduction means accepting that some harm is inevitable, whereas the zero tolerance approach of the United States is an example of a policy that, by definition, excludes all compromise (cf. Hawks, 1993). Canada, like the United States, has inherited the abstentionist morality where total abstinence is seen as the only acceptable goal of treatment for "abuse" of legal drugs and the only acceptable normal state with respect to illicit drugs. In North America, the drug war mentality has built additional serious barriers: Any seeming support for drug users has been construed by some as support for drug use. Although realism and pragmatism of the harm reduction approach would view total elimination of harm as unlikely, to seek to reduce harm does not preclude the elimination of harm; idealism and harm reduction are not mutually exclusive.

Society's failure to accept drug use as a legitimate form of risk taking poses a significant barrier. Whereas societies tolerate and even encourage some forms of risk that are associated with much greater likelihood of harm than drug use (such as car racing, mountain climbing, and jet-skiing), harm reduction is viewed as promoting something that is necessarily bad and evil.

Another barrier is that of the relative ease of applying the different approaches. The supply reduction approach is the easiest to apply because in the current political climate, it has more support than does harm reduction.

Religious and other beliefs that hold that people should be punished for committing sins against morality stand in the way of harm reduction. AIDS and other drug-related harms are viewed as just deserts (as long as they are someone else's problem).

Another obstacle is an increasing distrust in paternalism and state control (cf. Hawks, 1993). More and more, the state is seen as having no role in controlling health except for that of providing information and leaving the rest to the individual. Objections to intervention of the state undermine some harm reduction efforts, such as the removal of alcohol tariff barriers in the European Economic

Community and the General Agreement on Tariffs and Trade. Thus, harm reduction efforts are falling behind as economic issues become of greater concern and social and environmental programs take second place.

Legal barriers, such as paraphernalia and other drug laws, can stand in the way of harm reduction. In some cases, these barriers are more perceived than real. In such cases, rewriting of the relevant legislation to explicitly allow for syringe exchanges would make it easier for communities all over to open sites. In many other cases, however, the barriers of legislation are very real indeed: In Canada, for example, despite claims to have a harm reduction drug strategy, the primary mode of response to drug problems is still criminalization. To decrease this barrier to harm reduction, we need to change either the laws on drug use, or the enforcement of these laws, or both. Where current laws and policies do act as barriers, enabling strategies can sometimes be put into place that allow these barriers to be effectively overcome so that, for example, condoms or clean needles are still made available (see Tawil, Verster, & O'Reilly, 1995, for a review).

Another impediment is lack of public education regarding the nature and effects of drug policy. For example, one of the chief obstacles in setting up a syringe exchange is lack of public education on injection drug use and AIDS. Once the public is aware that syringe exchanges help to significantly reduce the spread of AIDS, they are much more supportive of them (although not in their own backyards).

The lack of treatment and other services for drug users in many countries stands in the way of significant progress in the area of harm reduction. This criticism is particularly true of our correctional systems. Until more user-friendly services are available, we are unlikely to be able to put harm reduction into practice, and we will continue to be hypocritical in our overall approach to drug users. To maximize contact with drug users, services can no longer afford to work only with those who seek to stop using drugs. It has been estimated that only 5% to 10% of the drug-using population is prepared to consider entering an abstinence-oriented program at any time. Clearly, we have to find ways to work with the other 90%.

With respect to prescribing drugs, it is indeed unfortunate that the kinds of prescribing options available in the United Kingdom are available in so very few countries. The majority of countries have said "no" to prescribing as a viable option, although the AIDS crisis is causing a number of them to reevaluate the situation.

CONCLUSION

The popularity of harm reduction on an international scale is evidenced by the increasing support for the International Conference on the Reduction of Drug

Related Harm, now in its tenth year, and by the recent formation of the International Harm Reduction Association (IHRA). Despite the increase in popularity among workers in the field, many health and addiction agencies in North America and elsewhere remain ambivalent about harm reduction as it pertains to alcohol and other drugs. Some have positioned it closer to primary prevention and demand reduction, thus avoiding its more controversial applications.

Harm reduction raises some difficult questions, but it is evident that debating these questions openly is better than ignoring them, as has been done all too often in the past. Comprehensive harm reduction programs that are culturally sensitive are necessary; harm reduction must be multifaceted, not just a singular intervention. The data regarding such drug-related consequences as AIDS make it clear that we need a long-term plan for harm reduction. Risk reduction is a social process; it is not something that public health officials can impose. An effective program must provide multiple means for behavior change and needs to be conducted on a long-term basis.

Although effective in reducing a number of the negative consequences associated with drug use, harm reduction has several limitations:

- The development and promotion of harm reduction strategies has to take into account the particular drug problem prevalent in a community, as well as the ethnic, socioeconomic, and legal characteristics of that community, or they will have limited applicability. For example, methadone maintenance programs are not applicable to stimulant problems. In these cases, other measures, such as ready access to clean equipment or distribution of stimulants in a noninjectable form, might be more effective.

- New interventions must be designed to reach all segments of the drug-using population. For example, at present, needle exchanges have had less success attracting young or female IDUs than older males. They are also less effective at reducing high-risk behavior in constituencies where greater legal restrictions apply.

- Harm reduction for injection drug use results in increased use of clean needles but not of condoms, and so, obviously, it cannot prevent sexual transmission of HIV (Stimson, 1997). In many communities around the world, the rate of increase in heterosexual AIDS has equaled or overtaken the rate for injection drug use-related AIDS.

- Harm reduction approaches are used mainly in the developed world. To be truly effective on a global level, they need to be applied in developing countries and to rich and poor alike.

As noted above, the most obvious question raised by the harm reduction approach is the meaning of the term *harm* itself. In deciding what constitutes harm, which are to be reduced, and in what order, scientific, political, moral, and other factors are obviously brought to bear. There are as many applications of harm reduction as there are harms to be reduced, but one person's harm may be another's benefit—and there's the rub. It would be all too easy for the harms that are selected for reduction to become only society's harms and not those of the individual and the community as well. Indeed, there are many who believe that sending drug users to jail is a form of harm reduction. We need to clarify the nature of the harm reduction approach sufficiently in order to prevent such arbitrary designation. At the same time, we must be careful that harm reduction does not get taken over by the temperance mentality, of which it is but an extension (why *harm* reduction and not *benefit* augmentation?). In so doing, we must be careful that the harms to be reduced are those that are truly relevant and not, as has happened all too often in the past, just those that are politically or morally correct. Harm reduction, in the final analysis, is concerned with ensuring the quality and integrity of human life in all of its wonderful, awful complexity. Harm reduction does not portray issues as polarities but sees them as they really are: somewhere in between. It is an approach that takes into account the continuum of drug use and the diversity of drugs, as well as of human needs. As such, there are no clear-cut answers or quick solutions. Harm reduction, then, is based on pragmatism, tolerance, and diversity. In short, it is both a product and a measure of our humanity. Harm reduction is as much about human rights as it is about the right to be human.

REFERENCES

Advisory Council on the Misuse of Drugs. (1988). *AIDS and drug misuse* (Part 1). London: HMSO.

Advisory Council on the Misuse of Drugs. (1989). *AIDS and drug misuse* (Part 2). London: HMSO.

Ball, J. C., & Ross, A. (1991). *The effectiveness of methadone maintenance treatment.* New York: Springer-Verlag.

Berridge, V. (1993). Harm reduction and public health: An historical perspective. In N. Heather, A. Wodak, E. Nadelmann, & P. O'Hare (Eds.), *Psychoactive drugs and harm reduction: From faith to science* (pp. 55-64). London: Whurr.

Brettle, R. P. (1991). HIV and harm reduction for injection drug users. *AIDS, 5,* 125-136.

Buning, E. (1990). The role of harm reduction programmes in curbing the spread of HIV by drug injectors. In J. Strang & G. V. Stimson (Eds.), *AIDS and drug misuse* (pp. 153-161). London: Routledge.

Buning, E. (1993, March). Presentation made at St. Lawrence Forum on harm reduction, Toronto.

Buning, E., van Brussel, G. H., & van Santen, G. (1988). Amsterdam's drug policy and its implications for controlling needle sharing. In *Needle sharing among intravenous drug abusers: National and international perspectives* (NIDA Research Monograph 80, pp. 59-74). Rockville, MD: NIDA.

Buning, E., Coutinho, R. A., van Brussel, G. H., et al. (1986). Preventing AIDS in drug addicts in Amsterdam. *Lancet, i,* 1435.

Centers for Disease Control and Prevention. (1993, April 19). *HIV/AIDS Prevention Bulletin.* Atlanta, GA: Author.

Dole, V. P. (1989). Methadone treatment and the AIDS epidemic. *Journal of the American Medical Association, 262,* 1681-1682.

Drucker, E. (1986). AIDS and addiction in New York City. *American Journal of Drug and Alcohol Abuse, 12,* 165-181.

Erickson, P. (1992, Summer). Political pharmacology: Thinking about drugs. *Daedalus,* pp. 239-267.

Fazey, C. S. J. (1992). Heroin addiction, crime and treatment. In P. A. O'Hare, R. Newcombe, A. Mathews, E. C. Buning, & E. Drucker (Eds.), *The reduction of drug-related harm* (pp. 154-161). New York: Routledge.

Gossop, M. (1978). Review of the evidence for methadone maintenance as a treatment for narcotic addiction. *Lancet, i,* 812-815.

Haemig, R. (1997, March). *The Swiss heroin trials: The second intermediary report.* Paper presented at the Eighth International Conference on the Reduction of Drug Related Harm, Paris.

Hart, G. J., Carvell, A. L. M., Woodward, N., et al. (1989). Evaluation of needle exchanges in central London: Behaviour change and anti-HIV status over 1 year. *AIDS, 3,* 261-265.

Hawks, D. (1993). Impediments to the adoption of harm reduction policies. In N. Heather, A. Wodak, E. Nadelmann, & P. O'Hare (Eds.), *Psychoactive drugs and harm reduction: From faith to science* (pp. 93-102). London: Whurr.

Heather, N., Wodak, A., Nadelmann, E., & O'Hare, P. (Eds.). (1993). *Psychoactive drugs and harm reduction: From faith to science.* London: Whurr.

HIT. (1996). *Reducing drug related harm in the Mersey region.* Liverpool, UK: Author.

Jurgens, R. (1996). *HIV/AIDS in prisons: Final report.* Montreal: Canadian HIV/AIDS Legal Network and Canadian AIDS Society.

Jurgens, R., & Riley, D. (1997). Responding to AIDS and drug use in prisons in Canada. *International Journal of Drug Policy, 8*(1), 31-39.

Kirby, J. (1996, July). *Opening address.* The Harm Reduction Satellite to the XIth International Conference on AIDS, Vancouver, BC.

Lurie, P., & Drucker, E. (1997). An opportunity lost: HIV infections associated with the lack of a national needle-exchange program in the United States. *Lancet, 349,* 604-608.

Lurie, P., & Reingold, A. L. (Eds.). (1993). *The public health impact of needle exchange programs in the United States and abroad.* Berkeley: University of California Press.

Merseyside Police Force. (1990). *Responsible demand enforcement: A summary.* Unpublished report. Liverpool, UK: Author.

Nadelmann, E. (1993). Progressive legalizers, progressive prohibitionists and the reduction of drug-related harm. In N. Heather, A. Wodak, E. Nadelmann, & P. O'Hare (Eds.), *Psychoactive drugs and harm reduction: From faith to science* (pp. 34-35). London: Whurr.

Nadelmann, E. (1995). Beyond needle park: The Swiss maintenance trial. *The Drug Policy Letter, 27,* 12-14.

Newcombe, R. (1992). The reduction of drug-related harm: A conceptual framework for theory, practice and research. In P. A. O'Hare, R. Newcombe, A. Matthews, E. C. Buning, & E. Drucker (Eds.), *The reduction of drug-related harm* (pp. 1-14). New York: Routledge.

Newman, R. G. (1976). Methadone maintenance: It ain't what it used to be. *British Journal of Addiction, 71,* 183-186.

Newman, R. G. (1987). Methadone treatment. *New England Journal of Medicine, 317,* 447-450.

O'Hare, P. A. (1992). Preface: A note on the concept of harm reduction. In P. A. O'Hare, R. Newcombe, A. Matthews, E. C. Buning, & E. Drucker (Eds.), *The reduction of drug-related harm.* New York: Routledge.

Palombella, A. (1990). Prescribing of smokeable drugs. *International Journal of Drug Policy, 1,* 31.

Rana, S. (1996). Harm reduction in Asia. *AHRN Newsletter, 1,* 4-6.

Rhodes, T., Myers, T., Bueno, R., Millson, R., & Hunter, G. (1998). Drug injecting and sexual safety. In G. Stimson, D. Des Jarlais, & A. Ball (Eds.), *Drug injection and HIV infection* (pp. 130-148). London: University College London.

Riley, D. M. (1993). *The policy and practice of harm reduction.* Ottawa, Canada: CCSA.

Riley, D. M. (1994). *The harm reduction model.* Toronto: The Harm Reduction Network.

Riley, D. M. (1995). Methadone and HIV/AIDS. *Canadian HIV/AIDS Policy & Law Newsletter, 2,* 1-14.

Riley, D. M. (1996). Drug testing in prisons. *International Journal of Drug Policy, 6*(2), 106-111.

Riley, D. M., Sawka, E., Connley, P., Hewitt, D., Poulin, C., Room, R., Single, S., & Topp, J. (1999). Harm reduction: Concepts and practice. *Substance Use and Misuse 34*(1), 9-24.

Riley, D. M., & Oscapella, E. (1997). Canada's new drug law: Some implications for HIV/AIDS prevention in Canada. *International Journal of Drug Policy, 7*(3), 180-182.

Robertson, J. R. (1990). The Edinburgh epidemic: A case study. In J. Strang & G. V. Stimson (Eds.), *AIDS and drug misuse* (pp. 95-107). London: Routledge.

Schneider, W. (1993). How my city charted a new drug policy course. *The Drug Policy Letter, 21,* 7-9.

Schneider, W. (1996, July). Presentation at the Harm Reduction Satellite of the XIth International Conference on AIDS, Vancouver, BC.

Springer, E. (1990). AIDS prevention with drug users supplanted by the war on drugs, or what happens when you don't use harm reduction models. *International Journal on Drug Policy, 2,* 18-21.

Stimson, G. V. (1989). Syringe exchange programs for injecting drug users. *AIDS, 3,* 253-260.

Stimson, G. V. (1997, March). *Harm reduction in practice: How the UK avoided an epidemic of HIV infection in drug injectors.* Paper presented at the Eighth International Conference on the Reduction of Drug Related Harm, Paris.

Stimson, G. V., Alldritt, L., Dolan, K., et al. (1988). *Injecting equipment exchange schemes.* Final report. London: Monitoring Research Group, Goldsmiths' College.

Stroneburner, R. L., DesJarlais, D. C., Benezra, D., et al. (1989). A larger spectrum of severe HIV-1 related disease in intravenous drug users in New York City. *Science, 242,* 916-918.

Tawil, O., Verster, A., & O'Reilly, K. R. (1995). Enabling approaches for HIV/AIDS prevention: Can we modify the environment and minimize the risk? *AIDS, 9,* 1299-1306.

van den Hoek, J. A. R., van Haastrecht, H. J. A., & Coutinho, R. A. (1989). Risk reduction among intravenous drug users in Amsterdam under the influence of AIDS. *American Journal of Public Health, 79,* 1355-1357.

Wille, R. (1983). Processes of recovery from heroin dependence: Relationship to treatment, social change and drug use. *Drug Issues, 13,* 333-342.

Wodak, A. (1990). AIDS and injecting drug use in Australia: A case control study in policy development and implementation. In J. Strang & G. V. Stimson (Eds.), *AIDS and drug misuse* (pp. 132-141). London: Routledge.

Wodak, A. (1996, July). *Harm reduction works.* Paper presented at the Harm Reduction Satellite to the XIth International Conference on AIDS, Vancouver, BC.

World Health Organization. (1986). *Consultation on AIDS among drug abusers.* Stockholm: World Health Organization Regional Office for Europe.

World Health Organization. (1989). *The uses of methadone in the treatment and management of opioid dependence.* Geneva: Author.

World Health Organization. (1990). *The content and structure of methadone treatment programs: A study in six countries.* Geneva: Author.

2

From Morphine to Methadone: Maintenance Drugs in the Treatment of Opiate Addiction

Ernest Drucker

By the end of the 19th century, millions of Americans and Europeans were regularly using patent medicines, tonics, salves, potions, and commercially available beverages containing some combination of opiates, cocaine, and alcohol (Berridge & Edwards, 1987; Courtwright, 1985; Musto, 1987). These substances were the frontline medicines of the time—almost universally prescribed by doctors and sold over the counter by pharmacists to remedy a wide range of real and imagined maladies and to treat the pain of injuries and chronic illnesses. Their psychoactive properties were also well recognized and exploited to relieve sleep disturbances, anxiety, and depression. These drugs had been known to have these beneficial effects for centuries—in some cases (such as alcohol), for

AUTHOR'S NOTE: The author would like to thank Ethan Nadelmann and the Lindesmith Center/ Open Society Institute for their generous support of my work, as well as the members and friends of the Princeton Working Group on Drug Policy for their productive inspiration and clarity on this very complex business. And a special thanks to Norman Zinberg, who bothered to come to the Bronx, and to Andy Weil, whose books *The Natural Mind* and *From Chocolate to Morphine* both served as a model of clear thinking and writing about drugs and (obviously, in the latter case) as a basis of this chapter's title.

millennia—and they were among the few effective tools of early medical practice.

The great 19th-century advances of chemistry spawned the modern pharmaceutical industry (aspirin was discovered and marketed as the first "wonder drug" in 1897), and this industry quickly turned its attention to the old botanical products already in such wide use. These were reprocessed and made more widely available in highly refined and far more potent forms—among them morphine and heroin (refined from opium poppies) and cocaine (from coca leaves). In both Europe and America, these products were heavily promoted, and they quickly developed huge markets because little else was available and they had such a powerful effect on symptoms—especially the opiates for pain (as they still do). But with increased use of these potent drugs, both within and outside medicine, came growing public awareness of their addictive qualities.

This growing awareness of the addictive potential of narcotics led governments to begin to regulate their production and sales. This was done with a view to continuing their useful role in medicine (e.g., as painkillers) but eliminating the open market in the many commercial products containing them. However, although the professed goal of the new drug regulations associated with the Pure Food and Drug Act (1906) and the Harrison Narcotics Act (1914) was to retain narcotics' still singular medical benefits and minimize the problem of addiction, these regulations quickly became part of a campaign for the prohibition of all drugs.

The same period also saw a surge of popular revulsion at the problem of addiction and growing hostility toward the addict—a demonization of drugs and those who used them. These sentiments were engendered and vigorously stoked by the lurid pulp journalism of the late Victorian age, with its overheated moralistic tales of "enslavement and depravity" associated with drug use, often with racial stereotypes of drug users (e.g., the Chinese and opium). It was also a period of moral crusades aimed at extirpating all sorts of "sinful" behavior from American society. Complicating matters further, these moral campaigns were also part of a powerful (and mostly positive) historical movement of the Progressive era, promoting social betterment and public health—ideas we take for granted in developed societies, even if we often have difficulty acting upon them.

ADDICTION

Although the word *addiction* does not appear in medical usage until the mid 19th century, by that time, millions of Americans and Europeans were habitual users of these substances, and many were considered dependent on them (Berridge & Edwards, 1987; Courtwright, 1985). Although this group represented only a minority of all those who used these drugs, even of those who used them often, "drug addicts" (generally a pejorative term) came to occupy the most prominent place in the public debate about drugs. It was clear that dependent individuals not only used a given drug to relieve the symptoms of illness and for the beneficial effects they undoubtedly produced as painkillers, stimulants, and mood alterers, but they also came to require their regular use in order to maintain a sense of well-being, to "feel themselves." And, in the absence of these drugs, these dependent users suffered prolonged anxiety, restlessness, sleep disturbance, and other symptoms we now call withdrawal or the "abstinence syndrome." Sometimes called "chemical dependency," drug addiction today is defined in the standard textbooks and diagnostic manuals of both medicine and psychiatry as a *disease* (American Psychiatric Association, 1995; WHO, 1995).

THE DISEASE CONCEPT OF ADDICTION

We now know that addictive phenomena are associated with certain drug actions within the nervous system and changes that occur in the regulation of the information that nerve signals carry—known as neurotransmission (Gardner, 1997). Biologically speaking, addiction may be understood as a disorder of neurotransmission associated with the effects of such drugs (including alcohol and tobacco) on particular parts of the brain. These areas normally produce similar substances, at minute levels, that are natural versions (called ligands) of most psychoactive drugs (e.g., endorphins)—a form of the opiates. Alterations of neurotransmission involving these ligands appear to form the basis for all of the long-term and short-term effects associated with externally administered psychoactive drugs. And, in the case of addiction (according to researcher Elliot Gardner), these drugs may hijack our natural systems and begin to alter the complex and subtle processes that normally regulate neurotransmission. These changes can endure for years, and the long-lasting (chronic) nature of addiction is one of its hallmarks. This can be seen in the tenaciousness of even self-destructive drug use that the addict sincerely wishes to stop, the great difficulty many people have in stopping, and the persistence of a felt need for the drug even after periods of complete cessation—often leading to a return to drug use (relapse).

The disease model of addiction includes the development of a very specific set of problems often associated with the regular use of certain drugs; chief among them are tolerance, withdrawal, and craving (Lowinson, Ruiz, Millman, & Langrod, 1997).

Tolerance. With the regular use of an addictive drug, some people need more and more of the drug to produce the same effect or, conversely, get less of an effect from the same dose. When opiates are used as painkillers for a long period, it is frequently necessary to increase the dose to produce the same analgesic effect. The regular coffee drinker may develop tolerance to caffeine and drink several cups at night without affecting his or her sleep, whereas the nontolerant coffee drinker will be up all night from a single espresso; likewise for the ciga- rette smoker who develops tolerance to nicotine and smokes several packs a day. With illicit drugs (whose cost is high), tolerance drives the addict to need more of the drug and to obtain more money to get enough of the drug just to feel nor- mal (i.e., to avoid withdrawal).

Withdrawal (abstinence syndrome). This is the other face of tolerance and a clear marker of the body's memory of drug effects. In withdrawal, a regular user reacts adversely to the absence of the drug to which he or she has become toler- ant. The withdrawal from most drugs has two phases: short term (acute) and long term (chronic). Withdrawal symptoms differ for the specific drug. The coffee drinker will experience headaches (which are quickly relieved by a cup or two), whereas the heroin addict, depending on the history of use, can suffer painful cramps, itching, sweating, and emotional jumpiness (once again reliably and quickly reversed by a dose of *any* opiate). But for most addictive drugs, the acute stage of withdrawal is characterized by a pervasive and highly distract- ing unease, often accompanied by sleep disturbance and diffuse anxiety that makes it difficult to think about much besides obtaining the drug (and instant relief). When in withdrawal, the dependent user has great difficulty in resist- ing the drug when it is available. The power of this need is formidable: Think about the cigarette smoker who will brave a winter storm to buy a pack in the middle of the night as an indication of the strength of what is often called "drug craving."

Drug craving. If addiction can be understood as a complex set of biological cues in which the body (in essence) says, "I need this drug to feel normal," crav- ing is the person's psychological experience and conscious awareness of that fact. It is perhaps the most important phenomenon of addiction because it moti- vates the addict so powerfully and for so long to use the drug in order to get re- lief. Although the use of a drug to feel at ease or to create a sense of well-being is not alien to most of us (think of the morning coffee or the social use of alcohol or cigarettes to relax), in the case of dependence, one does not feel normal without regular doses. And for illicit drugs, where society demands total abstinence and the drug is difficult and dangerous to obtain, this virtually dictates insufficient doses and frequent periods of prolonged craving.

LIMITATIONS OF THE DISEASE MODEL

But viewing addiction as a disease is a two-edged sword—useful but potentially dangerous. Its usefulness comes from the value of having a consistent physiological explanation of what are clearly powerful biological phenomena, grounded in scientific research in both pharmacology and brain functioning.

However, that is not the whole story, and our biological understanding of addiction (as a disorder of neurotransmission) does not mean that the social and psychological issues in drug use and addiction are unimportant. Indeed, in an environment freighted with powerful moral and legal reactions to the use of drugs, the stigma attached to drugs may come to be a more important factor than the biology of addiction; the demonization of drugs and the criminalization of the drug user (i.e., the war on drugs) could be more damaging to the individual and society than drug use or addiction. Despite great advances in our scientific understanding of drug actions, the view of drug use and addiction as a primarily moral (and legal) problem still persists and shapes the public discourse on their meaning. These negative perceptions powerfully determine our social and political responses to addiction—usually at the expense of the biological or disease model and of the drug user (Peele, 1990, 1993; Szasz, 1985). Thus, although the disease model may be in all of the medical textbooks, it is still not the basis of our overwhelmingly punitive response to the addict. Today, most addicts spend more time behind bars than in treatment for their "disease."

Another shortcoming of the disease model is that it easily overlooks the beneficial effects of many of the same drugs that it calls *pathogenic* (i.e., that are seen as the *cause* of the disease of addiction). Some form of drug use is virtually universal, and we often fail to distinguish between drug use and abuse or addiction. Although there is the potential for many drugs to produce adverse outcomes (among them addiction and toxic poisoning), these represent the minority of outcomes associated with even the use of some of the most powerful drugs, such as heroin and cocaine. And although the phenomena of addiction may be understood biologically in a disease model, this model is much less useful for understanding the full spectrum of drug use, which includes individual experimentation and recreational use, the highly structured and socialized patterns of psychoactive drug use seen in many tribal peoples, and the widespread use of alcohol in Western society. Even though alcohol use is generally accepted in our society today, we can still recognize that alcoholism is a disease and only a part (albeit an important part) of the normal pattern of use of this particular drug. At this time, we have difficulty accepting this broad range of patterns of use for the illicit drugs (like the opiates and marijuana), and we tend to forget that alcohol was prohibited in the United States from 1920 to 1934, a time when marijuana use was quite legal.

THE NATURAL HISTORY OF ADDICTION

Most users of most drugs do not become addicted to them. In the United States, it is estimated that more than 20 million people have tried heroin and that 40 to

50 million have tried cocaine, but fewer than 3% are current users. And even addiction itself can be understood in less pathological ways than the rather hopeless view implied in the (incurable) disease model.

Addiction may be conceptualized as a long-term process lasting 10 to 20 years with a predictable series of stages (a natural history). The good news is that the natural history of addiction tends toward reduction and often ends in cessation of use with middle age.[1] At each of these stages of addiction, there are opportunities for the affected individual to reduce or entirely cease the use of the drug—and this is what occurs in the majority of cases, even without treatment. Surprising as it may seem, even among those with prolonged use of opiates and cocaine, a favorable outcome is the norm (Courtwright, Des Jarlais, & Joseph, 1989; Reinarman & Levine, 1997; Waldorf & Biernecki, 1984; Waldorf, Reinarman, & Murphy, 1991). Accordingly, many now believe that drug treatment should be oriented to take advantage of this long-term natural history of drug use and exploit the multiple opportunities that it presents for effective intervention to help the addict through a long but finite period of "disease" with minimum harm to his or her health and social well-being.

ADDICTION TREATMENT

Early in this century, a wide range of treatments for the still poorly understood problem of addiction were considered and tried, but with little success—dependence on opiates appearing particularly intractable. Soon, it became clear that once dependency had been established, doing without these drugs was extremely difficult for many regular users. Thus began the search for medications and strategies for using them that might loosen the bonds of addiction.

At first, doctors tried to deal with the most apparent symptoms of acute withdrawal by prescribing gradually reducing doses of opiates over a period of weeks or months. The goal here was to soften the most unpleasant symptoms of acute withdrawal as the individual moved toward an abstinent state. This is called short-term detoxification (or tapering), and it is still an important tool for helping addicts gain control over their levels of use; it is also the most common form of initial treatment. Today, we are accustomed to celebrities entering expensive rehab centers (like The Betty Ford Center) for a few weeks to dry out and clear the drugs from their system. Often, detoxification is a prelude to attempts at drug-free treatment. But as often as not, relapse occurs, and the entire cycle recurs. Thus, although this approach can help those who have a life situation supportive of abstinence and can lessen the size and destructive potential of a drug habit, it is often inadequate in the longer term to prevent craving and a return to regular use of illicit drugs, especially in the case of the long-term user of opiates.

THE CONCEPT OF NARCOTIC MAINTENANCE

Among the very first approaches attempted for long-term treatment of dependency to opiates was the provision of controlled dosages of some form of the addictive drug itself. On the face of it, giving an opiate to one already addicted to its use seems a contradiction—"like giving alcohol to an alcoholic," some say. But this analogy does not really apply to opiate addiction. Unlike alcohol (which, in sufficient dosages, almost always adversely affects the individual's health and well-being), the opiates are not themselves physiologically damaging. Indeed, it is hard to make a case for opiates as pathogens: They cause no direct harm to any major organ system, nor do they affect mental functioning adversely if taken in the right dosages. Therefore, instead of limiting our treatment goal to abstinence, we may ask if it is possible for the opiate addict to continue to take some form of opiates on a regular basis. And if there is a natural history of opiate addiction that tends toward reduction and eventual cessation of use after many years, what may we do to ease this passage and reduce the health and social risks associated with the dependency on illicit drugs?

Despite much posturing about addiction as a moral weakness (whose sole remedy is abstinence), one alternate solution has been to reorient drug treatment toward better managing the natural course of addiction through the use of safer maintenance drugs rather than attempting to stop drug use altogether. In this approach, the goal of addiction treatment is primarily interrupting or reversing the pathological social processes that go along with heavy use of an illicit substance and eliminating the damaging consequences of an endless cycle of withdrawal and drug craving (i.e., reducing drugs' harm rather than ending their use).

Maintenance treatment attempts to replace more dangerous illegal drugs with safer legal ones that are medically prescribed. Maintenance can interrupt the progressively worsening processes of addiction by permitting the drug-dependent individual to end his or her reliance on illicit drug markets (with all of their dangers), and it can effectively neutralize the most negative physiological aspects of addiction—the endless cycles of craving and avoidance of withdrawal. Maintenance can permit addicts to get on with their lives even though their addiction has not been "cured."

Long-term maintenance treatment using medications similar to the substances to which the individual is addicted (opioids) is aimed at achieving permanent abstinence from *illicit* opiates by transferring the dependency to a more readily controlled dosage and safer forms of legal opiates. In addition to reduced reliance on more dangerous illicit drugs, effective drug maintenance also reduces the individual's exposure to the legal risks associated with obtaining them and the health risks from illicit use of drugs of unknown purity and potency (with the dangers of overdose) and use of unsterile injecting equipment. Most heroin addicts in the United States and Europe inject the drug, and sharing needles spreads infectious diseases like AIDS and hepatitis.

NARCOTIC MAINTENANCE IN PRACTICE

In Great Britain and the United States, some doctors recognized the value of this approach and instituted narcotic maintenance treatment early in the century. The British medical profession, under the leadership of Sir Humphrey Rolleston, President of the Royal College of Physicians, took pains to articulate a set of principles for the medical provision of opiates as a humane approach to "incurable" addiction. In 1926, they set up a Royal Commission that established the right of British practitioners to prescribe any and all drugs (including heroin in its injectable form) to their patients who were addicted and unable to cease all use on their own. This British system served them well for more than 40 years until changes in the drug scene of the 1960s led to its revision and the institution of greater controls. However, in the face of the AIDS epidemic, even the Conservative government of Margaret Thatcher saw the wisdom in maintenance programs and loosened the reins on medical prescribing, which led to a threefold increase in narcotic prescribing in Great Britain. This and other public health measures (such as needle exchange) may account for the low rate of HIV infection among heroin addicts in Britain for the past 10 years—less than 10% of the U.S. rates.

By contrast, in the United States, the drug maintenance approach has a troubled past, and the historical role of the American medical profession was less laudatory. In part, this was because American doctors were, at the time, members of a much lower-prestige profession than we know today. Furthermore, the medical profession was in large part held responsible for the problem of addiction in this country. No less a personage than Supreme Court Justice Oliver Wendell Holmes (writing in 1856) blamed the drug problem on the "constant prescription of opiates by certain doctors" (Musto, 1987, p. 328). Although many American practitioners (out of a humane motive) quietly provided these drugs to their patients as needed, others (often referred to as "dope doctors" and regularly vilified in the press) exploited these same patients' dependency, reaped substantial profits, and discredited the approach. Nevertheless, in the period from 1914 to 1924, some morphine maintenance programs were established in the United States in Shreveport, Louisiana; Jacksonville, Florida; and in New York City, where more than 7,000 patients were dispensed narcotic drugs under the auspices of the city's prestigious Department of Health.

But the general public reaction to this approach was negative, and soon, American medicine sought to distance the profession from narcotic maintenance and from the problem of addiction altogether. In 1910, the American Medical Association (still in its infancy) described the provision of drugs to the addict as "immoral" and declared the condition outside of its responsibility. Accordingly, the Harrison Act (passed in 1914 to regulate the manufacture and sale of narcotics) was soon interpreted as banning the medical prescription of opiates as addiction treatment. And this view, when challenged by concerned practitioners, was upheld in the U.S. Supreme Court throughout the 1920s. The effect was to outlaw this form of medical practice and to shut down the still young and inexperienced drug maintenance treatment programs that had begun to emerge in this country.

Just as medicine became the sole legitimate source of narcotic drugs (and their previous wide public availability began to contract dramatically in the early years of the 20th century), doctors began to shy away from prescribing narcotics outside of a very narrow range of uses as painkillers. And even there, narcotics were often prescribed at inadequate doses, which is a problem that perseveres in the medical use of opiates to this day and is one of the most troubling legacies of the old negative association of medicine with these important drugs.

METHADONE

It was not until 40 years later that we would see a reemergence of these old ideas of drug maintenance treatment within U.S. medical practice and the rediscovery and legitimation of maintenance treatment. In part, this change was due to renewed alarm about the heroin "epidemic" of the 1960s, where, for the first time in modern memory, heroin use moved out of the sequestered ethnic groups and the artistic urban bohemian subculture and jazz scenes that had for decades characterized drug use in American society. Working in New York's Harlem, Dr. Marie Nyswander (a young psychiatrist and jazz fan) was trying to help her addict patients, often prescribing (unorthodoxly) various opiate compounds to help them gain control of their use of illicit heroin. She was soon joined by Dr. Vincent Dole, a well-respected metabolic researcher at the prestigious Rockefeller University and New York Hospital. Together, they pioneered the use of a particular form of synthetic opiate, called Levoacytal (methadol, or methadone), for narcotic maintenance.

Methadone is a synthetic drug having the same basic molecular structure as heroin and all naturally occurring opiates. As a long-term maintenance drug, however, methadone has two important advantages over heroin that make it well suited for maintenance prescription: It can be given orally, and it is long lasting—24 to 36 hours for a single dose, compared to 2 to 3 hours for heroin (Ball & Ross, 1991; Newman, 1977).

A series of careful studies of methadone maintenance soon demonstrated that it did not lead to escalating tolerance and could therefore be used to achieve a stable daily dose without the ups and downs of shorter-acting opiates like heroin or morphine—especially when these are taken in uncertain doses and unpredictable schedules. This meant that a single daily oral dose of an inexpensive medication could eliminate withdrawal, narcotic craving, and the destructive need for illegal heroin. Importantly, in the proper dose for an already tolerant user, methadone did not produce intoxication (a high). This permitted relatively normal functioning, despite the fact that the user was taking large daily doses of a narcotic that would affect a nontolerant individual profoundly, perhaps even lethally.

Given the American medical profession's long antagonism to maintenance prescribing, the initial demonstration of the clinical efficacy of methadone had to convince the most skeptical of audiences. Accordingly, the first clinical trials of methadone selected the worst cases: several hundred heroin addicts who had tried every other option and failed repeatedly to become drug free. Most had 10 years or more of addiction, five or more previous treatment failures, and a multitude of problems linked to the criminalization of their addiction (i.e., long prison records, failed work histories, and shattered families). If methadone could help these hard-core addicts, it was reasoned, it would be taken seriously in America.

The initial results were spectacular—more than 90% retention in treatment and the virtual cessation of heroin use. The first was critical because staying in the program is the necessary prerequisite to a positive outcome in any form of chronic treatment. Second, these patients' maintenance on methadone made the use of illicit opiates unnecessary, and the use of street heroin quickly dropped to virtually zero. At the levels of methadone dosage used in maintenance (60 to 120 mgs per day), the corresponding level of tolerance meant that street doses of heroin (generally smaller in dose) had little effect and would be a waste of money. After a few attempts to use heroin, methadone patients quickly came to realize that because their narcotic tolerance had adjusted to the often higher dosages and regular administration of methadone, a "narcotic blockade" had been created, and they stopped buying and using heroin. Arrest rates dropped precipitously because there was no longer a need to engage in acquisitive crime to get money for illicit drugs. More critically, as they began to relocate their source of drugs from the street drug scene to the clinic, and shift their dependency from illegal to prescribed drugs, addicts began to reorient their lives away from drug seeking and back to the worlds of family, work, and the community (i.e., to "get a life").

The landmark clinical trial of methadone maintenance (first published in the *Journal of the American Medical Association* in 1964) captured widespread public attention. This led to its rapid acceptance and to a certain amount of oversell (i.e., methadone as a miracle cure). But the results of Nyswander and Dole's first series of clinical studies firmly established methadone maintenance as safe, effective, and feasible for large-scale implementation—indeed, this success was recognized by the award of the prestigious Lasker prize for its discovery. In the late 1960s, the United States saw a rapid expansion of methadone maintenance treatment programs, with clinics opening in dozens of cities and more than 75,000 patients in treatment by 1975 (115,000 by 1992). Today, methadone is the preeminent and (still) most successful treatment for heroin addiction, ending 40 years of therapeutic "nihilism" about addiction treatment in this country.

HOW METHADONE TREATMENT WORKS

The Patients

Methadone treatment is meant for adults who have used opiates continuously for at least 2 years and wish to stop its use. Most commonly, heroin is the drug upon which they have become dependent, but methadone is appropriate treatment for dependency to any narcotic (Preston, 1996; Ward, Mattick, & Hall, 1992).

The Treatment Program

In the United States, methadone treatment is organized around specialized methadone maintenance treatment programs (MMTPs), which are clinics (both public and private) that treat anywhere from 100 to 700 patients. These methadone clinics are mandated by federal and state regulations to provide counseling and social services, and some (a minority) also provide medical services. However, the main business is getting each patient the correct daily dose of methadone. Although methadone is long lasting (relative to heroin), missing a day's dose (or two) will destabilize a patient's blood level of the drug and may precipitate withdrawal. Accordingly, reliable access to the medication at the correct dose is the essential feature of methadone maintenance. Patients generally come into the clinic between one and seven times per week (the average is three to four), where they take the day's dose and get take-home doses for the other days of the week.

New patients' dosages are slowly built up over a few days or weeks to maintenance levels that may vary depending on the level of use of opiates on the street in the previous period of use and metabolic differences between individuals. The recommended minimal dose (by the FDA and NIDA) is 60 mg per day. The pharmacological objective is to find and establish a stable blood level of methadone such that the patient is neither too high (intoxicated) nor too low (in withdrawal). Study after study indicates clearly that when this proper dosage level is found and maintained, there is a precipitous and enduring decrease in heroin use.

Effect on the Abuse of Other Drugs

Methadone has no directly analogous effect on drugs other than the opiates, but by helping the heroin addict to leave the drug scene, the use of methadone often leads to reduction in use of or abstinence from other drugs. However, the heroin addict on methadone can still use cocaine or alcohol or marijuana and experience their effects fully. Random urine tests (originally used to verify that the patient was, in fact, taking his or her methadone) have come to be used to detect the concurrent use of other illicit drugs; in the United States, concurrent use can be grounds for dismissal from treatment and withdrawal from methadone.

Medical Care

Methadone is a potent narcotic, and careful monitoring and a close clinical relationship between doctor and patient is essential to its proper use. Side effects may include sweating, constipation, and sexual dysfunction—all of which are also evident in heroin use—and the prescribing physician must be sensitive to the patient's experience with the medication and be prepared to alter dosage as needed. Methadone may be safely continued during pregnancy, but there is some disagreement over dosages. However, reflecting a widespread belief by both women in treatment and many of the caregivers (who should know better) that more methadone is "bad," some expectant mothers are persuaded to cut down their dose—a decision that often leads to using other, more dangerous drugs to compensate for the inadequate dosage of methadone. The many medical problems associated with heroin addiction dictate a closer integration of methadone treatment with routine and specialized medical care. For example, modern AIDS care involves complex and changing medical needs, and some of the most common tuberculosis drugs appear to affect the metabolism of methadone (which is highly variable from individual to individual anyway). For example, patients taking one tuberculosis drug (Rifampin) may need their methadone dosage doubled.

Ending Methadone Treatment

At the present time, we have no medical cure for addiction (in the narrow, biological sense). But methadone is a vastly preferable way to take a class of drugs upon which so many are dependent, thus allowing users to live normal lives and to stop using heroin. From this perspective, getting off methadone is *not* a goal of methadone treatment, any more than getting a successfully managed diabetic off a regime of insulin is the correct treatment goal for that condition. Studies following even the most successful methadone patients (i.e., those who have readjusted to community life, job, and family) have determined that many of these patients relapse to use of heroin—experiencing debilitating craving despite years of successful maintenance and very gradual tapering off. This is a testament to the long and tenacious grip of opiate addiction. On the other hand, fully 25% of admissions to methadone treatment are individuals who have been in methadone treatment in the past—often several times. In New York State, which has more than 40,000 patients in an MMTP system established in the 1960s, more than 120,000 different patients have used methadone at some point in their long struggle with opiate addiction. This suggests that, over time, many methadone patients do, in fact, become drug free, using methadone as a tool for achieving total abstinence from opiates. This is powerful evidence of the eventual assertion of the natural history of addiction and its trend toward reduction of dependency with age.

SNATCHING DEFEAT FROM THE JAWS OF VICTORY

Although the United States was the pioneer in establishing methadone treatment, old attitudes that were hostile to maintenance approaches were never totally abandoned in America and soon began to reassert themselves with methadone as the target. It is important to realize that in addition to creating methadone treatment, the United States was also the birthplace and is still the spiritual center and home of the worldwide movement of drug-free therapeutic communities (TCs). Programs such as Synanon, Phoenix, and other self-help approaches draw on the peer group and 12-step methods of Alcoholics Anonymous—programs that sprang up in America in the face of the vacuum in medical services for addiction. Total abstinence from the use of all mind-altering drugs was the principal goal of treatment and the only acceptable terms for drug users' participation. A sharp division between this philosophy and methadone maintenance increasingly took its toll on the conception and practice of drug treatment in this country. And because of the inordinate U.S. influence in international narcotics matters, this polarization was also replicated in treatment services abroad.

The dominance of this drug-free abstinence orientation grew further under the auspices of the U.S. war on drugs. This moral crusade soon found a natural ally in the TCs and among recovering addicts, who often became the most articulate and persuasive spokespeople for the "Just Say No" approach. Its founding principle was the "evil of drugs" and the demonization of drug users, and this view soon undermined the credibility of methadone in this country. Although the successful methadone patient generally kept it a secret, the worst cases were all too evident around their overly large and often conspicuous clinics in the midst of some of our nation's most embattled communities. Methadone treatment was commonly and publicly held in contempt, and an urban folklore of methadone's evil qualities soon became the conventional wisdom in the drug treatment world. Subsequent cutbacks in the funding of addiction treatment in the urban health centers that had originally sponsored many of the first methadone treatment clinics, as well as its continued marginalization within medicine, all contributed to methadone's problems in the United States.

Predictably, the quality of methadone treatment began to suffer. This could be seen in the steady lowering of dosages, below therapeutically recommended levels, and in the increasingly punitive and controlling character of many MMTPs, which were often large clinics of the inner city that became associated with concentrations of unemployed and (often) still-active users of other illicit drugs. When the crack epidemic arrived, in the mid to late 1980s, it amplified the role of sex and drugs in the AIDS epidemic and produced a whole new group of drug users with particularly difficult-to-treat patterns of compulsive cocaine use. Crack also served to reinforce the strong attitudes already antagonistic to the use of methadone and further distracted attention from the treatment needs of the much older cohort of heroin addicts. The once rapid expansion of MMTPs in the United States ground to a halt, and stagnation set in; there has been little growth or innovation of methadone treatment in the United States since the 1970s.

Unfortunately, all of the old prejudices and antagonisms toward drug maintenance are still evident in the regulation of methadone maintenance in the United States. Methadone treatment is subject to many influences beyond the purely clinical responsibilities of getting the patient the right daily dose. Thus, a law enforcement agency (the DEA) rather than a health care agency controls many important aspects of the treatment program—and a set of government regulations, some of which are inordinately punitive, still governs methadone treatment in the United States. In response to this domination of methadone treatment by nonmedical forces, the National Association of Methadone Advocates (NAMA) was formed in 1980. It has been long in coming, but an active consumers' group of methadone patients and their advocates now exists that is fighting to normalize methadone treatment in the United States.

HARM REDUCTION: AIDS AND THE
REINVENTION OF METHADONE

In the early 1980s, the AIDS epidemic appeared in the United States, Europe, Asia, and the Pacific—immediately changing the significance of drug use and addiction (Mann & Tarantola, 1997). Although it had always been true that drug addiction and public health were linked, the appearance of AIDS set the stage for a reconsideration of injection drug use and addiction, now seen as a method of spreading AIDS, and a reconsideration of drug treatment as a tool of AIDS prevention. This led to the birth of harm reduction, which was the modern public health model for dealing with addiction as a global public health problem. Harm reduction offers an alternative to abstinence as the sole objective of drug treatment. With harm reduction, the goal is the prevention of collateral health and social damage associated with drug use, as well as the limitation of the other medical conditions that rampant and poorly treated addictions foster—especially AIDS and other infectious diseases (e.g., hepatitis) associated with sharing injection equipment and other sexually transmitted diseases via prostitution by addicts. Methadone has emerged as the ideal tool for harm reduction among heroin addicts (Erickson, Riley, Cheung, & O'Hare, 1997; Heather, Wodak, Nadelmann, & O'Hare, 1993; O'Hare, Newcombe, Buning, & Drucker, 1992).

In the case of AIDS, it soon became clear that drug addiction was the ignition point of a worldwide chain of transmission from addict to sex partner to newborn—a cycle that has already demonstrated the capability for the explosive spread of HIV in many areas around the world and especially the cities of the United States and Europe and throughout Asia, where this pattern was occurring in new populations for whom intravenous drug use had never been an issue. Faced with a burgeoning global heroin trade of huge proportions, and despite decades of massive expenditures on interdiction (supply reduction), the support of corrupt regimes (narcodictatorships), and the wholesale incarceration of drug users (up 400% in the United States since 1970), many governments and their public health and medical officials have realized the risk and adopted harm reduction as their national AIDS prevention strategy—with the notable exception of the United States.

Whereas the United States had embraced methadone maintenance early, other countries were slower to accept it, and it often faced prejudices similar to those of morphine maintenance in the United States during the 1920s. But in Great Britain, methadone maintenance was widely adopted in addiction treatment and was even provided in injectable forms in some instances. Hong Kong, which had no history of addiction treatment other than the residuals of the old Communist regimes approach and had brutally suppressed the drug trade and its addicts, as well as several other former British Commonwealth states (e.g., Australia, Canada, and New Zealand), also instituted modest methadone programs under state health department auspices. But continental Europe, with a few exceptions, had resisted the use of methadone, often at the insistence of their psychiatric associations—in Germany, France, and Belgium, its use by nonpsychiatrists was barred by law—and most psychiatrists disapproved of the maintenance approach.

NEW DIRECTIONS IN
MAINTENANCE TREATMENT

The experience of the AIDS epidemic among injection drug users in the United States (which was fully documented in thousands of studies) served to alert health authorities around the world to the link of drugs to AIDS. Soon, they began to massively expand treatment programs for the addictive disorders, which differed greatly from place to place. However, most European and many Asian countries already had developed substantial heroin-using populations, and their health ministries and public health authorities rediscovered methadone, which was still the most effective and well-proven treatment available for heroin addiction.

The period from 1985 to 1995 was the first decade of the AIDS epidemic among drug users in these parts of the world, whereas in the United States, HIV had entered the population in the mid 1970s. In response to this threat to public health, many countries instituted the rapid expansion of methadone treatment. Australia increased its availability of methadone tenfold, and in the Netherlands, methadone treatment services today reach more than 70% of Dutch addicts (compared to less than 15% in the United States). In addition to increases in treatment capacity, the international public health community developed new ways to improve the reach and efficacy of methadone treatment by breaking with the narrow, one-size-fits-all methadone clinic as the sole way of using this medication. A key step was the inclusion of methadone treatment as a part of the care rendered by primary care doctors within routine practices or medical clinics. In Europe and Australia today, the majority of methadone is prescribed by an ordinary doctor and dispensed by an ordinary pharmacy. In addition, new ways were devised to reach those who did not want to come to clinics but did want to use methadone to help control their addiction. Low-threshold approaches, such as The Methadone Bus in Amsterdam, extended treatment to new groups of addicts.

A recent study in Leicester, England suggests the direction that addiction treatment using maintenance drugs may take in the future—combining the pharmacological supports of maintenance drugs with the environment and psychological rehabilitation aspects of many drug-free programs. In this case, a therapeutic community, where no maintenance drugs were used, introduced methadone within the framework of the residential program. Whereas the program previously had a dropout rate of more than 60% (much of it in the first few months of the stay, when drug craving would be at its peak), retention jumped to more than 80% when maintenance doses of methadone were introduced. This example demonstrates that maintenance approaches can be used to support a range of treatment goals, including the more comprehensive life changes and rehabilitation that so many stigmatized and criminalized addicts now need, as much in response to our punitive and cruel reactions to their addiction as to any properties of heroin or of their biological dependency.

Furthermore, new forms of maintenance treatment for the opiates (and some other drugs) are emerging from the growing clinical experience with addiction treatment outside of the United States, fueling renewed confidence in medicine's ability to help control the worst aspects of addiction with the help of a range of medications—most of which are already available. Thus, in Germany (which, a decade ago, imprisoned physicians for prescribing methadone), methadone clinics now serve 5,000 patients. More than 200 physicians maintain another 25,000 addicts on oral codeine syrup, which is a shorter-acting opiate than methadone (i.e., one that is easier for the user to titrate, or control, the dosage according to his or her perceived need, as with any mood-altering medications). France, which had only 50 patients on methadone in 1990, now has 5,000 in care and another 5,000 coming in the next 2 years. Furthermore, many French physicians are now learning how to prescribe buprenorphine—a complex oral opiate that has both maintenance (agonist) and blocking (antagonist) actions that some doctors and their patients are finding helpful.

And in Switzerland (which has the highest AIDS rate in Europe), a bold experiment of injectable heroin maintenance is now in its second year, with more than 1,000 patients being seen in 20 clinics operated by the national Health Ministry. The program's careful evaluation already tells us that these patients are doing as well as Nyswander and Dole's first methadone patients in New York City, to whom they compare in terms of their long addiction histories and multiple treatment failures. But in this case, these are patients who had also tried methadone and still continued to use heroin. The preliminary studies of these patients indicates a high success rate as measured by retention in treatment (more than 80%) and a sharp reduction in their use of illicit drugs, with associated improvements in their reintegration into normal life (i.e., work, home, and family)—all while injecting an average of 400 mg of pharmaceutical heroin up to three times a day within a clinic setting.

CONCLUSIONS

Today, our scientific knowledge places us on the threshold of a comprehensive understanding of the neurophysiology of all drugs' actions in the brain and the biological basis of addiction. We are also beginning to understand potential genetic differences in susceptibility to addiction, which may explain, in part, why only a small minority of those who try these drugs become dependent upon them. These developments and important advances in pharmacology prefigure the development of a multitude of new and exquisitely specific psychoactive agents (Prozac is one of the first of these new drugs) that will someday help us to better treat and perhaps even "cure" addiction. But as long as we continue to view drug addiction primarily as a moral or psychological failing, rather than as a disorder of neurotransmission, we will continue to be handicapped in our ability to appreciate its biological reality and to fully employ the best tools of clinical medicine and public health that are at our disposal to minimize opiates' potential harms and take full advantage of their many real benefits. Until then, narcotic maintenance treatment offers a powerful tool for reducing the harms of opiate addiction and the array of public health and social problems that accompany it.

NOTE

1. For detailed discussions of normative and "controlled" drug use, see Vaillant (1968) and Zinberg (1984). For less pathological views of drugs and their widespread uses, see Brecher (1974); Weil (1974); Weil and Rosen (1993); and Zimmer and Morgan (1997).

REFERENCES

American Psychiatric Association. (1995). *Diagnostic and statistical manual* (4th ed., rev.). Washington, DC: Author.

Ball, J., & Ross, A. (1991). *The effectiveness of methadone maintenance treatment.* New York: Springer-Verlag.

Berridge, V., & Edwards, G. (1987). *Opium and the people.* New Haven, CT: Yale University Press.

Brecher, E. (1974). *Licit and illicit drugs.* New York: Consumers Union.

Courtwright, D. (1985). *Dark paradise.* Cambridge, MA: Harvard University Press.

Courtwright, D., Des Jarlais, D., & Joseph, H. (1989). *Addicts who survived.* Knoxville: University of Kentucky Press.

Erickson, P. G., Riley, D., Cheung, Y. W., & O'Hare, P. A. (1997). *Harm reduction: A new direction for drug policies and practices.* Toronto: University of Toronto Press.

Gardner, E. L. (Ed.). (1997). Brain reward mechanisms. In J. Lowinson, P. Ruiz, R. Millman, & J. Langrod (Eds.), *Substance abuse: A comprehensive textbook* (3rd ed.). Baltimore: William and Wilkins.

Heather, N., Wodak, A., Nadelmann, E., & O'Hare, P. A. (Eds.). (1993). *Psychoactive drugs and harm reduction: From faith to science.* London: Whurr.

Lowinson, J., Ruiz, P., Millman, R., & Langrod, J. (Eds.). (1997). *Substance abuse: A comprehensive textbook* (3rd ed.). Baltimore: William and Wilkins.

Mann, J., & Tarantola, D. (1997). *AIDS in the world* (Vol. 2). New York: Oxford University Press.

Musto, D. F. (1987). *The American disease.* New York: Oxford University Press.

Newman, R. G. (1977). *Methadone treatment in narcotic addiction*. New York: Springer-Verlag.

O'Hare, P. A., Newcombe, R., Buning, E., & Drucker, E. (Eds.). (1992). *The reduction of drug related harm*. London: Routledge.

Peele, S. (1990). *Love and addiction*. Lexington, MA: D. C. Heath.

Peele, S. (1993). *The diseasing of America*. Lexington, MA: D. C. Heath.

Preston, A. (1996). *The methadone briefing*. Liverpool: HIT.

Reinarman, C., & Levine, H. (1997). *Crack in America*. Berkeley: University of California Press.

Szasz, T. (1985). *Ceremonial chemistry*. Holmes Beach, FL: Learning Publications.

Vaillant, G. E. (1968). *The natural history of addiction*. Cambridge, MA: Harvard University Press.

Waldorf, D., & Biernecki, P. (1984). *Pathways from addiction*. Philadelphia: Temple University Press.

Waldorf, D., Reinarman, C., & Murphy, S. (1991). *Cocaine changes*. Philadelphia: Temple University Press.

Ward, J., Mattick, R., & Hall, W. (1992). *Key issues in methadone maintenance treatment*. Sydney, Australia: University of New South Wales Press.

Weil, A. (1974). *The natural mind*. Cambridge, MA: Harvard University Press.

Weil, A., & Rosen, W. (1993). *From chocolate to morphine*. New York: Houghton Mifflin.

World Health Organization. (1995). *International classification of diseases*. Geneva: Author.

Zimmer, L., & Morgan, J. (1997). *Marijuana facts, marijuana myths*. New York: Lindesmith Center.

Zinberg, N. (1984). *Drug, set, and setting*. New Haven, CT: Yale University Press.

3

The Coming of Age of Needle Exchange: A History Through 1993

Sandra D. Lane

Peter Lurie

Benjamin Bowser

Jim Kahn

Donna Chen

Needle exchange programs (NEPs) emerged in the mid to late 1980s as a strategy to address rapidly increasing rates of HIV and other infections among injection drug users (IDUs). In many parts of the United States, when they began, NEPs were illegal, often unwelcome in the very communities that were hardest hit by injection drug use and opposed by leaders in public health and drug treatment. The social history of how and why these programs developed not only provides a context for evaluating the public health costs and benefits of NEPs but also illustrates the interaction of public health officials, community and activist groups, the legal system, and the government in establishing health policy on a very controversial issue.

This chapter outlines the context in which needle exchange emerged in North America, traces the history of needle exchange from its inception in the mid-1980s to 1993, and identifies social and policy trends in the development of

NEPs. Because of the complex social history of NEPs, this chapter provides only an overview rather than a detailed description of each of the NEPs. Although there are now NEPs in Europe, Asia, and South America, this chapter primarily describes programs in North America. General trends in the evolution of NEPs are also identified, and selected examples of each trend are discussed.

Research for this chapter was part of a larger study on the public health impact of needle exchange programs in the United States and abroad (Lurie et al., 1993) that was conducted by a research team from the University of California at Berkeley and at San Francisco in 1992-1993.[1] Semistructured interviews were conducted with 25 needle exchange staff; 22 IDU researchers; 47 community leaders (law enforcement, ethnic minority groups, religious groups, local businesspeople, elected officials, and neighborhood groups); 14 public health officials; and 129 IDUs. Research was conducted in 15 cities—10 in the United States (San Francisco, CA; Santa Cruz, CA; Berkeley, CA; Portland, OR; Seattle, WA; Tacoma, WA; Boulder, CO; New York, NY; Boston, MA; and New Haven, CT); three in Canada (Vancouver, Toronto, and Montreal); and two in Europe (Amsterdam and London). The purpose of the study was explained to interview subjects, who were asked for permission for direct attribution of their comments. Except for one individual in the Boston area who had operated an illegal NEP, such permission was always granted, although some respondents provided additional, off-the-record information that was used as background material only. Permission to record the interviews on audiotape was sought; in only two cases was permission denied. Interview subjects were chosen in order to represent a diversity of views in support of and in opposition to needle exchange. Interviews, focus groups, and NEP site observations used the Rapid Assessment Procedure (RAP) method as a general framework. RAP is a collection of qualitative research strategies used for quick evaluation of health interventions (Scrimshaw et al., 1987). A total of 23 NEPs were visited and observed. Twenty additional NEPs in the United States were surveyed using a mail questionnaire. This information was supplemented with published reports, including journal and newspaper articles.

EARLY HISTORY

Distribution of clean needles to IDUs, but not exchanging them, was considered long before NEPs were formally established. Lt. Reggie Lyles, of the Berkeley Police Department, recalled first hearing discussions advocating the distribution of sterile needles to IDUs in 1970 at San Francisco State University. "In those days," he explained, "giving away needles was a way to deal with yellow jaundice and abscesses from shooting heroin" (R. Lyles, interview, August 27, 1992). One of the San Francisco NEP's early organizers, Patricia Case, recalled the early days of the HIV epidemic at San Francisco General Hospital. Doctors and nurses would leave a 10-pack of syringes in view of someone they knew to be injecting drugs and walk out of the room (P. Case, interview, August 7, 1992).

As the HIV epidemic progressed during the 1980s, many IDUs began to seek ways to obtain clean syringes. A study in New York City in the mid-1980s indicated that a growing number of IDUs were becoming concerned about their risk of injection-related HIV transmission, and that more than half of those studied were employing various strategies, such as more careful selection of injecting partners, to avoid infection (Des Jarlais et al., 1988; Friedman et al., 1987). The demand for clean injection equipment became so great that in New York City, an underground market developed. In some cases, used syringes were rinsed and repackaged to appear as if they were sterile and then sold to unsuspecting customers (Des Jarlais et al., 1985). In addition, even before the AIDS epidemic, many IDUs obtained syringes from diabetics (D. Des Jarlais, personal communication, 1993).

The First NEP: Amsterdam

The first formal NEP, established in Amsterdam by IDUs themselves, was concerned with preventing the spread of hepatitis B rather than HIV, which was not a recognized threat to IDUs at that time. Opened in the summer of 1984 by the Junkie Union, an Amsterdam-based drug users' advocacy group, the NEP also had support from the Municipal Health Service. Although Dutch law permits the sale of syringes without a prescription, members of the Junkie Union became concerned that an inner-city Amsterdam pharmacist's decision to no longer sell syringes to IDUs would result in an outbreak of hepatitis B (Buning, 1991). In 1986, the Municipal Health Service took over and expanded the NEPs, and by 1988, there were 11 different NEP locations in Amsterdam (Buning, 1991). News of Amsterdam's NEP spread via international conferences, where evaluations of the NEPs were widely discussed among health professionals, researchers, and AIDS activists in North America and elsewhere (Buning et al., 1986).

The Amsterdam program's objective was harm reduction rather than the promotion of abstinence from drugs. Some observers date the origins of the harm reduction concept to the approach to the drug problem adopted in Amsterdam, where injection drug use is considered a chronic, relapsing condition, and harm reduction involves providing medical and social services for IDUs who continue to inject. Members of the Junkie Union felt that total abstinence was an unrealistic, and perhaps impossible, goal for many IDUs. Instead, their efforts focused on decreasing the risk that an IDU posed to him- or herself or to others (Van Ameijden et al., 1992). A second objective of the program was to provide anonymous, accessible service; this has become known as a "low-threshold" approach to service provision.

Harm reduction is a concept that has influenced NEPs to varying degrees. It implies a respect for the choices people make, even unhealthy choices like injecting drugs, and is sometimes posited in opposition to approaches that emphasize drug treatment or punitive criminal justice measures. Pat Christen, director of the San Francisco AIDS Foundation, describes the distinction:

> I think that exchange should never, ever be linked to a demand to go into [drug] treatment, that [treatment] should be just an option that is presented and that it should be presented in the most neutral, nonjudgmental fashion possible. And that it should be made very clear to the IDUs that if they never go into treatment, they will still have access to the [NEP], . . . that they are really important in our community and we want them alive and well, healthy. . . . If you believe that IDUs are not capable of making decisions in their own best interest, in essence [it implies that] they are almost subhuman. (P. Christen, interview, June 10, 1992)

Many drug treatment providers and others view this argument with considerable skepticism. Such critics contend that harm reduction implies a tolerance for, and in some cases an acceptance of, drug use, and they fear that this approach will condone or even promote drug use. Even NEP staff vary quite widely in their definitions of harm reduction, and NEPs thus differ according to the extent to which entry into drug treatment is a major objective (Sorge, 1990). Some hold a civil libertarian view, that the "personal choice" of the individual must be respected, even if it involves drug use (Caravan staff, interview, July 15, 1992). Others see harm reduction more as a strategy to help IDUs remain uninfected and healthy while encouraging them to enter drug treatment and give up drug use. Michael McCrimmon, who runs a small NEP for HIV-infected clients at the Addiction Research Foundation, a government-sponsored agency in Toronto, disagrees with what he sees as an approach of "license." He described his disagreement with the civil libertarian approach:

> It's not everyone's right to be stoned if it's affecting other people. . . . If someone is out of control, and there's no way that an . . . addicted individual is in control, then they are not responsible any longer. . . . Most of the individuals who we are seeing have gross psychosocial problems. (M. McCrimmon, interview, September 3, 1992)

Rather than an either/or choice between license and abstinence, most researchers and NEP staff have come to see harm reduction as a continuum. Harm reduction implies graded levels of intervention to decrease the harm caused by drug use. In practice, this means a focus on incremental increases in healthy behavior, with a goal for many of being drug free, but also with a realistic understanding of the difficulties in attaining that goal.

Bleach-Based Outreach Programs:
A Precursor to Needle Exchange in the United States

Although news about NEPs in Europe and Australia was widely discussed among North American IDU researchers during the mid-1980s, there was a general consensus that government opposition would preclude such an effort in the United States. Nevertheless, the very rapid spread of HIV among IDUs in cities like New York alarmed researchers and activists (J. Watters, interview, June 5, 1992). In a number of cities, this led to street outreach efforts based on the disinfection of injection equipment with bleach; condom distribution; and referrals for health care, drug treatment, and HIV testing—a strategy that was popularly known as "bleach and teach" (Newmeyer, 1988). Although bleach outreach programs came to be quite widely accepted, and more than 40 have been funded by the Department of Health and Human Services since 1987 (Martinez, 1992), there was substantial opposition to these programs when they began in the mid-1980s (Des Jarlais et al., 1990; J. Watters, interview, June 5, 1992). Some raised questions about the safety of bleach: Would it be used as directed? Who would be liable if bleach was injected? Who would pay for the bleach? Many of the same arguments that are now applied to NEPs—that it would send the wrong message and encourage drug use—were expressed by opponents of bleach outreach, including then-Attorney General Edwin Meese (Des Jarlais et al., 1990).

Many NEPs emerged both indirectly and directly from street-based outreach efforts, including some that promoted bleach disinfection. In some cases, street outreach was the first opportunity that researchers and public health providers had to interact with IDUs outside of a treatment facility, hospital, public health clinic, or prison. Through this less formal, personal interaction, some health professionals and researchers became convinced that many IDUs cared about their health and wanted to prevent HIV transmission. In some cases, street outreach workers themselves were the organizers of early underground NEPs. Other NEPs, such as New Haven's program, which is run by the local Department of Health, grew directly out of street outreach programs, even employing the individuals who had staffed them (E. O'Keefe, interview, August 18, 1992).

Early NEPs in the United States

The earliest NEPs in North America followed the first NEPs in Europe by more than 2 years. Often established by activist groups or individuals, NEPs in the United States frequently started as illegal, privately funded efforts that generated enormous controversy in some cities. With legal changes in some states to allow pilot NEPs, and the growing involvement of selected local governments, many exchanges are now operated by more established, community-based organizations, and several are run directly by local health departments. By the third quarter of 1993, at least 37 NEPs in 27 cities were operating in the United States (see Table 3.1).

The first person to distribute sterile injection equipment to IDUs publicly in the United States was Jon Parker. A former IDU, Mr. Parker was a Master of Public Health student at Yale University when one of his professors commented that IDUs should not be the focus of HIV prevention efforts because they would not change their behavior. This comment so angered Mr. Parker that he began to meet with IDUs to warn them of the dangers of HIV transmission. During one of these meetings in Boston in 1986, an IDU brought in seven sterile syringes and gave them to other IDUs. In late 1986, Mr. Parker began distributing and later exchanging syringes on the streets of New Haven and then Boston (J. McGrath and J. Parker, interview, August 13, 1992; E. O'Keefe, interview, August 18, 1992; D. Waldorf, personal communication, September 1, 1997).

Several of the early NEPs were established as explicit acts of civil disobedience to publicly test the prescription law, which requires a doctor's prescription to possess a syringe, and to call public attention to the issue of AIDS among IDUs (P. Case, interview, August 7, 1992). Jon Parker has most vividly lived up to this description; by 1993, he claimed to have been arrested 27 times in seven states (California, Massachusetts, Illinois, New Hampshire, Rhode Island, New York, and Delaware) and to have publicly challenged the prescription law in all 11 states that had them (J. McGrath and J. Parker, interview, August 13, 1992). Mr. Parker founded the National AIDS Brigade, which, as of September 1993, continued to operate activist-run NEPs in Boston, New Haven, and New York City.

The first NEP to operate with some community support and formal structure was organized by Dave Purchase in Tacoma. In April 1988, Mr. Purchase, an activist with extensive experience in directing drug rehabilitation programs, informed the mayor, public officials, and others whom he thought might be politically affected that he planned to begin an NEP. In August 1988, he set up a table in downtown Tacoma to exchange syringes. Originally funded by the Mahatma Kane-Jeeves Memorial Dope Fiend Trust, made up of Mr. Purchase and other private donors, the program grew into the Point Defiance AIDS Project and is today operated under a contract with and supported primarily by the Tacoma/Pierce County Department of Health (D. Purchase, interview, August 4, 1992). A second NEP run by the Department of Health itself opened in a Department of Health pharmacy in March 1989 and was, as of 1993, the only pharmacy NEP in the United States.

Two additional NEPs emerged in November 1988, in San Francisco and in New York City. San Francisco's Prevention Point opened on the Day of the

TABLE 3.1   NEPs in the United States Through August 1993

State	City	Month and Year Opened
Alaska	Fairbanks	August 1989
California	Berkeley	November 1990
	Los Angeles	June 1992
	Monterey County	April 1992
	Novato	October 1992
	Oakland	July 1992
	San Diego	January 1992
	San Francisco	November 1988
	San Jose	July 1992
	San Mateo	September 1990
	Santa Cruz	December 1989
Colorado	Boulder	May 1989
Connecticut	Bridgeport	May 1993
	Hartford	March 1993
	New Haven	November 1990
	Willimantic	March 1990
Hawaii	Honolulu (3 programs)	September 1991
		November 1991
		July 1990
Illinois	Chicago	January 1992
Indiana	Indianapolis	October 1992
Massachusetts	Boston (2 programs)	February 1991
		November 1986
New York	Buffalo	April 1992
	New York City (5 programs)	December 1992
		February 1990
		September 1992
		February 1990
		August 1990
Oregon	Portland	November 1989
Pennsylvania	Philadelphia	December 1991
Washington	Olympia	April 1992
	Seattle	March 1989
	Spokane	May 1991
	Tacoma (2 programs)	August 1988
		March 1989
	Yakima	November 1992

Dead, November 2, 1988, as an underground program staffed by activists. From its beginnings with two teams, one mobile and one stationary, Prevention Point had expanded to five teams by 1993. Its low-technology model consists of five or six volunteers standing in a row on the sidewalk, while hundreds of clients each week move past exchanging syringes and collecting condoms, cotton, alcohol wipes, and bleach.

The first New York City NEP opened on November 7, 1988 as an experimental program. Because it was run by the Health Department, the NEP was designed to satisfy the numerous concerns of opponents in city and state government. IDUs were accepted into the program only if they were already on a waiting list for drug treatment, and they could participate in the NEP only until a treatment slot was found for them (Joseph, 1992). They were given one syringe, imprinted with a Health Department logo, and they could exchange only that one syringe at each visit. Because of difficulties in housing the NEP, it was located in the Health Department headquarters. This location was far from most of the clients' neighborhoods but quite close to both the court buildings and the police department. Despite the obstacles, 294 NEP clients attended during the program's year of operation, although few IDUs obtained large numbers of syringes (New York City Department of Health, 1989).

Although legal, the New York City NEP was a source of tremendous controversy, especially among community groups. Leaders in the African American community argued that they had not been consulted about setting up the NEP and felt that the Health Department had not sufficiently addressed the many social and health problems caused by drug use, particularly in poor and minority communities. The program was closed in 1990 by newly elected Mayor David Dinkins, who had promised its closure during his election campaign.

Immediately following the program's closure, two activist groups, the National AIDS Brigade and ACT-UP, began distributing syringes in Manhattan's Lower East Side. Members of these groups were arrested for possession of drug paraphernalia in March 1990 but were subsequently acquitted of the charges (Drucker, 1990). In addition to this public activity, activists from the Association for Drug Abuse Prevention and Treatment (ADAPT), ACT-UP, the Gay Men's Health Crisis, and other organizations met with community groups and lobbied Mayor Dinkins in an effort to gain support for needle exchange. An important strategy in building community support was explicitly linking needle exchange with drug treatment, housing, and other services. These efforts were aided in part by the 1991 publication of the evaluation of New Haven's NEP, which estimated a 33% decrease in HIV transmission among NEP clients (Kaplan et al., 1993), and by statements favoring NEPs by the National Commission on AIDS (National Commission, 1991). The result was that in 1991, the Dinkins administration's policy shifted from adamant opposition to cautious support for pilot NEPs (Anderson, 1991). The community response, particularly of African American and Latino community leaders was a defining aspect of the debate over NEPs in New York City.

During 1989, NEPs opened in the states of Washington and Oregon. ACT-UP Seattle informed the health department in March 1989 that they would be starting an NEP and that they wanted the Health Department to take it over. After 6 weeks, the King County Department of Public Health did just that, and it now runs and funds the NEP, which had five sites and five paid staff members at the time of our site visit (NEP staff, interview, June 3 and 11, 1992). Outside-In, a Portland social service agency for homeless youth directed by Kathy Oliver, would have opened its NEP prior to Tacoma's, but unexpected problems with liability insurance delayed its opening until November 1, 1989. Although Outside-In's NEP operated legally, the insurance company explained in its letter withdrawing coverage that it did not want to go against the wishes of the President of the United States. Ms. Oliver identified a new insurance carrier and sought help from the County Board of Commissioners to cover the additional $30,000 that liability insurance would cost. The program began with one site in an Outside-In building and subsequently added a second site in a downtown cafe (K. Oliver, interview, June 15, 1992).

Canadian NEPs

While the debate over NEPs raged in the United States, the programs were increasingly accepted abroad. By the first quarter of 1993, at least 23 countries on three continents had active NEPs (see Table 3.2) (Brenner et al., 1991; Rezza et al., 1992).

Canada's NEPs were inspired in part by data presented at the 1988 International AIDS Conference in Stockholm describing the very high rates of HIV infection among IDUs in Edinburgh and New York City (B. MacKenzie, interview, October 5, 1992). Public health leaders felt that the low rates of HIV infection among Canada's IDUs offered a window of opportunity. In 1989, the Canadian federal government offered to co-fund for 2 years some comprehensive pilot IDU HIV prevention programs that would include NEPs. The federal government also required that the projects be independently evaluated and offered to fund the evaluations. Five provinces accepted federal matching funds (Ontario, British Columbia, Quebec, Alberta, and Manitoba) (B. MacKenzie, interview, October 5, 1992). In Toronto, Vancouver, and Montreal, the three Canadian cities that were visited as a part of the research for this chapter, NEPs have been co-funded by a combination of city, provincial, and, for the first 2 years, federal sources. Vancouver's NEP had been established with private support in 1989, a few months before the federal government's offer of funding;

TABLE 3.2   Countries With NEPs Through August 1993

North America
  Canada
  United States

Europe
  Austria
  Belgium
  Czech Republic
  France
  Germany
  Ireland
  Italy
  Luxembourg
  Malta
  Netherlands
  Norway
  Poland
  Slovenia
  Spain
  Sweden
  Switzerland
  United Kingdom

Asia
  Australia
  Nepal
  New Zealand
  Thailand

SOURCES: Brenner et al. (1991); Rezza et al. (1992).

Toronto's and Montreal's major NEPs were established in 1989 with this federal co-funding. The programs operate legally, mostly through community-based organizations that subcontract with the local health department, except in Toronto, where the NEP is run directly by the Department of Public Health. By 1993, a total of 28 Canadian cities had active NEPs.

Canada's experience with NEPs differs greatly from that in the United States. Discussions of needle exchange in Canada were generally not as politically charged as in the United States. Many Canadian NEPs began with local, provincial, and/or federal support, and relatively few were started by activists. There were some Canadian groups that opposed needle exchange—notably the Diabetic Association, which opposed IDUs receiving free syringes while its members were obliged to pay for them—and a few public health and community leaders. The majority of Canadian public health leaders, however, including the Canadian Public Health Association, supported pilot NEPs. NEPs are conceptualized as a part of a multifaceted approach that combines education; prevention of initiation into drug use; counseling; the support of local law enforcement; and linkage to other services, including drug treatment (B. MacKenzie, interview, October 5, 1992).

TRENDS IN THE EVOLUTION OF NEEDLE EXCHANGE PROGRAMS

A number of trends can be identified in the development of U.S. NEPs. These include (a) movement from an adversarial to a cooperative relationship with city officials, police, and community leaders; (b) changes in laws governing needle exchange and availability; (c) changes in funding sources; (d) greater institutionalization; and (e) increasing federal government involvement in research on NEPs. These trends are not absolute stages through which each program has passed; in some cases, they exist within programs (e.g., some NEPs have moved from activist-run operations to community-based organizations). In other cases, they represent a shift that affects subsequent NEPs as they begin. For example, newer NEPs have tended to begin operations with greater legitimacy than did earlier programs.

From Civil Disobedience to Community Consultation

As mentioned previously, some of the earliest programs—the National AIDS Brigade in Boston, New Haven, and New York City, and Prevention Point in San Francisco—were begun by activists or activist groups as explicit acts of civil disobedience (Downing et al., 1991). One of the most visible activist groups in the United States has been ACT-UP, which established NEPs in Seattle, New York City, Boston, and Los Angeles. These individuals were willing to risk arrest (a few actively courted arrest) to challenge laws that limit needle availability. One of the original staff members of San Francisco's NEP explained how this factor may have contributed to the program's effectiveness in gaining trust in the IDU community:

> The clients observed us taking a risk of arrest, which in the [drug-using] community has tremendous social meaning. And we did it night after night. The night after the earthquake in San Francisco, we were there with flashlights. . . . So, when they saw this behavior with people they perceived [as having] something to lose, they perceived that we were more like them. They were carrying heroin in their pockets, they were illegal; we were carrying needles, we were illegal. And there was a reduction in the social distance. (P. Case, interview, August 7, 1992)

Activists who were arrested were usually defended pro bono by lawyers who were themselves members of activist legal groups, including the Civil Liberties Union of Massachusetts (CLUM), Gay and Lesbian Advocates and Defenders (GLAD), and the American Civil Liberties Union (ACLU). Members of these groups have also been active in helping to draft legislation that would create pilot NEPs or would allow over-the-counter sales of syringes, and in providing legal advice regarding needle exchange to elected officials.

By July 1993, there had been 14 arrests of 31 individuals in 11 cities in the United States for exchanging syringes. Nine of the 14 arrests were of National AIDS Brigade members, including eight arrests for Jon Parker (J. McGrath and J. Parker, interview, August 13, 1992). Seven arrests led to acquittal or charges being dropped, two trials ended in hung juries, two cases are still pending, and three cases led to convictions. Two convictions were in the Boston area; in Buffalo, the defendants pleaded guilty to reduced charges of disorderly conduct (R. Sorge, personal communication, August 10, 1993).

Activists who established the earliest NEPs had a sense of urgency, and some felt that the effort to establish community consensus would take precious time away from what they perceived to be life-saving efforts. The original staff of San Francisco's Prevention Point explained, "We felt that, in the midst of an epidemic, waiting for permission to implement a life-saving measure was unethical" (Downing et al., 1991). John Turvey, who began the DEYAS NEP in Vancouver before federal government and public health support launched Canada's other programs, said he felt that it was better to act first and consult second (J. Turvey, interview, August 10, 1992). He pointed out that NEPs in Toronto and Montreal, whose staff had sought government, police, and community consensus first, took 12 to 18 months to open. In both San Francisco and Vancouver, NEP staff sought and gained critical government and community support only after the programs were under way.

After the phase of civil disobedience, the staff of many NEPs forged alliances with local public health and elected officials, community leaders, and police departments as part of their efforts to gain community consensus. In Tacoma, Dave Purchase met with the mayor, health department officials, city and county council members, and the chief of police to discuss his intention to set up an NEP (D. Purchase, interview, August 4, 1992). Mr. Purchase also went to Seattle to help ACT-UP set up its NEP. ACT-UP Seattle established lines of communication and forged an agreement with Seattle's chief of police not to arrest the NEP staff (NEP staff, interview, June 3 and 11, 1992). Elaine O'Keefe, former director of New Haven's NEP, and others on the New Haven Mayor's Task Force on AIDS consulted with city officials, community leaders, and drug treatment providers for more than 3 years to gain support for the NEP (A. Novick, interview, August 17, 1992; E. O'Keefe, interview, August 18, 1992). New Haven's Chief of Police, Nicholas Pastore, sat on the Protocol Committee that designed the Department of Public Health's NEP and has become one of the program's strongest supporters (N. Pastore, interview, August 19, 1992).

Cooperation between police departments and NEPs seems to have developed in areas where police departments were receptive to community-based initiatives. In several cities—Tacoma, Portland, New Haven, Montreal, and Toronto—police departments in the mid to late 1980s had reorganized their approach to law enforcement to conform to a policy of community policing. This newer approach to policing focuses on greater personal contact with the community, including police officers walking through neighborhoods, attending community meetings, and getting to know the residents of their assigned areas. Community policing appears to have shifted the police view of injection drug use as solely a criminal problem to somewhat more of a public health problem. This shift may well have allowed some police departments to be more receptive to needle exchange.

Forging such links with police departments, however, has not eliminated the problems faced by NEP clients from line officers who may not agree with departmental policies. Even in cities where police chiefs are on record as supporting the NEP, and sometimes in areas where needle exchange is legal, NEP clients have reported having clean needles confiscated or broken by police officers, and some report having been arrested while going to or from the NEP (San Francisco client focus group, August 26, 1992; Toronto client focus group, September 2, 1992; Tacoma client focus group, August 4, 1992).

Changes in Laws Governing Needle Exchange and Availability

A second trend involves changes in the laws governing needle exchange and needle availability. Several different types of laws affect the legal status of needle exchange in the United States, including (a) paraphernalia laws, restricting syringe possession; (b) prescription laws; (c) drug- and prostitute-free zones, operating in cities in Washington State and Oregon; and (d) restrictions on the use of federal funds to support needle exchange activities. Analysis of data from the 33 programs visited or surveyed by telephone for this research resulted in the following NEP definitions regarding legal status: (a) legal, in which no prescription law restricted needle exchange activities, or in which state laws have been issued to allow such activities; (b) illegal-tolerated, in which a local elected body (e.g., city council) in a state with a prescription law has voted to support or approve the NEP; and (c) illegal-underground, which operates in violation of state law. Of the 33 programs studied, 19 were legal, eight were illegal-tolerated, and six were illegal-underground.

There has been a trend toward increasing legalization of needle exchange, using local ordinances and changing state laws to allow NEPs. In certain states, these legal and legislative efforts include challenging and, in two states, Connecticut and Maine, modifying or revoking existing prescription and paraphernalia laws. During 1990, two states (Hawaii and Connecticut) passed bills authorizing the establishment of pilot NEPs (L. Bowleg, personal communication, August 5, 1993). Also in 1990, Rhode Island's legislature requested the state Department of Health to compile and evaluate data on the efficacy of NEPs in slowing HIV transmission (Debuono et al., 1990).

In November 1990, following the July 1990 passage of a bill allowing a pilot NEP in Connecticut, the Department of Health in New Haven opened its pilot NEP. In May 1992, in part as a result of the evaluation of New Haven's NEP (O'Keefe et al., 1991), the Connecticut General Assembly passed additional legislation allowing the sale by a pharmacist of up to 10 syringes without a prescription and the possession of up to 10 clean syringes without drug residue (B. Weinstein, personal communication, August 4, 1993). Additional legislation passed in Connecticut in 1992 allowed the Connecticut Department of Health Services to establish and fund NEPs in Hartford and Bridgeport and authorized the establishment of three more unfunded NEPs. One of these unfunded programs was established in Willimantic, and in 1993, the Connecticut General Assembly approved funding for that program.

The trend toward legally operating NEPs has not been straightforward or smooth in many cases. In New York City, for example, the first NEP operated legally and was run by the health department. After it closed, activist groups distributed needles illegally in acts of civil disobedience and were arrested. Following this period of civil disobedience, and after gaining critical community support, the state agreed to funnel money from the American Foundation for AIDS Research (AmFAR) to five community-based organizations (CBOs) that now operate legal NEPs in New York City.

San Francisco's NEP is illegal according to state law, but it has the official support of the city and county government. In 1991, California State Senator Diane Watson and Assembly Speaker Willie Brown introduced two similar pilot NEP bills into the California State Senate and Assembly. The bills were voted down in 1991. Watson and Brown introduced the bills again in 1992, and both passed votes in the Senate and Assembly but were vetoed by Governor Pete Wilson in September 1992 (Lucas, 1992). In his veto message, Governor Wilson stated that there was "insufficient evidence to demonstrate the efficacy of these programs" and that "we cannot afford to threaten the credibility of our ongoing anti-drug efforts" (Wilson, 1992).

Between 1990 and 1993, San Francisco took several independent measures regarding needle exchange. In 1990, San Francisco voters approved a Libertarian Party-sponsored ballot initiative calling for the repeal of all laws prohibiting the sale, possession, use, and distribution of syringes (M. Valverde, personal communication, September 9, 1993). In 1992, the San Francisco Board of Supervisors and the San Francisco Health Commission adopted resolutions urging the Department of Public Health to implement a comprehensive plan, including needle exchange services, to prevent HIV transmission among IDUs (Gordon, 1992; "Minutes," 1992). In March 1993, in a direct challenge to Governor Wilson's veto, then-Mayor Frank Jordan declared a public health emergency in connection with the HIV epidemic among IDUs (Jordan, 1993). In doing so, he directed the city and county Department of Public Health "to take immediate steps to implement a needle exchange program by entering into a contract for the provision of needle exchange services" (Jordan, 1993).

Some programs that began legally have faced legal challenges to their continued operation. When Tacoma's Point Defiance began, the Washington State Drug Paraphernalia Act made possession or distribution of needles illegal ("Needle Exchange," 1989). However, a second state law, the Omnibus AIDS Act, authorized syringe sterilization programs, and existing laws gave public health officials certain powers to combat the AIDS epidemic. The Tacoma-Pierce County Board of Health voted to fund the NEP in January 1989. In April 1989, the Omnibus Drug Bill, which would have made needle exchange illegal, passed the Washington State legislature (Wilson, 1989a), but the section covering NEPs was vetoed by Governor Booth Gardner (Purchase et al., 1989; Wilson, 1989c). In vetoing the bill, Gardner stated, "The needle exchange pilots being pursued in certain counties appear to be having a positive effect" (Wilson, 1989c).

In July 1989, Washington State Attorney General Ken Eikenberry released a legal opinion that the Omnibus AIDS Act did not preempt the paraphernalia law, and that needle exchange was therefore illegal in the state (Wilson, 1989b). In order to force a legal decision to clarify the NEP's legal status, the city of Tacoma withdrew funding from the NEP. By prior agreement of all parties, this withdrawal prompted Dr. Alfred Allen, then-director of the Tacoma-Pierce County Health Department, to file a "friendly" suit against Pierce County and Tacoma in the Pierce County Superior Court (Hagan, 1991; H. Hagan, interview, August 3, 1992; D. Purchase, interview, August 4, 1992; Severson, 1990). In February 1990, Superior Court Judge Robert Peterson ruled that needle exchange was legal, citing the authority given health officers to fight the AIDS epidemic (Abe, 1990; Hagan, 1991). This decision was never appealed (Hagan et al., 1991). A similar ruling in a subsequent case held the Spokane NEP to be legal as well (Abe, 1990; McKee, 1991; Severson, 1990). The Spokane case was appealed, however, and the NEP was found to be legal by the Washington State Supreme Court, setting a binding precedent on the matter for the State of Washington (Paulson, 1992).

In 1992, seven U.S. states introduced legislation to legalize pilot NEPs, and five states introduced legislation governing the sale and possession of syringes (Bowleg, 1992). Of all of the 1992 legislation, only that in Connecticut became law. In 1993, seven states (California, Illinois, Maine, Maryland, Massachusetts, Rhode Island, and Texas) again introduced legislation to legalize pilot NEPs. The Massachusetts pilot NEP legislation passed on July 19, 1993. The legislation did not become law in the remaining five states (L. Bowleg, personal communication, August 5, 1993). In 1993, the New Hampshire legislature passed a bill revoking the state prescription law that was subsequently vetoed by Governor Stephen Merrill, who described it as a bill that "winked at illegal activity" (Merrill, 1993). The Maine legislature, however, subsequently passed a statute revoking their state's prescription law.

In terms of the legal status of the 33 U.S. NEPs that were visited or surveyed by mail for this research, two conclusions may be drawn: (a) All NEPs that opened prior to 1990, many of which were underground at the time of opening, are now either legal or illegal-tolerated; and (b) of the 12 NEPs that opened in 1992, only five were legal in September 1993. Thus, although there is a trend toward increasing legalization of NEPs, many newer NEPs are still illegal (Curie et al., 1993).

Funding

The earliest NEPs in the United States were funded privately, often by individual donations; in some cases, the exchange staff paid for the needles they gave out. Such private donations still provide at least some support to many NEPs. In addition, private foundations have awarded grants to several NEPs. The largest of these contributors has been AmFAR, which has provided funds for NEPs in Portland, Boulder, San Francisco, and New York City. In 1992, the Robert Wood Johnson Foundation made a 3-year grant to allow the New Haven NEP to expand its services.

NEPs that have relied on private sources for most or all of their operating costs have experienced periods of considerable financial instability. San Francisco's Prevention Point NEP, for example, which relied primarily on private donations from its inception in 1988 until March 1993, when the City and County Department of Public Health began providing support, frequently had inadequate funds with which to purchase syringes. According to Prevention Point's director, George Clark, in May 1992, the group owed $13,000 to a syringe manufacturer and was unsure, at that time, how they were going to obtain enough syringes to distribute (G. Clark, interview, June 3 and 11, 1992).

Even programs that have received some local governmental funds have experienced periodic funding crises. For example, statewide budget cuts early in 1992 in Oregon severely reduced Outside-In's funding at the same time their

AmFAR grant was ending. Just before the program was preparing to close, it received a grant from Photographers and Friends United Against AIDS in New York City. With this funding and a second grant from AmFAR, it has remained open.

Although federal policies prohibit the use of federal funds for needle exchange services, programs are increasingly receiving city and even state funds. The Tacoma and New Haven programs, for example, are primarily funded by their city and/or county health departments. Hawaii's NEPs have received State Department of Health and private funding (State of Hawaii Department of Health, 1992), and, as mentioned, San Francisco's program has received Department of Public Health funding (Russell, 1993).

Institutionalization

As NEPs in many areas have gained greater community support and more regular funding sources, there has been a trend toward greater institutionalization. Some activist-run NEPs, such as Tacoma's Point Defiance AIDS Project, have evolved into CBOs. In other cases, established CBOs, such as Outside-In in Portland, have added needle exchange to their other services. These NEPs often have formal or informal linkages with health departments. A few (New Haven, Seattle, Boulder, and Toronto's The Works) are run directly by health departments. As mentioned previously, Seattle's NEP was started by ACT-UP and subsequently taken over by the health department. Others (New Haven, Boulder, and Toronto's The Works) have been run by health departments from their inception.

Whereas many programs were started by committed volunteers, more programs now employ paid staff and must deal with such issues as health insurance, union policies, overtime pay, and vacation coverage. In a few programs, such as New Haven, liability concerns limit the ways in which volunteers can assist the program. In San Francisco and Tacoma, the activists continue to work with the NEP, and instead of worrying about getting arrested, they now worry about writing quarterly reports. With greater institutionalization, NEP staff have often gained specialized experience with the IDU population or, in some cases, professional training in public health or social work. The NEP with the most highly trained staff is CACTUS in Montreal, where all staff are registered nurses.

Many of the early programs started by handing out needles on the street, thus avoiding the costs of vehicles and office rentals. In the transition from activist-run to more established organizations, these infrastructure expenses grew as well, sometimes greatly increasing the operating costs of the programs. More formal linkages with drug treatment facilities, social services, and health care providers have often come with increasing institutionalization. For example, in 1993, New Haven's NEP and the Yale/New Haven Hospital AIDS Care Program linked services. The AIDS Care Program van now follows the NEP van on a regular schedule and offers HIV and tuberculosis testing and primary medical care to NEP clients (Altice et al., 1993; E. O'Keefe, interview, August 18, 1992). With greater institutionalization, a community potentially has the more control over the activities of the NEP and can insist on evaluation reports that show whether the NEP has met its stated objectives.

One of the potential costs, however, may be the widening of the social distance between clients and staff, leading to more formal, professional relationships. Although this is a risk, it is not inevitable. New Haven's NEP, for example, is quite institutionalized. Nevertheless, by hiring some former IDUs, and by providing service through a mobile van that stops in accessible locations, it has tried to combine the informal warmth of the activist groups with the institutionalization of a formal public health intervention.

Greater Federal Funding of NEP Research

Five laws passed by Congress from 1988 to 1991 prohibited the use of federal funds for the provision of needle exchange services. These were the Comprehensive Alcohol Abuse, Drug Abuse, and Mental Health Amendments Act of 1988, the Health Omnibus Programs Extension of 1988, the Ryan White Comprehensive AIDS Resources Emergency Act of 1990, and the Departments of Labor, Health and Human Services, and Education, and Related Agencies Appropriations Acts of 1990 and 1991 ("General Provisions," 1993). In 1993, the Departments of Labor, Health and Human Services, and Education, and Related Agencies Appropriation Act continued the ban on the use of federal funds for needle exchange services "unless the Surgeon General of the United States determines that such programs are effective in preventing the spread of HIV and do not encourage the use of illegal drugs" ("General Provisions," 1993).

A 1989 memorandum issued by Barry S. Brown, NIDA's Chief of Community Research, warned that federal funding would be withdrawn from any program that "is engaged in, or . . . supports" NEPs ("US Sending Mixed Signals," 1989, p. A24). Brown later modified the restrictions so that any individual receiving federal funding could work on needle exchange on his or her own time. Brown's original statement made researchers doing work in the area of drug use reluctant to become involved with needle exchange. One of the reasons that activists played such prominent roles in establishing NEPs may have been that researchers and health professionals were unwilling to jeopardize their funding. Some of the NEP staff members described how this issue has caused continuing friction between activists and researchers, because the activists were willing to take certain risks that researchers were not willing to take (San Francisco NEP staff, interview, June 3 and 11, 1992).

By 1992, the federal government began funding research evaluating NEPs, although the ban on federal support for NEP services continued. Early federally supported research on NEPs included the present study, funded by the CDC in April 1992; research conducted for the Office of National Drug Control Policy by ABT Associates, a research consulting firm from Cambridge, Massachusetts; and a General Accounting Office evaluation requested by Representative Charles Rangel of New York City that assessed the New Haven research and the research cited in the National Commission on AIDS report ("Needle Exchange Programs," 1992). In addition, the July 1992 bill reorganizing the Alcohol, Drug Abuse and Mental Health Administration approved $5 million, of which $2 million were appropriated, for research on needle exchange by the National Academy of Sciences ("General Provisions," 1993). The National Institute of Drug Abuse also funded research on New Haven's Syringe Tracking and Testing System as well as on the NEPs in San Francisco and Seattle. By 1993, there were seven federally funded studies of NEPs. Four of these, including the present study, were concerned primarily with the synthesis of existing information, and three studies entailed the collection of new data.

CONCLUSION

Needle exchange has been one of the most controversial public health issues in the United States during the past decade. The crisis of the AIDS epidemic, and its spread to IDUs, their partners, and their infants, has inspired a social movement led in its earliest phases by committed activists guided by a philosophy of civil disobedience. Like most social movements, there has been a trend toward greater institutionalization, and with it greater legal and policy acceptance in many states and localities. This trend toward greater institutionalization of NEPs has forged better links between NEPs and other public health services, in some cases creating more comprehensive services.

The growing public acceptance of needle exchange, however, has not been universal or unequivocal. Needle exchange as a strategy has seemed to many to be in direct opposition to the concurrent war on drugs being waged by federal and local law enforcement. These two deeply held social values—eliminating all illicit drug use versus reducing the social harm of drug use to the greatest extent possible—have meant that public health policy on this issue has often been made amid bitter, contentious debates.

NOTE

1. Material included in this chapter is drawn from Chapters 3, 4, and 5 of Lurie et al. (1993).

REFERENCES

Abe, D. (1990, February 17). Needle exchange ruled legal. *Tacoma News Tribune*, p. A1.

Altice, F. L. et al. (1993). *Provision of health care and HIV counseling and testing for clients of the New Haven needle exchange program.* Abstract PO-D17-3927 presented at the IX International Conference on AIDS, Berlin.

Anderson, W. (1991). The New York needle trial: The politics of public health in the age of AIDS. *American Journal of Public Health, 81,* 1506-1517.

Anon. (1993, March 23). *Needle exchange programs: Research suggests promise as an AIDS prevention strategy.* U.S. General Accounting Office.

Anon. (1993). Impact of new legislation on needle and syringe purchase and possession— Connecticut, 1992. *Morbidity and Mortality Weekly Report, 42,* 145-148.

Bowleg, L. (1992, April). Straight to the point: State legislatures revisit the needle exchange and prescription-for-needles controversy. *Intergovernmental AIDS Reports,* pp. 1-5.

Brenner, H. et al. (1991). *AIDS among drug abusers in Europe: Review of recent developments.* Geneva: World Health Organization.

Buning, E. C. (1991). Effects of Amsterdam needle and syringe exchange. *International Journal of the Addictions, 26,* 1303-1311.

Buning, E. C. et al. (1986). Preventing AIDS in drug addicts in Amsterdam [Letter]. *The Lancet, i,* 1435.

Debuono, B. B. et al. (1990, December 10). *Needle exchange programs: An examination of existing data and relevant issues.* Office of Disease Control, Rhode Island.

Des Jarlais, D. C. et al. (1985). "Free" needles for intravenous drug users at risk for AIDS: Current developments in New York City [Letter]. *New England Journal of Medicine, 313,* 1476.

Des Jarlais, D. C. et al. (1988). The new death among IV drug users. In I. B. Coless & M. Pittman-Lindeman (Eds.), *AIDS: Principles, practices, and politics* (pp. 135-150). Washington, DC: Hemisphere.

Des Jarlais, D. C. et al. (1990, August). *Almost banning bleach.* Paper presented at the annual meeting of the American Psychological Association, Boston.

Downing, M. et al. (1991). *Establishing a street-based needle exchange: Prevention Point's experience.* San Francisco: Prevention Point Research Group.

Drucker, E. (1990). The trial of Jon Parker. *International Journal on Drug Policy, 1,* 8-9.

Friedman, S. et al. (1987). AIDS and self-organization among intravenous drug users. *International Journal of the Addictions, 22,* 201-219.

General Provisions of the Department of Labor, Health and Human Services, and Education and Related Agencies Appropriations Act, 1993. (1993). P.L. 102-321.

Gordon, R. (1992, April 25). Supes mull needle swap plan. *San Francisco Independent,* pp. 1-2.

Hagan, H. (1991). Syringe exchanges struggle to carry out HIV prevention. *Washington Public Health, 9.*

Hagan, H. et al. (1991). The Tacoma syringe exchange. *Journal of Addictive Diseases, 10,* 81-88.

Jordan, F. M. (1993, March 15). *Declaration of a local emergency.* Unpublished report, Office of the Mayor.

Joseph, S. (1992). The needle exchange. In *Dragon within the gates: The once and future AIDS epidemic* (pp. 191-220). New York: Carroll & Graf.

Kaplan, E. H. et al. (1993). Let the needles do the talking! Evaluating the New Haven needle exchange. *Interfaces, 23,* 7-26.

Lucas, G. (1992, October 1). Wilson vetoes legislation legalizing needle exchange. *San Francisco Chronicle,* p. A15.

Lurie, P., Reingold, A., Bowser, B., Chen, D., Foley, J., Guydish, J., Kahn, J., Lane, S. D., & Sorenson, J. (1993). *The public health impact of needle exchange programs in the United States and abroad* (Vols. 1 & 2). San Francisco: University of California, San Francisco, Institute for Health Policy Studies.

Martinez, R. (1992). Needle exchange programs: Are they effective? *ONDCP Bulletin, 7,* 1-7.

McKee, M. (1991). Needle exchange advocates gaining ground nationwide. *The Recorder.*

Merrill, S. (1993, June 15). Letter to members of the General Court, New Hampshire.

Minutes of the January 21, 1992 Health Commission Meeting. (1992, January 21). San Francisco Health Commission.

National Commission on Acquired Immune Deficiency Syndrome. (1991, July). *The twin epidemics of substance abuse and HIV.* Washington, DC: Author.

Needle exchange is still in legal twilight [Editorial]. (1989, May 1). *Tacoma News Tribune.*

Newmeyer, J. A. (1988). *Why bleach? Development of a strategy to combat HIV contagion among San Francisco intravenous drug users* (NIDA Research Monograph #80, pp. 151-152). Rockville, MD: National Institute on Drug Abuse.

New York City Department of Health. (1989, December). *The pilot needle exchange study in New York City: A bridge to treatment.* New York: Author.

O'Keefe, E. et al. (1991, July 31). *Preliminary report: City of New Haven needle exchange program.* New Haven, CT: City of New Haven.

Paulson, T. (1992, November 6). Needle exchange upheld. *Seattle Post-Intelligence,* p. 1.

Purchase, D. et al. (1989). *Historical account of the first North American syringe exchange.* Abstract ThDP 74 presented at Final Program and Abstracts of the Vth International Conference on AIDS, Montreal.

Rezza, G. et al. (1992). *HIV prevention strategies in injection drug users.* Lausanne, Switzerland: Institut Universitaire de Medicine Sociale et Preventive Lausanne.

Russell, S. (1993, March 13). S.F. to challenge state, start needle exchange. *San Francisco Chronicle.*

Scrimshaw, S. et al. (1987). *Rapid assessment procedures for nutrition and primary health care.* Los Angeles: University of California, Los Angeles, Latin American Center.

Severson, K. (1990). Suit tests legality of needle program. *Tacoma News Tribune.*

Sorge, R. (1990, Fall). Drug policy in the age of AIDS: The philosophy of "harm reduction." *Health/PAC Bulletin,* pp. 4-10.

State of Hawaii Department of Health. (1992). *Needle exchange programs: A report to the Needle Exchange Oversight Committee.* Honolulu: Author.

US sending mixed signals on trade-ins of dirty needles. (1989, March 15). *New York Times,* p. A1.

Van Ameijden, E. J. et al. (1992). The harm reduction approach and risk factors for HIV seroconversion in injecting drug users, Amsterdam. *American Journal of Epidemiology, 136,* 236-243.

Wilson, P. (1992, September 30). Letter to California Assembly.

Wilson, S. (1989a, April 8). Attorney general: Needle exchange violates state law. *Tacoma News Tribune.*

Wilson, S. (1989b, May 20). Lawmakers outlaw needle program; veto looms. *Tacoma News Tribune,* p. A7.

Wilson, S. (1989c, May 8). Veto gives needle exchange a better shot. *Tacoma News Tribune,* pp. B1-B2.

4

The Medicalization
of Marijuana

Lana D. Harrison

Writing a chapter on medicalized marijuana for a book that will stand the test of time is quite a challenge, because the societal response to medicalized marijuana is in a state of flux. For many years, therapeutic effects in cases of nausea, pain, epilepsy, asthma, and hypertension have been documented both for marijuana plant extracts and purified cannabinoids (Synder, 1971). After several failed challenges to the Drug Enforcement Administration (DEA) to reschedule marijuana in recognition of its potential medicinal uses, there was a surprising and well publicized turnaround with the passage of Proposition 215 in California and Proposition 200 in Arizona in November 1996. In their respective states, these propositions permit the use of marijuana for medical purposes with a physician's prescription. The Arizona initiative went even further in allowing physicians to prescribe a number of currently illegal drugs for medical purposes— although it still required the endorsement of two physicians and citations from relevant scientific research. The propositions did not make marijuana or other drugs legal, nor was the issue of availability and access to the illegal drugs dealt with. Rather, the intent was to prevent the prosecution of individuals who, with the tacit consent of their physician, used or possessed marijuana (and other controlled substances in Arizona). The problem is that neither proposition can really be implemented without violating federal law.

There was a swift response to the passage of these state propositions by the federal government. The President's Office of National Drug Control Policy

(ONDCP) issued immediate press releases decrying the legislation, declaring it simply a ruse to legalize marijuana. They suggested that voters did not know what they were voting for, especially in Arizona. The Community Anti-Drug Coalitions of America brought 1,000 leaders of its local chapters to Washington within 2 weeks of the passage of the propositions to discuss how to prevent similar initiatives from reaching the ballot in other states. The president of the organization said, "They're using AIDS victims and terminally ill as props to promote the use of marijuana" (Wren, 1996, p. 16). On December 30, 1996, the Departments of Justice and Health and Human Services sent letters to physicians and licensing boards, as well as local, state, and national medical associations, stating that the DEA will revoke the registration of any physician who recommends the prescription of marijuana or other illicit drugs. The federal government's official response, released on February 11, 1997, said that "these measures pose a threat to the National Drug Control Strategy goal of reducing drug abuse in the United States" ("Administration Response," 1997, p. 6164). The official response was basically that the federal government would do all that it could to effectively keep the propositions from being implemented; that they would work to "limit the states' ability to rely on these and similar medical use provisions" ("Administration Response," 1997, p. 6166).

It is obvious that these propositions were not well received by the federal government. Yet a majority of voters in the states of California and Arizona thought that the time was ripe for compassionate use of marijuana. There were relatively well-financed campaigns in both states to encourage the populace to approve these propositions, but were the voters duped, as the federal government suggests? Perhaps the best way to understand the polarity in this debate is to explore some of the history leading to current developments.

HISTORY OF MEDICAL APPLICATIONS WITH CANNABIS

The earliest record of human cannabis use may be a description of the drug in a Chinese compendium of medicines, dated 2737 B.C. according to some sources, but 400 to 500 B.C. by others (Grinspoon & Bakalar, 1993). Records on the medicinal use of cannabis appear in the Egyptian Ebers papyrus of the 16th century B.C. (Zias et al., 1993). Cannabis use is documented in the four Vedas (from India), the oldest completely preserved religious texts on earth, dating back to about 1000 to 1500 B.C. It appears that marijuana was used in a religious ceremony for freedom from distress or anxiety. There is also information that hemp was used as an anesthetic during the second century in China. Greek and Roman healers recommended cannabis for its ability to cure earache and assorted pains in the first and second centuries. A thousand years later, we find hemp or cannabis included in the Latin herbal of Rufinus (c. 1287 A.D.). The first English herbal by Nicholas Culpeper (ca. 1645) recommends it for a variety of ailments including jaundice, coughing, worms, gout, and rheumatism (Aldrich, 1971).

In 1839, Dr. William B. O'Shaughnessy, a British physician working in Calcutta, introduced the therapeutic values of cannabis into Western medicine. He reported on the analgesic (pain relief), anticonvulsant (antivomiting), and muscle-relaxant properties of the drug. American doctors began using cannabis tincture and extracts around 1850 (Aldrich, 1971; Grinspoon & Bakalar, 1993). Between 1840 and 1900, European and American medical journals published more than 100 articles on the therapeutic use of cannabis. It was recommended as an appetite stimulant, muscle relaxant, analgesic, hypnotic (sleeping aid), and anticonvulsant. As late as 1913, it was recommended as the "most satisfactory remedy for migraine" (Grinspoon & Bakalar, 1995, p. 1875).

By the late 1930s, the chemical structure of delta 9-tetrahydrocannabinol, or THC, was sufficiently well known for drug companies to synthesize analogues in the hope of retaining therapeutic effects but eliminating psychoactivity. However, the Marijuana Tax Act in 1937 virtually terminated all research on the drug (Snyder, 1990). Modeled after the Harrison Act, it essentially placed marijuana into the same category as cocaine and opium drugs. The Harrison Act, which became federal law in 1914, effectively outlawed opiates and cocaine without a physician's prescription. In 1915, California became the first state to pass a law prohibiting marijuana possession unless prescribed by a physician. Other states followed suit over the next two decades such that when the Marijuana Tax Act became federal law in 1937, 43 of the then 48 states had already passed anti-marijuana legislation. The passage of the Marijuana Tax Act had been fought by the American Medical Association (Brecher, 1986). The medicinal use of cannabis declined in the early 20th century due to not only the Tax Act, but also the introduction of alternatives such as injectable opiates and, later, synthetic drugs such as aspirin and barbiturates. Furthermore, research had effectively been halted (it was illegal to import marijuana into the United States) (McWilliams, 1991), the potency of preparations was variable, and responses to oral ingestion were erratic.

The Recent History of Medicalized Marijuana

In October 1970, President Richard M. Nixon signed the Comprehensive Drug Abuse and Prevention and Control Act of 1970 into law. One aspect of the Controlled Substances Act defines a schedule for drugs. Schedule I lists those substances that have no accepted medical utility but have substantial potential for abuse. Found on this schedule are heroin, marijuana, and various hallucinogens. Schedule II lists substances having a high abuse liability but also having some accepted medical purpose. Found on Schedule II are morphine and cocaine. It is worth noting that under the scheduling provisions of the Act, marijuana was grouped with heroin, whereas cocaine, with its significant abuse liability and very limited medical use, still falls into Schedule II. Nevertheless, the Comprehensive Drug Abuse and Prevention and Control Act of 1970 also "lowered the maximum penalty for possession of an ounce of marijuana to one year in jail and a $5,000 fine, with the option of probation or a conditional discharge at the judge's discretion" (Slaughter, 1988, p. 421).

The long-awaited report of the National Commission on Marihuana and Drug Abuse (1972), which investigated the recent increases in the popularity of marijuana use among young people, recommended that more studies be conducted to evaluate the efficacy of marijuana in the treatment of physical impairments and disease. The report noted that historical references suggest the therapeutic usefulness of cannabis and recommended investigations concerning its usefulness in treating glaucoma, migraine, alcoholism, and terminal cancer. It is also noteworthy that the Commission recommended the decriminalization of cannabis possession.

In 1972, the National Organization for the Reform of Marijuana Laws (NORML) petitioned the DEA to transfer marijuana to Schedule II so that it could be legally prescribed. It was not until 1986 that the DEA acceded to the demands for the public hearings required by law (Grinspoon & Bakalar, 1995).[1] The hearings lasted 2 years, during which many patients and physicians testified and thousands of pages of documentation were introduced. In 1988, the DEA's chief administrative law judge, Francis Young, ruled that the federal government should reclassify marijuana so that doctors could prescribe it. However, his order to reclassify marijuana was overruled by the DEA administrator, who issued a final rejection of all pleas for reclassification on March 26, 1992. He stated that "Americans take their medicines in pills, solutions, sprays, shots, drops, creams and sometimes in suppositories, but never by smoking" (Federal Record, 1992, p. 10499). The only other way to change marijuana's scheduling is for the Food and Drug Administration (FDA) to tell the DEA that the drug has "currently accepted medical use."

The 1992 ruling by the DEA was appealed to the U.S. Court of Appeals for the District of Columbia by NORML, the Drug Policy Foundation (DPF), and the Alliance for Cannabis Therapeutics (ACT). The Court's decision was issued in February 1994, eliminating three of the eight criteria used by the DEA to determine if a drug was medically acceptable, yet upholding the 1992 DEA ruling (Schwartz & Voth, 1995). The decision not to reschedule marijuana was based on its failure to meet the following five criteria taken from the U.S. Court of Appeals (argued October 1, 1993 and decided February 18, 1994):

1. The drug's chemistry must be known and reproducible.

2. There must be adequate safety studies.

3. There must be adequate and well-controlled studies proving efficacy.

4. The drug must be accepted by qualified experts.

5. The scientific evidence must be widely available.

It is known that marijuana contains more than 400 chemicals, some of whose chemical properties are not completely known—which means that it does not meet the first criterion. In terms of safety studies, the DEA argues that marijuana's side effects are extensive, though not fully understood (Hecht, 1991). Because few well-controlled studies to document marijuana's risks or benefits have been conducted, it does not meet the last three criteria.

According to a June 20, 1995 press release by the DEA administrator, there are adequate procedures to permit qualified researchers to conduct studies using marijuana and other Schedule I drugs. The administrator reported that currently, there were 2,040 applications registered to engage in research activities with Schedule I drugs, of which 1,605 were for marijuana. The DEA sends the protocols to the FDA for medical and scientific evaluation as well. Independent decisions are made by both the FDA and the DEA to approve the application.

Dr. Donald Abrams, a professor of clinical medicine at the University of California, San Francisco and the chairman of San Francisco's Community Consortium, would argue that the procedures to gain access to marijuana for research studies are not adequate. He tried to get access to marijuana to conduct a pilot study to compare the efficacy of inhaled marijuana with synthetic THC (the major chemical metabolite in marijuana, available through prescription under the name of Marinol) as an appetite stimulant for patients with HIV wasting syndrome. Dr. Abrams's protocol was developed in consultation with and approved by the FDA. However, the DEA rejected Dr. Abrams's request to obtain marijuana from a company in the Netherlands licensed to cultivate cannabis for botanical and pharmaceutical research, nor would they grant him a legal supply of domestic marijuana for the research. There is a marked contrast between Dr. Abrams's experience, which was fairly widely publicized, and the statement of the DEA administrator indicating a relatively large number of individuals licensed to conduct research with cannabis. One would expect that based on the administrator's statement, the scientific knowledge about cannabis is continually increasing.

The Compassionate IND Program

In 1976, as a result of a settlement agreement in a lawsuit against the government, a procedure was devised to allow patients who needed marijuana (because no other drug would produce the same therapeutic effects) to receive marijuana cigarettes under the (compassionate) single-patient investigative new drug

(IND) procedure at the FDA. The initiator of the lawsuit was Robert Randall, who had been told in 1972 that he had 3 to 5 years before his glaucoma would result in blindness. Although Mr. Randall also takes prescription drugs, he is still alive and sighted, and he still receives monthly supplies of marijuana cigarettes grown on a government farm in Mississippi. Patients with cancer and chronic pain have also won access, but the application process was complicated, and between 1976 and 1991, only about 15 patients were awarded single-patient INDs for marijuana cigarettes (Grinspoon & Bakalar, 1995; U.S. Public Health Service, personal communication, July 12, 1994).

In 1990, a man known as Steve L. became the first AIDS patient to obtain marijuana through the single-patient IND program, 10 days before he died. On August 10, 1990, a judge found Kenny and Barbara Jenks guilty of possessing and cultivating two marijuana plants. They argued in court that the marijuana was of medical necessity—Kenny Jenks, a hemophiliac, had infected his wife with AIDS after receiving AIDS-infected blood in 1985. They applied for the Compassionate IND program for marijuana cigarettes after their arrest and were the last people to be accepted into the program (Hughes & Van Nattie, 1990)— 9 months after they applied (Hewitt, 1991). Both have since died.

The decision to close the Compassionate IND program for marijuana cigarettes appears to be the result of the anticipation of scores of applications from AIDS patients as they became aware of the value of marijuana in helping them to eat. In 1991, there was a tripling in the number of applications received, virtually all of them from patients with HIV wasting syndrome, which led to a review of the IND program for marijuana. When the U.S. Public Health Service chose to close the program in 1991, there was no public announcement, and the 28 patients whose applications had been approved by the FDA were held in limbo. The U.S. Public Health Service completed a review of marijuana's reported health benefits and dangers for symptoms associated with five diseases, and it decided that there was no evidence that smoked marijuana was better than available alternative therapies. Concern was also expressed that smoked marijuana could be harmful to people with impaired immune systems, particularly AIDS patients. The Secretary of Health and Human Services closed the program in March 1992, although the 13 people already smoking marijuana legally for medical purposes were allowed to continue (Cotton, 1992). Instead of marijuana, the U.S. Public Health Service recommended Marinol, a Schedule II capsule form of synthetic THC (U.S. Public Health Service, personal communication, July 12, 1994). Furthermore, the head of the U.S. Public Health Service said that providing marijuana as medicine might create the "perception that this stuff can't be so bad" (Cotton, 1992, p. 2573). He said he feared that AIDS patients using marijuana would be more likely to practice unsafe sex.

In 1985, the government recognized that the principal active metabolite in cannabis—THC—had medical use. In 1986, Marinol's use was approved as an antiemetic (antivomiting agent), and at the beginning of 1993, Marinol was approved under a Supplemental New Drug Application for anorexia found to be associated with appetite and weight loss in AIDS patients (Levine, 1993). These are currently the only approved uses of Marinol, although it is prescribed for a number of other indications. Thus, many experts argue that marijuana cigarettes are not necessary to the medical arsenal. However, other experts argue that Marinol does not substitute for smoked marijuana, and indeed, some of the other chemicals in marijuana may provide useful therapeutic functions individually or in concert with other chemicals in the plant. They point out that Marinol is absorbed into the blood through the gastrointestinal tract. Only about 15% to 20% in the blood reaches the brain, whereas smoked marijuana is absorbed in the lungs through the bronchia and goes immediately to the brain (Roxane Laboratories, personal communication, 1997). This appears to provide immediate relief from nausea, rather than waiting several hours for the effects of the oral capsule to take hold. Furthermore, many pharmacies prefer not to stock Marinol because of the difficulty of the records they have to keep, or the fact that it has to be stored differently. The cost of a monthly prescription varies, and in one Midwest city in 1995, the price was $165 to $185 per month, whereas in a West Coast city, the price was $350 to $370 per month (Roxane Laboratories, personal communication, 1997).

Although all drugs have side effects, two of medicalized marijuana's chief proponents, Dr. Grinspoon and Dr. Bakalar from Harvard, state that marijuana is far less addictive and far less subject to abuse than are many drugs now used as muscle relaxants, hypnotics, and analgesics (Grinspoon & Bakalar, 1995). One of marijuana's greatest advantages as a medicine is its remarkable safety. There are no known cases of lethal overdose. Based on animal models, the ratio of lethal to effective dose is estimated at 40,000 to 1 (Grinspoon & Bakalar, 1995). The chief health concern is the effect of smoking on the lungs.

When the U.S. District Court handed down its decree on medicalized marijuana in 1995, it noted that "not one American health association accepts marijuana as medicine" ("Marijuana Scheduling Petition," 1992, p. 10499). Marijuana has been rejected as medicine by the American Medical Association, the National Multiple Sclerosis Society, the American Glaucoma Society, the American Academy of Ophthalmology, and the American Cancer Society ("Marijuana Scheduling Petition," 1992). However, support was voiced by the American Public Health Association at its annual meeting in October 1995, when its 30,000 members passed a policy statement encouraging research on the therapeutic properties of cannabis and alternative methods of administration to decrease the harmful effects related to smoking. It urged the Clinton administration and Congress to move expeditiously to make cannabis available as a legal medicine where shown to be safe and effective and to allow immediate access to therapeutic cannabis through the Compassionate IND program. The policy statement concluded that greater harm is caused by the legal consequences of marijuana's prohibition than the possible risks of medicinal use. The California Medical Association and the American Bar Association also say that the ban on medical marijuana should be lifted.

A fairly well publicized 1991 survey completed by 1,035 members of the American Society of Clinical Oncology found that 48% would prescribe marijuana to some patients if it were legal. Thirty percent said that they needed more information before deciding if they would prescribe it. Perhaps surprisingly, 44% said they had already recommended its illegal use to patients to control vomiting (Doblin & Kleiman, 1991). The authors caution that the survey response rate of 43% makes it difficult to project the results to U.S. oncologists more globally, but they suggest that the results demonstrate that oncologists' experience with marijuana is more extensive and opinions more favorable than would have been believed. A subsequent survey of every third member of the American Society of Clinical Oncology, with a 72% response rate, showed that about 30% believed that marijuana should be rescheduled, and 32% said that they would prescribe it (Schwartz & Voth, 1995).

RECENT RESEARCH ON MARIJUANA'S MEDICAL UTILITY

In 1993, at the request of members of Congress, the U.S. Public Health Service conducted a review of marijuana's medical utility. The major conclusion was that there is no clinical evidence to suggest that smoked marijuana is superior to currently available therapies for glaucoma, weight loss and wasting associated with AIDS, nausea and vomiting associated with cancer chemotherapy, muscle spasticity associated with multiple sclerosis, or intractable pain (U.S. Public Health Service, personal communication, July 12, 1994). However, a review of the statements of the various National Institutes of Health (NIH) that participated in the review are sprinkled with the use of words like "may" or "probably." For example, the National Institute on Allergy and Infectious Diseases (NIAID), writing on HIV wasting syndrome, and the National Institute of Neurological Disorders and Stroke, writing on multiple sclerosis, used identical language in stating that "Drug absorption is dependent on deep inhalation of marijuana smoke and *may* [emphasis added] be impractical or unacceptable for non-smoking patients." The report of the National Cancer Institute (NCI) actually states: "In general, NCI scientists believe that marijuana-related compounds can be useful for certain cancer patients" (U.S. Public Health Service, personal communication, July 12, 1994).

The NIH, which is the umbrella organization for the institutes listed above, again held an (albeit short) scientific meeting on February 19-20, 1997 to review the scientific data concerning the potential therapeutic uses for marijuana and the need for and feasibility of additional research. The Expert Group reviewed research with respect to the potential efficacy of cannabinoids, including smoked marijuana, in the areas of analgesia, neurological and movement disorders, nausea and vomiting associated with cancer chemotherapy, glaucoma, and appetite stimulation. They found that most of what is known about the clinical pharmacology of marijuana is actually the results of experiments with pure THC, which, although similar, is not always the same as the clinical pharmacology of smoked marijuana containing the same amount of THC (National Institutes of Health [NIH], 1997, p. 9).

The Expert Group basically concluded that the

> scientific process should be allowed to evaluate the potential therapeutic effects of marijuana for certain disorders, dissociated from the societal debate over the potential harmful effects of nonmedical marijuana use. All decisions on the ultimate usefulness of a medical intervention are based on a benefit/risk calculation, and marijuana should be no exception to this generally accepted principle. (NIH, 1997, p. 2)

The Expert Group concluded that the availability of Marinol does not fully satisfy the need to evaluate the potential medical utility of marijuana and that "for at least some potential indications, marijuana looks promising enough to recommend that there be new controlled studies done" (NIH, 1997, p. 5), including (a) appetite stimulation/cachexia, (b) nausea and vomiting following anticancer therapy, (c) neurological and movement disorders, (d) analgesia, and (e) glaucoma. The following paragraphs contain information taken from the Report to the Director, National Institutes of Health, by the Ad Hoc Group of Experts, February 19-20, 1997.

Appetite stimulation/cachexia. Research demonstrates a strong relationship between smoking marijuana and increased frequency and amount of eating, although no long-term studies have been conducted. Significantly, a survey examining physicians' choice of drugs to treat HIV wasting syndrome, or cachexia, found that the first line of choice (80%) was megestrol, with Marinol being used by 54%. Marinol was also the second choice of most physicians.

Nausea and vomiting. There is a large body of scientific research on the use of primarily oral THC on chemotherapy-related nausea and vomiting. However, none of the studies has compared either oral THC or smoked marijuana with current state-of-the-art medications. These medications are effective in about 80% of patients, and the investigation of the efficacy of smoked marijuana on those for whom current medications are not effective might be an initial starting point.

Neurological and movement disorders. There is substantial animal research showing that cannabinoids have anticonvulsant effects in the control of epilepsy, although there is little information on humans. The spasticity and nocturnal spasms produced by multiple sclerosis (MS) and partial spinal cord injury have been relieved by smoked marijuana and oral THC in numerous anecdotal reports, but no large-scale controlled studies have been conducted. There is evidence from animal research that cannabinoids may be of value in altering the root cause of a disease such as MS rather than simply treating its symptoms. Neither smoked marijuana nor oral THC have been found to be successful in the treatment of Parkinson's disease or Huntington's chorea.

Analgesia. Results of animal and human studies have been conflicting. The recent identification of cannabinoid receptors suggests some evidence that they are part of a natural pain control system. There have been no controlled studies of smoked marijuana in patients with naturally occurring pain. It is likely that smoked marijuana, because of its rapid absorption, is more effective in pain relief than oral THC.

Glaucoma. Glaucoma is a condition of the eye in which the fluid pressure within the eyeball (the intraocular pressure) increases beyond normal range and causes damage to the optic nerve with a very real possibility of blindness. Scientists agree that the chronic smoking of marijuana may alleviate the elevation of intraocular pressure, but marijuana also decreases blood pressure (and thus blood flow) to the eye and may interfere with blood supply to the optic nerve. Thus, even though intraocular pressure is reduced, the glaucoma process may still occur (Drug Enforcement Administration, 1994). The American Academy on Ophthalmology's Committee on Drugs, as well as the National Eye Institute of the National Institutes of Health, believes that a long-term clinical study appears appropriate. They would like to investigate whether marijuana offers any advantages over the 24 currently approved medications in the form of both eye drops and pills for the treatment of glaucoma, when used singly or in combination.

In summary, the NIH has recently come forward to suggest that there are adequate reasons to expect that smoked marijuana has utility in the therapeutic treatment of certain conditions, and it proposes that research be conducted. Another part of the federal government's response has been to ask the National Academy of Science's Institute of Medicine (IOM) to conduct a comprehensive, 18-month study and evaluation of the scientific research regarding the medical uses of marijuana. They asked the IOM to examine all medical and scientific evidence, identify gaps in knowledge, determine whether further research could answer these questions, and determine how that research could be designed and conducted ("Administration Response," 1997). The government has committed nearly a million dollars to the IOM to provide a comprehensive assessment on the state of scientific knowledge of the existing clinical, medical, and scientific evidence on the following topics: (a) neurological mechanism of action of marijuana; (b) effects of marijuana on health and behavior; (c) marijuana's "gateway" characteristics; (d) efficacy of therapeutic use of marijuana for specific medical conditions (e.g., glaucoma, multiple sclerosis, wasting diseases such as AIDS and cancer, nausea, and pain) compared with approved alternative pharmacotherapies; and (e) adverse effects of marijuana compared with approved alternative pharmacotherapies (J. Crist, personal communication, January 3, 1997). The Federation of American Scientists (FAS), sponsored by 45 Nobel Prize winners, urged President Clinton to instruct the NIH to conduct research on the possible medical uses of cannabis in every instance where there are indications of possible efficacy, rather than wait for the completion of the 18-month research of the existing literature by the Institute of Medicine (FAS, 1997). Incidentally, Dr. Abrams, the researcher at the University of California, San Francisco who fought unsuccessfully with the federal government for a pilot study comparing smoked cannabis with Marinol and a placebo in the treatment of AIDS patients, received approval from the NIH in 1997 to carry out his 2-year study.

Of course, all of these responses are subsequent to the passage of Proposition 215 in California and Proposition 200 in Arizona in November 1996. The passage of the propositions appears to be a leading indicator of change rather than lagging. Remember that the federal response was that voters were "duped." In Arizona, the proposition, in addition to permitting doctors to prescribe Schedule I drugs, includes providing parole/probation and treatment as alternatives to incarceration for people convicted for possession for the first and second offenses, required people who were on drugs and committed violent crimes to serve their entire sentence, and created a drug-related fund and commission. Thus, there were other factors that may have helped to sway public opinion in support of the proposition. However, in California, the proposition pertained solely to medicalizing marijuana. And in fact, recent events help to document the changes in public opinion in California toward permitting the use of marijuana for medical purposes.

The Passage of Propositions 200 and 215

Six years prior to the passage of Proposition 215 in California (November 1990), a referendum was passed in San Francisco urging California to permit doctors to prescribe marijuana to the seriously ill (Isikoff, 1990). Although it had no legal effect, the referendum, endorsed by 79.5% of the city's voters, was significant in reflecting growing public sentiment on the issue. A year later, a 1991 referendum urging the legalization of medical marijuana was approved by about 80% of San Francisco's voters. The California Medical Association endorsed therapeutic marijuana use in 1992. In August 1993, both houses of the California state legislature passed a resolution calling for an end to federal restrictions on the medical use of marijuana (Gebhart, 1994). The state legislature has repeatedly expressed support for the idea by large margins, as have county and city boards of supervisors around the state. Major California newspapers, including the *San Francisco Chronicle* and the *Oakland Tribune,* have editorialized in favor of medical marijuana (Christie, 1996). A March 1996 poll by David Binder Research found that 66% of registered voters in California support medicalized marijuana. Nevertheless, Governor Wilson vetoed medical marijuana bills twice.

California's Proposition 215 was passed by a popular vote of 56% to 44%. The proposition was based on a 1995 bill that passed the legislation but was vetoed by the governor. The passage of Proposition 215 overruled the governor's veto (Raine, 1996). The proposition mandates that the state cannot impose any civil or criminal penalties on any parties with any illness for which marijuana provides relief if the patient is possessing or growing marijuana for personal use. To verify a medical need, the patient must have an oral recommendation from a physician. Proposition 215 was endorsed by the California Nursing Association, the California Academy of Family Physicians, the San Francisco Medical Society, the Older Women's League of California, and the California Legislative Council for Older Americans. The American Cancer Society took a neutral position after a Sacramento Superior Court judge ordered changes in pamphlets that erroneously suggested that the American Cancer Society was against Proposition 215 (Raine, 1996).

Dennis Peron, the initiator of the proposition, did not help his cause by immediately lighting up a marijuana cigarette after the proposition was passed, proclaiming that a legitimate medicinal use for marijuana includes stress reduction. He has been quoted as stating that because stress relief is a medical purpose, any adult who uses marijuana does so for medical reasons. Unfortunately, comments such as this from the leadership provides the federal government with their platform, exemplified in 1994 by U.S. Public Health Service spokesman Bill Grigg, who said, "The only reason we're having the medical marijuana debate is because [advocates] want it legalized for recreational use" (Voelker, 1994).

After the passage of Proposition 215, despite its support for medicalized marijuana, the California Medical Association advised the state's 75,000 physicians not to recommend the use of marijuana for medical purposes to patients. The American Medical Association issued a similar statement on December 30, 1996, following the federal government's announcement that the DEA would revoke the registrations of any physicians who recommended marijuana or other illicit drugs for medical purposes, given that their use is still illegal under federal law. Both medical associations support increased research to determine the effectiveness of marijuana as a medical treatment.

A U.S. Federal District Court judge issued a preliminary injunction on April 30, 1997, that bars the Clinton administration from prosecuting doctors who recommend marijuana to their patients under Proposition 215. The preliminary injunction will remain in effect until the lawsuit is resolved in federal court, although the administration is expected to appeal the decision (Wallace, 1997).

In Arizona, the legislature passed three bills that significantly altered Proposition 200 before the summer recess in 1997. Approximately 1,000 nonviolent drug offenders were to be granted the possibility of parole, but on March 6, the governor signed an emergency bill changing the standard established by the proposition that was used to determine parole eligibility. Instead of determining whether the prisoner would be a danger to the public if early release were granted, the new criteria are the probability that the prisoner will not violate the law and whether the release is in the best interests of the state. Those with prior felony convictions are exempted from the new law, reducing the number of prisoners eligible for early release to about 200. On April 8, the Arizona Senate passed a bill that eliminated the provision in Proposition 200 that prohibited incarceration for first-time offenders who violate probation. On April 22, 1997, the Arizona state legislature passed a bill prohibiting doctors from writing prescriptions for illegal drugs *unless there is FDA approval*. This effectively nullified Proposition 200 (Mattern & Mayes, 1997). However, 2 months later, on July 16, 1997, supporters of Proposition 200 submitted about 100,000 signatures to block the two new laws that dismantled the proposition. This delayed the implementation of the two new laws until voters could vote on the referendum in the November 1998 general election.

In Arizona, where the proposition passed 65 to 35, the proposition was supported by some conservatives, including former Senator Barry Goldwater as honorary chairman. Former Democratic Senator Dennis DeConcini, who was a finalist to become national drug czar in both the Bush and Clinton administrations, was a key adviser to the committee. One contributor, John Sperling, donated $480,000 to the campaign. Other financial backers included New York billionaire investor George Soros, who gave $430,000, and billionaire Ohio insurance company owner Peter Lewis, who donated $330,000. Opponents were only able to raise $5,100 (Sahagun, 1996). Joseph Califano Jr., former Secretary of Health, Education and Welfare in the Carter administration, gives different figures, saying that of the $300,490 contributed to support the proposition, only $490 came from the state, with $200,000 from the Drug Policy Foundation and $100,000 directly from Soros (Califano, 1996). Califano says that of the $1.8 million in donations for California's Proposition 215, $1.4 million came from out of state, with $550,000 coming from Soros. Califano states that "a moneyed, out-of-state elite mounted a cynical and deceptive campaign to push its hidden agenda to legalize drugs" (p. A25).[2]

Buyers Clubs

There has also been an unusual development in California in the form of Cannabis Buyers Clubs that provide access to cannabis for medical purposes. The clubs make marijuana available for a fee to approved individuals, although the fee may be based on a sliding scale that is based on ability to pay. The San Francisco-based Cannabis Buyers Club is the largest and most conspicuous of the cannabis buying clubs. It was born in the city's gay Castro District, and most of its referrals are from the gay community. The headquarters is a 29,000-square-foot commercial building on Market Street, near city, state, and federal buildings. It enjoys the tacit approval of City Hall. Non-enforcement not only saves the city money, but it also saves the San Francisco Police Department (SFPD) from the bad publicity of arresting and jailing people with terminal conditions, many of them members of the city's politically powerful gay community (Christie, 1996).

In April 1995 ($1\frac{1}{2}$ years before the passage of Proposition 215), the DEA and FBI put the San Francisco Buyers Club under surveillance. Their request to the SFPD to become involved was declined, and the investigation was ultimately called off. However, on August 4, 1996, agents of the California Bureau of Narcotic Enforcement raided the Cannabis Buyers Club. The club was ordered closed the next day, but the sheriff said he did not "wish to spend precious law enforcement dollars busting people engaged in distributing marijuana for medical purposes" (McCabe, 1997, p. A1). Interestingly, the raid was staged about 3 months prior to the passage of Proposition 215 and 1 day before the Republican National Convention in San Diego. The club is headed by Dennis Peron and serves as the headquarters for Californians for Compassionate Use, which initiated Proposition 215 in California. The city's district attorney and local U.S. attorney were unwilling to prosecute the case (McCabe, 1996). San Francisco's mayor and the head of the Board of Supervisors basically decried the actions. The Cannabis Buyers Club in San Francisco reopened on January 15, 1997, following a San Francisco Superior Court judge's order to allow medical marijuana sales to patients under the provisions of Proposition 215 (Lepsch & Kempner, 1997). The club has reorganized as the San Francisco Cannabis Cultivators Club.

On March 25, 1997, San Jose, California became the first municipality in the United States to monitor and permit medical marijuana distributors. The zoning ordinance requires that medical marijuana dispensaries be at least 500 feet from schools, day care centers, and churches, and at least 150 feet from residential areas. The clubs may open no earlier than 9:00 a.m. and close no later than 9:00 p.m. Owners must post signs indicating that only adults are allowed, and no one is permitted to smoke marijuana near the business. The Cannabis Buyers Club must apply for a city permit to operate a medical marijuana club

(Mowatt, 1997). In San Mateo County, California, one of the supervisors also proposed that the county assume the responsibility of obtaining and distributing marijuana for medical purposes through its hospital and health clinic pharmacies (Simon, 1997).

Few buyers clubs have attempted to operate (above ground) outside of California, and those that have appear to have links to the San Francisco club. In fact, even within the state of California, most are linked to the San Francisco club. A Cannabis Buyers Club in Seattle (Green+Cross Patient Coop) was raided and closed in May 1995. It had been up and running for a little less than 2 years. One of the owners had tried unsuccessfully to lobby the Bainbridge Island City Council (east of Seattle) for a resolution urging police to deprioritize arrests of medical marijuana users. A judge threw out the case in September 1995 on the grounds that the police overstepped their search warrant (Christie, 1996).

The buyers clubs are a unique phenomenon, yet it is obvious that their history is intertwined with the larger issue of medicalized marijuana, especially in California. The developments in California may indeed become a model for the distribution of medical marijuana in other states that have such legislation, but this is not the expectation. On December 12, 1997, the California First District Court of Appeals ruled that medical marijuana clubs cannot legally sell the drug despite the passage of Proposition 215 (Schwartz, 1997). The California Supreme Court left the ruling intact at a hearing on February 25, 1998. The key issue appears to be that a buyers club may not be legally considered a primary caregiver; a primary caregiver cannot be a commercial enterprise (Egelko, 1998). The ruling essentially holds that the intent of Proposition 215 was to allow people to cultivate and possess marijuana, or a primary caregiver to act on the behalf of those too ill or bedridden to do so. Obviously, there is no easy solution, even with the advent of Proposition 215, to supply marijuana to those with a medical need. There is not much incentive yet for pharmaceutical companies to become involved in growing, marketing, and distributing marijuana, but if research demonstrates that there are legitimate medical uses, this could change radically and rapidly.

THE FUTURE OF MEDICALIZED MARIJUANA

The medical marijuana propositions in California and Arizona have sparked a national debate. Perhaps this was long overdue in terms of helping to crystalize the issues and open up the debate to a much broader audience than the major players in the past few decades—the DEA and NORML. Research shows that cannabis has therapeutic value, and undoubtedly, there are sick people who could benefit from having access to it in smoked form. Virtually all drugs have side effects, and the intoxicating qualities of smoked cannabis may be preferable to the side effects from some standard treatments. Furthermore, compared to Marinol, many more of the active ingredients are realized through the absorption process, and the effects are more instantaneous.

Perhaps the most surprising finding following the passage of the medical marijuana propositions in California and Arizona was that legislation permitting patients with certain disorders to use marijuana with a physician's approval has been enacted in 36 states since 1978. However, 13 states have either repealed or allowed their laws to expire. Still, 25 states and Washington, DC have current medical marijuana laws. One of the first laws was enacted in Virginia in 1979, allowing physicians to prescribe marijuana for either glaucoma or the side effects of chemotherapy. A bill was introduced in 1997 expanding the conditions for which marijuana can be prescribed to include AIDS and neurological disorders. Other than California and Arizona, the most recent state to legally allow physician-prescribed marijuana was Louisiana in 1991.

The state marijuana laws generally can be categorized into three groups: therapeutic research, physician prescription and the medical necessity defense, and the rescheduling of marijuana. Thirteen states currently have laws authorizing therapeutic marijuana research programs; however, all of the research programs had ceased operating by 1991. Massachusetts and Washington have enacted legislation in recent years that would reestablish research programs on the therapeutic effects of marijuana. Nine states have laws that allow physicians to prescribe, dispense, or distribute marijuana to be used as medicine. Most indicate that marijuana is to be used for the treatment of serious illnesses such as cancer and glaucoma. Currently, three states—Iowa, Montana, and Tennessee—have laws that reschedule marijuana to something other than a Schedule I drug.

In November 1998, voters in Alaska, Nevada, Oregon, and Washington passed medical marijuana initiatives. Medical marijuana was also on the ballot in Washington, DC, but the vote count was not released because Congress prohibited any city funds from being spent on the initiative. An exit poll suggested that the voters approved the initiative. Voters in Arizona reapproved Proposition 200 by voting to maintain their 1996 medical marijuana law, which allows the prescription of other drugs for medical purposes as well.

Internationally, the British Medical Association's Board of Science and Education called for the legalization of certain cannabinoids for medical use in July 1997 (Murray, 1997). Also, the French government announced that it will approve the experimental use of cannabis in hospitals in 1998 as a first tentative step toward a relaxation of the country's laws. The French government has also commissioned a study of the relative dangers of cannabis and other illegal drugs compared to the legal drugs such as alcohol and nicotine (Lichfield, 1997). On December 10, 1997, an Ontario judge ruled that certain sections of Canada's

Controlled Drug and Substances Act were unconstitutional in cases where marijuana is used for medically approved purposes; however, the Crown is appealing the judge's decision (Bannon, 1997). Nevertheless, a poll of Canadians found that 83% supported the legalization of marijuana for medical purposes (Bindman & Bronskill, 1997).

In the beginning of this chapter, I commented on the difficulty of trying to address the issue of medicalized marijuana because the societal response is in a state of flux. On one hand, although the research evidence clearly suggests its usefulness, the base of this research is not new and has not held up under scrutiny from the DEA, nor has it been convincing enough in the past to even convince the federal government to move forward with more research. Therefore, I am tempted to predict that little more will happen, even anticipating that the IOM will find merit to further research. Also, it is important to note that the IOM was not charged with simply examining medical efficiency, but with examining marijuana's gateway characteristics. Even more important, the 18-month IOM study basically just lays the groundwork for future research—research that may require following individuals over many years to gauge the effects of marijuana on health and behavior. Also, add to this mix the fact that the federal government commissions that have examined the issue of medicalized marijuana in the past few decades, including the National Commission on Marihuana and Drug Abuse in 1972 and the National Academy of Science in 1982, have recommended increased research, and yet few well-conducted studies have been completed. This reinforces my belief that the safest prediction is that the status quo with respect to medicalized marijuana will be maintained into the foreseeable future.

The reason that this prediction may be wrong is simply that there is evidence of growing grassroots support for medicalized marijuana. Consider the backers of Proposition 215 in California: the California Nursing Association, the California Academy of Family Physicians, the San Francisco Medical Society, the Older Women's League of California, and the California Legislative Council for Older Americans. Part of the appeal in California was to older Americans, who disproportionately are struck with cancer and chronic pain. Although Dennis Peron may not generate much sympathy or empathy for wanting to use marijuana to reduce stress, older Americans who choose to use it to cope with pain, or to relieve the side effects of cancer chemotherapy, will.

NOTES

1. In 1983, the National Association of Attorney Generals passed a resolution calling for the rescheduling of marijuana (Affidavit of Robert Stephan, DEA Administrative

Hearings, Judge Young presiding). In 1984, the American Bar Association enacted a similar resolution (Alliance for Cannabis Therapeutics, Miscellaneous, Volume 1, Tab 1, Administrative Hearings, Judge Young presiding).

2. It should be noted that in 1996, George Soros donated $40 million to the Emma Lazarus fund to help immigrants become U.S. citizens; $46 million to education, social, and legal reforms in Russia; $12 million to the Algebra Project for math education in the United States; and $10 million to South African ventures (Adler, 1997).

REFERENCES

Adler, J. (1997, February 3). He gave at the office. *Newsweek,* pp. 34-46.

Administration response to Arizona Proposition 200 and California Proposition 215. 62 Fed. Reg. 6164. (1997).

Aldrich, M. D. (1971). *A brief legal history of marihuana.* Phoenix, AZ: Do It Now Foundation.

Bannon, P. (1997, December 11). Medical use of pot is legal: Court upholds patient's challenge of drug laws. *Ottawa Citizen,* p. A1.

Bindman, S., & Bronskill, J. (1997, November 21). Justice minister calls for national debate on medical marijuana. *Ottawa Citizen,* p. A1.

Brecher, E. M. (1986). Drug laws and drug law enforcement: A review and evaluation based on 111 years of experience. *Drugs and Society, 1*(1), 1-28.

Califano, J. (1996, December 4). Devious efforts to legalize drugs. *Washington Post,* p. A25.

Christie, J. (1996, April). Club Medicine. *Reason,* pp. 54-57.

Cotton, P. (1992). Government extinguishes marijuana access, advocates smell politics. *Journal of the American Medical Association, 267,* 2573-2574.

Doblin, R., & Kleiman, M. A. R. (1991). Marijuana as antiemetic medicine: A survey of oncologists' experience and attitudes. *Journal of Clinical Oncology, 9,* 1314-1319.

Drug Enforcement Administration. (1994). *Drug legalization: Myth and misconceptions.* Washington, DC: U.S. Department of Justice.

Egelko, B. (1998, February 26). Decision barring pot club stands. *Orange County Register,* p. A1.

Federation of American Scientists (FAS). (1997). *Scientist urge presidential order for marijuana testing.* Press release.

Gebhart, F. (1994). California panel backs medical marijuana. *Drug Topics, 183*(2), 26.

Grinspoon, L., & Bakalar, J. (1993). *Marihuana, the forbidden medicine.* New Haven, CT: Yale University Press.

Grinspoon, L., & Bakalar, J. (1995). Marihuana as medicine: A plea for reconsideration. *Journal of the American Medical Association, 273*(23), 1875-1876.

Hecht, B. (1991, July 15 and 22). Out of joint: The case for medicinal marijuana. *New Republic,* pp. 7-10.

Hewitt, D. (Executive Producer). (1991). Smoking to live. *60 Minutes, 24*(11), 2-6.

Hughes, S., & Van Nattie, D., Jr. (1990, November 20). Medical necessity and marijuana use. *Washington Post* Health section, p. 9.

Isikoff, M. (1990, November 12). "Compassionate" marijuana use. *Washington Post* Health Section, p. 17.

Lepsch, P., & Kempner, P. (1997). NewsBriefs. *The Drug Policy Letter, 32,* p. 11.

Levine, K. (1993). Drug approved for treating appetite loss in AIDS patients. *Drug Topics, 137*(3), 28-32.

Lichfield, J. (1997, December 21). Cannabis campaign: France to ease drug laws and let doctors try dope. *The Independent,* p. 15.

Marijuana scheduling petition; Denial of petition. 57 Fed. Reg. 10499. (1992).

Mattern, H., & Mayes, K. (1997, April 16). Legislators approve delaying Prop 200, court battle likely over pot law. *Arizona Republic,* p. A1.

McCabe, M. (1996, August 5). State raids marijuana buyers' club. *San Francisco Chronicle,* p. A1.

McWilliams, J. C. (1991). The history of drug control policies in the United States. In J. A. Inciardi (Ed.), *Handbook of drug control policies in the United States.* New York: Greenwood.

Mowatt, R. (1997, March 26). S.J. OKs medicinal marijuana clubs. *San Jose Mercury News,* p. 1B.

Murray, I. (1997, July 3). Doctors back cannabis treatments. *London Times,* p. 2.

National Commission on Marihuana and Drug Abuse. (1972). *Marihuana: A signal of misunderstanding.* New York: NAL.

National Institutes of Health, the Ad Hoc Group of Experts. (1997, February 19-20). Report to the Director.

Raine, G. (1996, May 28). Push to put pot on the ballot. *San Francisco Examiner,* p. A1.

Sahagun, L. (1996). Arizona begins revolt against drug war politics. *Los Angeles Times,* p. 1.

Schwartz, R., & Voth, E. A. (1995). Marijuana as medicine: Making a silk purse out of a sow's ear. *Journal of Addictive Diseases, 14*(2), 15-21.

Schwartz, S. (1997, December 13). Medical marijuana clubs illegal. *San Francisco Chronicle,* p. A1.

Simon, M. (1997, October 16). San Mateo County-run dispensaries are proposed. *San Francisco Chronicle,* p. A17.

Slaughter, J. (1988). Marijuana prohibition in the United States. *Columbia Journal of Law and Social Problems, 21,* 417-475.

Snyder, S. H. (1990). Planning for serendipity. *Nature, 346,* 508.

Synder, S. J. (1971). *Uses of marijuana.* New York: Oxford University Press.

Voelker, R. (1994). Medical marijuana: A trial of science and politics. *Journal of the American Medical Association, 217*(21), 1645-1648.

Wallace, B. (1997, May 1). Doctors can recommend marijuana; Judge extends order until lawsuit is resolved. *San Francisco Chronicle,* p. A1.

Wren, C. (1996, November 17). Votes on medical marijuana are stirring debate. *New York Times,* p. 16.

Zias, J., Stark, H., Seligman, J., Levy, R., Werker, E., Vreuer, A., & Mechoulam, R. (1993). Early medical use of cannabis. *Nature Archive '92-'94* [CD-ROM]. New York: Macmillan.

5

Pregnancy, Drugs, and Harm Reduction

Marsha Rosenbaum
Katherine Irwin

Shortly after the National Institute on Drug Abuse (NIDA) was established, physicians and scientists expressed concern about the effects of drug use during pregnancy. In 1974, P.L. 94-371 was enacted, which "mandated that drug abuse and dependence *among women* [emphasis added] be given special consideration for treatment and prevention" (Kandall, 1996, p. 196). Subsequently, NIDA funded hundreds of research and demonstration projects that focused on the etiology, consequences, and treatment needs of drug-using women. Although interest in women's issues and federal funding for research continued through the 1970s, 1980s, and into the 1990s, recent substance abuse prevalence data indicate that change has not been positive (National Household Survey, 1994). Women's use of illegal (and legal) drugs has increased, along with drug use during pregnancy.

The increasing size and scope of the problem of women's substance abuse has been exacerbated, if not caused, by two national trends. First, poverty, homelessness, substandard education, and health care have increased since 1980 (Phillips, 1991). As members of America's ever-growing underclass, drug users' lives have become more chaotic, risky, dangerous, and violent (Currie, 1993). Second, for addicts without financial resources, access to drug treatment has become increasingly problematic because of a decline in federal funding of programs since 1976 (Gerstein & Harwood, 1990). Although the Office of

National Drug Control Policy advocates a shift in funding from enforcement to prevention and treatment (Brown, 1995), thus far, drug users have experienced little change in access (Wenger & Rosenbaum, 1994). Ironically, if monies and availability *were* increased, it seems unlikely that even the best form of drug treatment could reverse the deleterious effects of the social and political policies of the 1980s and 1990s. Lacking a chance at the American Dream and a stake in conventional life, drug abusers will continue to relieve their suffering through the use of pain-killing and euphoria-producing substances (Rosenbaum, 1989; Waldorf, Reinarman, & Murphy, 1991).

From 1991 to 1995 (along with Sheigla Murphy, Margaret Kearney, Kimberly Theidon, and Jeanette Irwin), we worked on a San Francisco-based, NIDA-funded study of pregnancy and drug use.[1] The research team interviewed in depth 120 women who used heroin, cocaine, and/or methamphetamine and were pregnant or immediately postpartum. We used the grounded theory method of data collection and analysis (Strauss & Corbin, 1990).

When the study began, we believed that the life circumstances of drug users, women, and especially pregnant women were dismal, and that innovative ways of thinking about the problem were necessary. It was clear that policies that advocated total abstinence or treatment as a cure for addiction were not effective. We were ripe for a new concept, a new framework, a new way of looking at what could be done given a social and economic system that, almost by definition, *fostered* the alienation, hopelessness, and boredom that perpetuated drug abuse. Despite the efforts of the war on drugs, drug abuse seemed here to stay and its consequences, such as AIDS, more dire than ever. A framework was needed that was more *pragmatic* and less idealistic; more *reality-based* and less moralistic; stressing what *could* be done rather than what ought to be done.

Harm reduction is a simple concept, not a camouflage for radical change in drug policy, first implemented in Europe and Australia and used primarily to deal with the AIDS crisis. In the United States, professionals have been using the harm reduction concept for some 30 years in the form of methadone maintenance treatment (Rosenbaum, 1995). Those who subscribe to a harm reduction perspective deplore, yet accept, the inevitability of drug abuse. They advocate for working *with* users to minimize the harms brought about by abuse, even if drug use itself cannot be stopped (Nadelmann et al., 1994).

Although according to prevailing stereotypes, drug users carelessly engage in practices destructive to themselves and others, our study population indicated that women regularly engaged in harm reduction strategies designed to protect themselves and their fetuses. These strategies were based on women's beliefs about the mechanisms and seriousness of fetal damage, procedures for drug screening in local health care agencies, and the likelihood of loss of custody. Sasha (045), for example, was a 24-year-old African American and one of the many women in our study population who defined harm reduction. She was a crack smoker in her seventh month of pregnancy at the time of the interview. She spoke freely about her attempts to reduce the impact of her crack use, for herself and her fetus. In the following passage, she explained her stance on the subject:

> I know I'm an addict and I do like to get high, but I don't want to die, you know what I'm saying? So in my mind—this is my own philosophy—if you're gonna do it, you need to know when you're getting close to the edge and try to back up a little bit.

Amanda, a 27-year-old African American, was in a similar position when we interviewed her in her sixth month of pregnancy. She had smoked crack intermittently during her pregnancy and described her harm reduction philosophies in this way:

> Okay, I got a problem with drugs. Okay, fine. I gotta do something. But in the moment when I'm doing this drug, I am aware of my life. I'm not just focusing on this drug. I'm not just focusing on this hit, because when your mind becomes so involved with that hit, you forget about somebody coming up on you killing you. You forget about all these things until something drastic happens like "I'm six feet under" or "God, my baby's dead. I'm going to jail or I just got stabbed." That's very, very dangerous. There's a way to do this. There's a way. If you're gonna do it, do it in the right manner as to where you're caring for your life.

For Amanda, harm reduction meant thinking about "all these things" and taking various measures to insulate herself from such occurrences. By developing an awareness of the dangers accompanying drug use, she strategized to avoid such hazards as death, incarceration, fetal damage, and victimization.

As the following discussion illustrates, the ways in which pregnant drug users strove to minimize the potential damage of their drug use challenges the image of the careless drug addict. We discuss the practices used by these women and examine the harm reduction trends that emerge from these data. We turn first to a discussion of the women's perceptions regarding the potential teratogenic effects of their drug use, followed by their efforts to "take care" and reduce harm.

THE PERCEPTION OF HARM

The concerns that the women expressed regarding fetal outcomes varied according to their primary drug. The women who were most frightened about the damage their drug might cause were those who used crack. At the time these interviews were conducted, the media blitz surrounding crack use was tremendous. By comparison, drugs such as heroin and methamphetamine failed to attract the level of condemnation reserved for crack cocaine.

To understand the women's perception of potential harm resulting from their drug use, it is important to examine the social context of drug use. The profile of those who use a particular drug greatly influences the moral panic generated about the substance. A quick overview of our study population provides insight into the factors that may have influenced the concern regarding crack. Most of the crack smokers (82%) were African American, the majority (70%) of the heroin users were white or Latina, and the methamphetamine users were nearly exclusively (92%) white. A number of researchers have suggested that the social construction of crack as a "demon drug" was certainly tied to those who were its primary users—namely, low-income blacks in urban settings. Additionally, central to this panic was the medical construction of the mother's body as toxic to her fetus (Chavkin, 1991; Fink, 1990; Harrison, 1991; Muraskin, 1991).

Consequently, with a few exceptions, the women most likely to express grave concerns about giving birth to an infant damaged by drug exposure were the crack users in our study. Although there were a few heroin users who articulated the same fears of causing serious fetal harm, they were by far the minority voice in that group.

Crack

Sasha and Amanda were representative of the women who used crack. Generally, they had used crack in a binge-and-purge style during their pregnancies. Binges were characterized by smoking one crack rock after another in a process called smoking "back to back." Such smoking could last for several days, during which women had minimal sleep and barely ate. Women referred to this pattern as "going on 24/7," which means smoking 24 hours a day, 7 days a week. Although 24/7 was a common term, women admitted that, in reality, they had never gone without sleep for an entire week. A crack binge generally lasted no longer than 3 or 4 days. Women often had periods of abstinence in between binges. Abstinence periods could be a few hours to a few months.

Crack-using women's fears of causing fetal damage were omnipresent in their interviews. Some women feared crack use would cause serious behavioral problems, whereas others worried that their infants would be deformed. Another common concern was that their babies would be born mentally impaired. Although the particular manifestations varied, the common theme for the crack users in our study was that their drug use would definitely cause some damage. For example, Amanda felt that crack-related damage was unavoidable and began to brace herself for the outcome early in her pregnancy:

This baby has been exposed to crack cocaine from the first—beginning of conception to about now, and that's what? Six months? I don't like that. That's a bad feeling, because this baby's suffered a lot of damage. Yeah, I'm mentally tripping because it's already bad enough my son's gonna suffer in his childhood. But there's no sense in me sitting here living in a fantasy world thinking that "Well, Amanda, you done smoke from one to six months, that amount of drugs from one to six months is not gonna have any effect on my baby even if I do quit right now." That's a lie—I know there's gonna be effects already.

Rhonda, a 30-year-old African American, had smoked $100 worth of crack every day in the beginning stages of her pregnancy. At 2 months, she saw a physician, discovered her pregnancy, and looked back in horror at the amount of crack she had smoked. She immediately quit using crack, but the fear of the possible physiological harms haunted her. In her third month of pregnancy, Rhonda had an abortion. She describes the factors in her decision:

> The baby was doomed from the start. I don't care what those doctors say when they say, "Oh you're pregnant and you can stop using drugs and your body will be okay." That's a lie. 'Cause my baby suffered after that and it was my fault, my own fault. I ain't blaming it on nothing. I'm not saying because the doctors didn't notice it or nothing. It was me.

Heroin

The heroin users in our study population tended to approach their pregnancies with far less anxiety than did the women who smoked crack. Heroin did not receive the sort of attention given to crack in the media in the late 1980s and early 1990s, and many heroin users were confident that they would deliver healthy infants. Again, it should be noted that the heroin users were primarily (70%) white and Latina, two groups who generally have better pregnancy outcomes than do African-American women in this country regardless of drug use. Moreover, heroin had been on the street longer than crack or methamphetamine. Consequently, many women had either delivered healthy babies previously or knew other women who had done so.

Chandra, a 40-year-old white woman, was representative of the women in this group. She was a heroin user in her fourth month of pregnancy who firmly believed that heroin caused few, if any, problems during pregnancy:

> The heroin does not hurt them at all. All my three babies had it. As long as you eat and you sleep. See, that's the reason we wanted to participate [in the study] is just to show people that it's not the drug, it's the situation.

Later in the interview, Chandra tried to illustrate the relative harmlessness of heroin during pregnancy as compared to other drugs. Crack, she felt, was the worst drug one could use while pregnant. As she stated this, she grabbed a piece of paper and began drawing a picture of the typical "heroin baby" and then a typical "crack baby." The crack baby sketch was thinner than the heroin baby. Additionally, to emphasize the compromised health of the crack-exposed infant, Chandra drew dark circles under the infant's eyes.

Lauren, a 19-year-old white heroin user, was much like Chandra. She had used heroin during both her pregnancies. When we interviewed her during her most recent pregnancy, she was convinced that heroin did not compromise her chances for a healthy pregnancy. Below, she described her philosophy about opiate use during pregnancy:

> I knew the heroin would relax the baby. And I would do codeine. I'd do Percodans [a prescription pain reliever classified as an opiate]. Those are all narcotics, Class II or III narcotics. And these are things that just mellow you out. It goes through the bloodline and stuff, but it doesn't really cause a birth defect. But when you do crack or you do LSD or something, then you start to worry.

Women in this group had used heroin for a number of years, often during past pregnancies. Because they felt that drug use did not compromise their health, they tended to focus more on *controlling* their drug use rather than quitting entirely. In contrast to the binges and abstentions described by the women who used crack, most women in this group chose to maintain their drug use at low levels during their pregnancies rather than go cold turkey.

Methamphetamines

The methamphetamine users in our study were white. This group was the most likely to express uncertainty regarding the potential impact of their drug use on either themselves or their fetuses. Most of these women were pregnant for the first time, thus having no prior experience by which to either assuage or magnify their concerns.

As with the women who used crack and heroin, perceptions of risk were dependent on information and context. Methamphetamine use has largely been overlooked in recent discussions of pregnancy and drug use. Very few studies have addressed the potential problems associated with methamphetamine use, and even fewer media stories have focused on the increased use of this drug. Although there is no *direct* connection between women's views on methamphetamines and public attention, it is probable that lack of negative *or* positive information has resulted in a set of ambivalent beliefs about its use.

Women's views on methamphetamine use vacillated. Although none of the women could cite specific harm that might result from their drug use during pregnancy, most imagined that some harm must ensue. Whereas the crack users had quivering incubator babies to envision and the heroin addicts sometimes imagined a baby in classic withdrawal, the methamphetamine users lacked specific information or images upon which to draw. For some women, the space of the unknown allowed them to imagine the worst. For others, the lack of research one way or the other allowed them to relegate their concerns to the background in their lives.

Emily, a 32-year-old white woman, and Pamela, a 39-year-old white woman, exemplify the range of responses to drug-related harm that characterized the methamphetamine users in our study. Emily had suspected she was pregnant during the first trimester. She had used methamphetamines intermittently for the previous 12 years, first as a recreational drug and then as a diet aid. At the time of the interview, she framed her methamphetamine use in terms of how alert the drug made her feel.

> It makes you feel exuberant. Makes you feel like you can see things a lot clearer, or your mind is working. It just makes you feel sharper, more on the ball or something like that.

Emily injected a small amount of methamphetamine three times a week. Although she wished she had more money for other things, she did not plan to quit using in the near future regardless of her pregnancy. As with most of the women who used methamphetamines, Emily told us that she could not fathom the amount of harm that might result from using methamphetamines during pregnancy. At one point during the interview, she asked,

> I would really like to find out more about why. This isn't really for the taped part, but any articles or stuff to read on the effects of the drug on the baby, you know, from the mother's use of drugs. I look reasonably healthy. I feel reasonably healthy.

Like many other women in this group, she did not know where to begin looking for detailed information on the possible impact of methamphetamine use. Although she felt healthy, her drug use made her question whether she was harming either herself or her fetus.

On the subject of fetal health and drug-related harm, Emily's concerns vacillated. She was unable to locate information on the impact of methamphetamine use during pregnancy in traditional educational materials such as health pamphlets, articles, or even the media. Consequently, she turned to her friends and other long-term methamphetamine users for health information. She told us:

> I mean, I definitely felt guilty about it [using methamphetamines during pregnancy]. Even though he [her partner] and other people kept trying to convince me that speed isn't really harmful. Other drugs are more harmful, like alcohol or LSD or something like that. I just can't think it is going to be harmless.

Like the other women in this group, Emily found it difficult to articulate a specific set of possible consequences, instead voicing a more general concern about negative effects.

Pamela was a methamphetamine user who also suspected that she was in the first few months of pregnancy. Like Emily, she had a long history of methamphetamine use and did not plan to quit using this drug anytime in the near future. She was keenly afraid of the possible harm of this drug on pregnancy and cited the lack of information as partial testimony to the dangerousness of the substance. Her stance was that methamphetamine users should not have children until more is known about the effects on fetal and maternal health. As she said,

> These people who are doing it now . . . it's really scary. Like I said, I know what happened to the children that were subject to their parents' drinking or their mother's drinking while they were pregnant with them. Just that alone scares me. Nobody knows really what the amphetamine or, see that's another thing why I'm so against it being so illegal, because when it's legal they'll study it more and it'll be more open and people will find out really. People are going to use it anyway, whether they say it's okay or not. But when the alcohol study started coming out, I know a lot of people who stopped drinking. A lot of people cut back on their drinking when they actually could see what damages . . . if you can't see what the damage is, it doesn't register. People should be able to see it. And if it's not open or it's not allowed—nobody knows what happens to the amphetamine use and pregnancy, and I've been doing those things for 20 years!

The possible harm of methamphetamine use seemed to plague Pamela's mind. Her pregnancy, she felt, was an accident, and she had definite plans to abort. Abortion was the only form of harm reduction she trusted, because the uncertainty of methamphetamine-related harm made her reluctant to gamble.

This group of women posed provocative problems and questions for health care providers and drug policymakers. On one hand, the lack of public attention allowed them to interpret and define their drug use and pregnancy experiences for themselves and without outside pressures. On the other hand, lack of knowledge about methamphetamine use during pregnancy limited their opportunity to use health information that would have given them more self-determination in regard to their pregnancy decisions and mothering experiences. In general, their health maintenance routines, like their feelings about the potential impact of their drug use, were vague and tenuous.

In sum, although the particular worries varied primarily according to the woman's primary drug, one common trend emerged: No woman approached her pregnancy without some apprehension. Although cessation of drug use was discussed as the ultimate goal, complete abstinence was difficult to achieve and maintain. Consequently, these women drew upon an extensive repertoire of strategies to manage their fears and minimize the potential damage of their drug use. These harm reduction techniques are the subject of the remainder of this chapter.

Harm Reduction Strategies

Women in our study population used several strategies for reducing drug-related harm. They included switching drugs, counteracting drug use, altering the drug-using lifestyle, and health care.

Switching Drugs

One method that women used to reduce drug use was to combine their primary drug with other drugs, or substitute a drug that they perceived as less harmful. This harm reduction strategy was most frequent among the crack users, reflecting their heightened concerns regarding the impact of crack on their babies.

Sasha, a crack smoker mentioned earlier, told us how difficult it was to stay away from crack during pregnancy. When she felt the urge to smoke crack, she smoked marijuana instead. She described her routine:

> Yeah, I couldn't do anything. I just smoked pot a little bit. You know, I smoked pot. He [her husband] knew I did have a drug problem, okay, so what he would do if he seen me getting edgy or what, he'd say, "Go in my closet, dear. I got some weed in there. Why don't you smoke some of that?"

Unlike Sasha, Darleen, a 22-year-old African American, mixed crack with marijuana as a way of lessening her crack intake. At the time of the interview, Darleen suspected she was in the first 5 months of pregnancy. Her crack smoking was "putting worry on her" because she felt that crack was the worst drug one could use during pregnancy. She told us she feared her child might be born with "a hole in its heart or something" as a result of her crack use. Below, she described her efforts to reduce her crack consumption:

> Well, so now I've got to smoke more weed than crack. And then I do get some crack, I'm gonna get like three rocks and maybe just roll up three rocks. And if I roll me some weed, it's gonna keep me high all day long.

In addition to drug switching, some women tried to have "on and off" days. As Denise, a 23-year-old African-American crack smoker, told us:

> I mean, with the baby I shouldn't be getting high anyway. We all know that's a no-no. I be, okay, that's 2 weeks I haven't smoked, so that's 2 weeks for the baby. Now I can get high. Then I'll have 2 more weeks. You gotta think like that.

Counteracting Drug Use

Because women's attempts to reduce or cease their drug use were not always successful, they employed other methods to reduce harm. Included in the array of techniques were strategies for counteracting drug use. A number of women had consumed substances they believed could counteract the harm of drugs or cleanse their system of drug toxins. Prenatal vitamins, niacin, pickle juice, and vinegar were some of the items women ingested during pregnancy. For example, Peggy, a 34-year-old African-American crack smoker, told us she wanted to be clean until she had her child. The night before her interview with us, she threw away all her crack pipes and began drinking pickle juice. As she told us:

> I been drinking a lot of pickle juice and eating a lot of pickles. 'Cause that cleans your system out. Yeah, I been drinking vinegar, too. I been drinking vinegar straight now with a little warm water. I'm gonna make sure there ain't nothing in my system with this one.

Many women expressed the belief that prenatal vitamins were very important. Even women who did not go to a health care provider often purchased prenatal vitamins and emphasized how faithfully they took them. Somehow, those pills functioned as "magic bullets," testimony to the powerful imagery of legal pharmaceuticals. One recurring scene that women described was injecting heroin or holding a crack pipe in one arm while reaching for vitamins with the other. Although the contradiction may seem glaring, women did make an effort to close the gap between "mother" and "addict."

Another example of counteracting drug use was Evania, a 33-year-old Latina who had been injecting heroin for 6 years and was 3 months into her third pregnancy. She had been trying to cut down on her use because she worried about what the drugs would do to her baby. She had used drugs throughout her pregnancies but mentioned some steps she took to insulate her children from harm. When breastfeeding, she would fill all her bottles with breast milk before using heroin so that her babies would not be exposed to the drug.

Altering the Drug-Using Lifestyle

Other harm reduction techniques included changing aspects of the drug-using lifestyle. Pursuing drugs, raising money for drugs, taking drugs, and coming down from drugs all involved health-compromising consequences. Although women acknowledged and frequently accepted these dangerous activities outside of pregnancy, during pregnancy, they sought to change as many unhealthy routines as possible. Despite the primary drug women used, most acknowledged that heavy immersion in the drug-using lifestyle accompanied poor eating habits. For crack smokers, loss of appetite was particularly pronounced and perceived as a dire problem during pregnancy. Consequently, women were particularly conscious of any health hazards that would compound the already harmful qualities of their drug consumption. Forcing oneself to eat on a regular basis was a common practice. Amanda struggled constantly with her lack of appetite. In the following excerpt, she explains her views on eating regularly as a harm reduction strategy:

> I had to eat. I had to put something in my baby's system so the drug won't affect him or hit him as hard, because I can't see that. I cannot see knowing you have a weakness and sitting up there smoking and knowing you have a life in you, too, at the same time and not feeding your child, because what that boils down to is "Yeah, I know I'm hurting my child." But if you know that your weakness is there, you're going to try to help your child at the same time. You're gonna feed it. Even though you're doing something wrong, even though you're doing something that is not basically right and you have no control over the drug or the weaknesses that you have, you have control whether you feed your child while he's inside you.

Other lifestyle changes included forcing oneself to sleep, moving away from friends or family members who were using drugs, or moving out of neighborhoods where drug use was rampant. Harm reduction for women of all groups was not static. Women mixed and matched different techniques at different times during their pregnancies. Sasha, for example, tried numerous times to reduce her crack use but continually failed because her husband and most of the people living in her building were avid crack smokers. She lived in one of the biggest projects in San Francisco that is well known for open drug sales and use. Before her pregnancy, people used her apartment to smoke in private or to sell crack. They often "kicked her down" a rock or two as payment for the use of her apartment. After discovering that she was pregnant, Sasha felt that this routine was compromising her chances for a healthy pregnancy, and she attempted to employ many of the above-mentioned techniques as a way to guard against the harm of continued crack smoking. The following excerpt describes her attempts to juggle life in a crack house with concern for her pregnancy:

> *Sasha:* I was approximately 4 months pregnant. And that's when it just, just being around it, easy access to it, not having to pay for it every day. People would [ask], "Hey, can I come in here and smoke?"
>
> *Interviewer:* And they'll pay you?
>
> *Sasha:* Drugs or money. It was like on every floor, and there's 20 floors. It's just easy access, and it was constantly every day [knocks on a glass to imitate a person

knocking on a door] somebody's knocking at my door. And from morning to night, I just had a little rock house. You know what I'm saying? But I didn't sell drugs.

Interviewer: So what were your eating and sleeping habits like at that time?

Sasha: Very poor. Very poor. I knew what I had to do was I had to eat before somebody knocked on the door. So, when I would get up in the morning, I'd rush to the kitchen and try to get stuff in me, food in me, take my prenatal vitamins, and that's about it. I just would take my vitamins and eat a little bit.

The Prenatal Care Dilemma

Health care, and, more specifically, *prenatal* care, was perceived as one of the best ways to improve one's health during pregnancy. Women who believed that their drug use posed grave threats to fetal well-being had very problematic relationships to health care. For women who sought prenatal care, the question of whether or not to disclose their drug use had to be addressed. Although the medical literature indicates that lack of prenatal care may put a woman at risk for a poor pregnancy outcome, for the drug-using woman, seeking prenatal care might also put her at risk of losing her child if her drug habit was detected. In short, the dilemma is as follows: not disclosing may result in a "damaged" baby; disclosing may result in loss of custody of that baby. Weighing these risks is a major challenge in these women's lives. The crack users, most fearful of fetal damage, focused on the importance of prenatal care as a *health concern.* Heroin users, on the other hand, were less concerned about fetal damage and more fearful of *loss of custody.* Methamphetamine users, having no information at all, were characterized by *uncertainty.*

Health Concerns

Overall, women were more likely to disclose their drug use to health care providers in order to enlist their cooperation in maximizing their health. Women saw providers' medical expertise and the various technological advances as very powerful harm reduction resources.

Maria, a 34-year-old African-American crack smoker in her seventh month of pregnancy, told us:

I told my doctor [about her crack use]. I said, "Please have all your important instruments near you, because I used [crack] with my baby."

Amanda told her doctor about her crack use as a way of alerting her doctor to the risks of her pregnancy. In addition to technological advances, she felt that her providers could give her valuable information that she could use to improve her health. In the following passage, she described her relationship to her provider:

> When I go to my prenatal care appointment, I'll tell the doctor, "I fucked up. I smoked. Is my baby okay? I don't want nothing to happen to my baby." I'm learning and wanting to know all these things so it'll help me further help my baby.

For Amanda and many other women in this category, telling providers about their drug use during pregnancy opened doors to what they believed were important resources. Although women felt that prenatal care could not take away the damages caused by crack, they viewed prenatal care as an essential step in monitoring and curtailing damages.

Unfortunately, women's attempts to improve their health through traditional heath care were problematic. Crack users often found that after disclosing their drug-using status, they received harsh judgments from health care providers. Jessie, a 33-year-old African American, had just given birth to her first crack-exposed child when we interviewed her. The uncomfortable memories of her hospital experiences were fresh in her mind. During Jessie's first two pregnancies, she had not smoked crack, nor had she missed a single prenatal appointment. At delivery, her doctors and nurses were very supportive. However, her most recent pregnancy was a markedly different experience. She smoked crack almost continually and managed to attend only two prenatal appointments. At delivery, the doctors and nurses treated her like "a dirty little crack addict." Looking back at her own experiences and those of others, she describes why women in her position fail to get prenatal care:

> I know a lot of mothers say that they don't get prenatal care 'cause they feel like as soon as they walk through the door they will be judged. "Oh, you're a crackhead. Why the hell did you get pregnant anyway?" So, they don't get prenatal care. They have those commercials about addicts that don't get prenatal care because they just don't give a shit. They do give a shit, but they are thinking about how they gonna be looked at when they walk in the hospital door, like they not good enough to be pregnant.

Jackie, a 30-year-old African American, had 3-year-old and 4-month-old sons. She had numerous miscarriages before giving birth to these children. She had been honest with the doctors about her drug use but finally stopped going because they kept giving her "funny looks." She disclosed her drug use because

> it was like no secret. I wasn't trying to hide it, 'cause soon as they took my urine they was gonna know anyway. Every time you go for your pregnancy, they take it, yeah, and they test it for drugs.

When women weighed the benefits and costs of seeking prenatal care, many factors influenced their decisions. The value of prenatal care was considered in terms of the risks of attendance and disclosure of drug use. As the following excerpts illustrate, the women had varied experiences with health care providers—some positive, and others devastating. Oprah, a 32-year-old African American, states:

> I'd go in one door and come out the other door, and I'd say I went to the doctor. I just didn't like them sitting up there all the time asking these same questions, and they don't check you. They just listen to the baby's heart and all that. I can listen to his heart cause he's inside me. I feel him. That was always good in case something was wrong. They wanted me to take a sonogram, but I didn't never go. I thought I had better things to do.

Moira, a 23-year-old African American, added:

> I don't think they help you out at all. It's like they push you on the stomach. They do a urine test every time you go in. "All right, you're doing fine. See you next month." So, I don't think I get no help from them at all.

As discussed earlier, the women frequently did not realize that they were pregnant until well into the second trimester. They discussed their fears, that late entry into prenatal care would be used against them.

Courtney, a 30-year-old African American, was 19 weeks pregnant with her first child. She smoked crack and drank beer. This pregnancy was not planned, but she was very excited about having a baby. The baby started moving a week prior to the interview, causing her to resolve to stop using drugs. She said the following about prenatal care:

> Now, if I waited till I was 5 months pregnant to start prenatal, they'll test [my urine] then. It's like, "Why didn't she come in? She should have come in."

Lavinia, a 32-year-old white woman, gave birth to her third son 4 months prior to the interview. A working-class San Franciscan, Lavinia did not start using heroin until she was 27 years old. She felt that her drug use was prompted by a rape that left her devastated for more than a year. Indeed, for 8 months following the rape, she was unable to leave the house. Although she abstained from drugs during the final 3 months of her pregnancy, Lavinia had used heroin and crack during the first two trimesters. She discussed her experience with health care providers. "Like, when I was in San Diego, it was hard even for me to find a doctor, because all they told me to do was get an abortion. They wouldn't deal with me." However, despite the punitive treatment she had experienced, Lavinia was determined to receive prenatal care: "I knew that if I wasn't getting prenatal care that would be a strike against me, since I was getting it so late."

Women who received harsh judgments during or immediately after pregnancy were reluctant to continue prenatal attendance and endure further ridicule. Therefore, women in this group were forced to navigate a precarious path between their efforts to reduce drug-related harms and their efforts to avoid persecution. Although very few women avoided health care altogether, many admitted that they did not get as much health care as they would have liked.

In contrast, Jocylene, a 26-year-old African American, was HIV positive. Whereas she had certainly experienced discriminatory health care in the past, during this pregnancy, the nurse practitioner had been extremely supportive. In a powerful endorsement of caring health providers, Jocylene told us, "I know she is worried about me. If it wasn't for her, I'd be dead right now. People just don't understand . . . just a little bit of kindness can do a fucking lot. It really can."

In light of past negative experiences with the health care system, difficulties with transportation or child care, and hours spent trying to obtain Medi-Cal and then locate a provider who would accept the woman as a patient, it was not surprising that prenatal care received mixed reviews. However, as Jocylene makes clear, one committed professional could heal more than just an ailing body.

What is most striking is the assertion that women are unaware of the dangers of using drugs while pregnant, or that they are not themselves concerned. This stands in sharp contrast to statements from the women in our study population. For example, Darleen, who was 5 months pregnant, was asked how she felt about going for prenatal care. She responded that she got tired of being told the same old thing:

> I mean, 'cause I know my mistakes, you know? I don't like people to tell me things 'cause I already know. Like, "You know you're not supposed to be doing that." I know that!! It's like, "Why are you telling me that?" I already know. Will you please stop? I can't stand it when somebody just keeps lecturing me about what I'm doing wrong. I already know in my heart what I'm doing wrong and I already know, you know. I already know.

Custody Concerns

Heroin users, like crack users, took vitamins, went to prenatal appointments, asked for providers' "important instruments," and maintained more regular eating and sleeping patterns. They engaged in these activities as a way to *improve* their health during pregnancy, as opposed to the crack-using women, who looked to these health routines to "clean their systems" or counteract perceived negative drug effects.

Prenatal care as a health-maintaining regimen was problematic for heroin-using women. Because they did not, on the whole, believe that their drug use compromised their health, they did not look to providers as helping agents in the battle to produce a healthy baby. These women were more likely to view health care providers as extensions of Child Protective Services (CPS), which could challenge the custody of their children.

Potential loss of motherhood was by far most threatening for women in the heroin group, and a more pronounced fear than a damaged baby. For these women, "harm" was defined as loss of custody. Consequently, their harm reduction efforts included reducing the chance of agency intervention in their lives. Specific techniques to avoid loss-of-motherhood harms included lying to providers about drug use, covering up signs of drug use, and avoiding health care altogether. Methods of avoiding custody loss, like all other harm reduction strategies, was not a static program. Below is a detailed description of some of the ways women in this group combined harm reduction techniques.

Mindy, a tall, slender, 29-year-old African American, had given birth shortly before the interview. Because she feared health care providers discovering her drug use, she avoided health care until delivery. Below, she describes how she managed her drug-using identity in the hospital:

> With L., the middle baby, the little boy, when I went to the hospital, I got my arm up in a bandage. [I said] that I had sprung my elbow or something. I made up something. I told them I just came out here from Arkansas and I had all my prenatal up there.

By "getting her arm up in a bandage," Mindy avoided exposing her injection scars to providers. Because the standard profile of a pregnant drug user includes a lack of prenatal care, Mindy avoided confessing that she had no prenatal care. Instead, she told her providers that she had just moved from Arkansas. This story provided her with a strong alibi and allowed her to allay their suspicions.

Unlike Mindy, Tanya, a 29-year-old white woman, did not feel comfortable avoiding prenatal care. However, like many women in this group, she desperately hoped to avoid having her drug use detected by nurses and physicians. Instead of covering up injection scars, she chose to inject in less noticeable areas of her body. She told us:

> Mostly now I muscle [injecting subcutaneously]. I just muscle it in my ass. But I mean, I've had enough to where if my doctors are gonna check me, they're not gonna tell me, "Okay, let me see your rear." I've even done it into my tongue.

Like many other women in this group, Tanya chose to avoid intentionally or unintentionally disclosing her drug use to providers. On the other hand, she also did not like lying to her doctor. Her preference was to avoid being asked about her drug use altogether. Injecting into her buttocks and tongue allowed her to look like a non-drug user to her health care providers.

At another extreme of harm reduction techniques are Sidney, a 31-year-old white woman, and Chandra, a 40-year-old white woman. Both chose to avoid prenatal care and planned to give birth outside of hospitals. Chandra had spent some time researching home births and felt confident that she and her friends could manage the birth on their own. She related her plans:

> I'm gonna have it at home, and then I'm gonna register the birth at about 3 or 4 months. I'm not going to—I didn't report this baby to welfare. I'm going to wait until it's born, and then they're gonna ask for a birth certificate, and at that point I'm gonna say—'cause they're not tied with CPS [Child Protective Services] in that sense. They're telling me what to do and that's the point where I go to a lawyer and I say, "I had a home birth. I need a birth certificate."

Sidney, a heroin user, also planned to give birth outside of the hospital. Unlike Chandra, these plans were not based on her knowledge or confidence in home births. Rather, these plans stemmed from past negative experiences with traditional health and human services agencies. She told us:

> I don't know. I might just go out in the woods and have it. Go to Mexico and have it. Maybe I can kick. I don't know. I mean, I just don't know anymore.

In addition to not trusting nurses and physicians, Sidney was also petrified of a custody case. A few years prior to her most recent pregnancy, she was arrested for drug possession. The baby's father had recently died, and Sidney's parents refused to take custody of her two children. Consequently, CPS intervened and placed her children in foster care. At the time of our interview, Sidney was still attempting to regain custody of her children. She felt that her chances looked bleak because of her difficulties in finding a job, locating permanent housing, and continuing use of heroin. In light of her past experiences, Sidney's plans to give birth in Mexico or in the woods seemed serious.

Uncertainty

Methamphetamine-using women were unsure of the possible harms associated with their drug use and, therefore, less decisive than cocaine and heroin users about which methods of harm reduction to employ. Far more of these women were unsure of what to do about terminating the pregnancy. Most felt positively about health care and admitted that they would love to attend prenatal care appointments if they could make a decision about the pregnancy, or if time permitted.

Pamela, mentioned earlier, did not change her health routines at all during the pregnancy. She had firmly decided to abort because this was the only effective harm reduction she could imagine. One month after the interview with Pamela, a member of the research team ran into her on the street. The two talked briefly, and Pamela revealed that her plans had unexpectedly changed. The following is an excerpt from the interviewer's field notes:

> When I spoke with Pamela last month, she planned on having an abortion. At that time she felt babies should be wanted and they should have responsible healthy parents who can afford to give them whatever they want. This month her feelings on parenting and pregnancy while using speed are being tested. Being a very thin woman, I trusted her calculations that she was in the first few months of pregnancy. Unfortunately, we were both wrong. After her initial appointment for an abortion, Pamela learned she is too far along in her pregnancy to abort legally.
>
> "It just goes to show you that you never know anything about the future," was the only rationalization she could make after explaining how completely distraught this news makes her. Pamela was very vague when I tried to probe into her future plans during the interview. Having an abortion was the only definite decision she could make. About other plans, she told me "things always come out differently than I expect. So I don't expect." Last month I viewed this as a limited response. This month I understand her statement better. She's attending regular prenatal appointments now but has not quit doing speed. This is the extent of the information she could share with me as she was late for an appointment and had to run (3/9/92).

Sally was a 31-year-old white woman with seven children, including a 2-month-old baby. She confirmed her pregnancy by purchasing an over-the-counter pregnancy test and, like Pamela, assumed she was in the first few months of pregnancy. In preparation for the baby, she and her boyfriend began moving to a larger room in their residence hotel, painting their new room, moving things out of storage, and collecting new baby clothes. In the midst of this move, she began the process of getting Medi-Cal so that she could begin prenatal appointments. Unfortunately, all of her work and plans were interrupted when she went into premature labor before she could attend her first appointment. Sally, too, was much further along in her pregnancy than she suspected. In the following, she describes her daughter's health, premature labor, and her experiences in the hospital:

> Yeah, the lungs weren't fully developed, and they had to put her on oxygen and everything. . . . She was lethargic, which is real groggy and everything, and they

said she wasn't sucking properly. You know, she wouldn't eat right. Well, I had that problem with [names second oldest child] and it didn't have anything to do with his birth or anything else. It was they were trying to give him a bottle and he didn't want the bottle. He was a breast baby, and that's all there was to it. He did not want the bottle. And we tried to talk to them at the hospital and see if maybe that was what it was with [names this baby], but they wouldn't, they didn't even want to try and find out . . . everything was on account of the drugs. And it's like the first child care worker, Social Services, she says something about, "Well, the baby's underweight, and the baby doesn't eat well." And I said, "Well, couldn't that be due to the prematurity?" "Yeah, or the use of drugs." And it was like they said, "Well, she's lethargic," and this, that, and the other thing, and I said, "[w]hich could be due to her not being fully developed," and she turned around [sarcastic tone], "Well, or the use of drugs." It's like they can't actually say it's the use of drugs, but—and it's like [names her husband] told them when the paramedics walked in the room that we had done the drugs, what exactly we had done . . . it's like nobody tried to hide the fact that—we didn't lie to them and say, "No, we weren't doing no drugs." That's the first thing he told them when they came to the door, told them what we did, how much we did. And it's like they acted like we were trying to hide it, but then they didn't want to believe that, "Well, you had to have known you were pregnant. Well, yeah, did you look at the size of her when she come into the hospital." I mean, I didn't look like I was. I just finally was getting to about that big [makes a gesture with her hand]. I looked like I was about 2 months pregnant.

In Sally's previous pregnancies, prenatal care was a positive part of her experiences. Like Pamela, she had made plans, but things did not go as she expected.

Drug Treatment

The majority of women in our study population were not in residential or methadone drug treatment when interviewed. Nevertheless, many had, at some point in time, tried various forms of treatment, including weekly drop-in meetings at local churches. Because of current social and political pressure to impose mandatory treatment on pregnant addicts, treatment was a force to be reckoned with and was an acceptable option for some women. The frequent comment regarding drug treatment was that it worked only if a woman had made an internal commitment to stop using drugs. However, even for those women who were receptive to the idea of drug treatment, the availability of a quality program was hardly guaranteed. Aside from a handful of tiny residential programs, there was little treatment for crack users. Methadone maintenance, of course, remained the most prevalent option for heroin users. In California, availability of methadone, even for pregnant women, was problematic. Finally, for methamphetamine users, there was absolutely no treatment modality for pregnant women.

CONCLUSIONS

Women in our study population expressed great concern about the levels of drug-related harm that occurred during their pregnancies. Their evaluations varied according to the particular drug they were using and were often based on what they had heard through the media. Contrary to popular myth, our interviewees cared very much about the outcomes of their pregnancies and used a variety of strategies to reduce drug-related harms. Perhaps most problematic in this potpourri of methods was prenatal care. These harm reduction efforts were made by the women in preparation for birth and delivery. At this time, the "product" of this troubled pregnancy would be presented to the woman herself and to professionals who had the power to decide whether she was worthy of retaining custody of her child.

Pregnant drug users often practice harm reduction in some form or another. Given their own efforts, what should be done in terms of intervention?

1. Women should have better *information* so that their efforts are more effective.

2. Those who intervene should stop punishing these women and instead *facilitate* their harm reduction efforts.

3. Women should have access to health care without (a) risk of losing their baby to CPS or (b) humiliation, as well as access to treatment that does not require total abstinence.

4. Finally, professionals in research and treatment must learn to settle for less, because insisting on perfection may exacerbate the problem.

NOTE

1. National Institute on Drug Abuse, Grant #R01 DA 06832, Marsha Rosenbaum, PhD, Principal Investigator; Sheigla Murphy, PhD, Co-Principal Investigator; Coryl Jones, PhD and Jag Khalsa, PhD, Program Officers.

REFERENCES

Brown, L. (1995, March 12). Top cop in the war on drugs. *San Francisco Chronicle*, p. 4.
Chavkin, W. (1991). Mandatory treatment for drug use during pregnancy. *Journal of the American Medical Association, 266*, 1556-1561.
Currie, E. (1993). *Reckoning: Drugs, the cities, and the American future.* New York: Hill & Wang.

Fink, J. R. (1990). Reported effects of crack and cocaine on infants. *Youth Law News, 11*(1), 37-39.

Gerstein, D., & Harwood, H. (Eds.). (1990). *Treating drug problems Vol. 1: A study of the evolution, effectiveness, and financing of public and private drug treatment systems.* Washington, DC: National Academy Press.

Harrison, M. (1991). Drug addiction in pregnancy: The interface of science, emotion, and social policy. *Journal of Substance Abuse Treatment, 8,* 261-268.

Kandall, S. (1996). *Substance and shadow: A history of women and addiction in the United States, 1850 to present.* Cambridge, MA: Harvard University Press.

Muraskin, R. (1991). Mothers and fetuses: Enter the fetal police. In A. Trebach & K. Zeese (Eds.), *New frontiers in drug policy* (pp. 211-214). Washington, DC: The Drug Policy Foundation.

Nadelmann, E., Cohen, P., Locher, U., Stimson, G., Wodak, A., & Drucker, E. (1994). *The harm reduction approach to drug control: International progress.* Working paper, The Lindesmith Center, 888 Seventh Avenue, New York, NY 10016.

National Household Survey on Drug Abuse: Population estimates 1993. (1994). DHHS Publication No. (SMA) 94-3017. Substance Abuse and Mental Health Services Administration (SAMHSA), Office of Applied Studies, Parklawn Building, Room 16C-06, 5600 Fishers Lane, Rockville, MD 20857.

Phillips, K. (1991). *The politics of rich and poor.* New York: Random House.

Rosenbaum, M. (1989). *Just say what: An alternative view on solving America's drug problem.* San Francisco: National Council on Crime and Delinquency.

Rosenbaum, M. (1995). The demedicalization of methadone maintenance. *Journal of Psychoactive Drugs, 27*(2), 145-149.

Strauss, A., & Corbin, J. (1990). *Basics of qualitative research: Grounded theory procedure and technique.* Newbury Park, CA: Sage.

Waldorf, D., Reinarman, C., & Murphy, S. (1991). *Cocaine changes: The experience of using and quitting.* Philadelphia: Temple University Press.

Wenger, L., & Rosenbaum, M. (1994). Drug treatment on demand—Not. *Journal of Psychoactive Drugs, 16*(1), 1-11.

6

Coffee Shops, Low-Threshold Methadone, and Needle Exchange: Controlling Illicit Drug Use in the Netherlands

Dirk J. Korf

Ernst C. Buning

HARM REDUCTION AS A MAINSTREAM CONCEPT

The first automobiles attracted many enthusiastic spectators, but car accidents soon led to protests. To reduce hazardous effects to motorists and others, safer cars were constructed. New measures were introduced to increase public safety: traffic lights, viaducts, speed limits, mandatory regular check-ups, safety belts, and so on. Recently, environmental awareness generated new protests against cars. In response, companies and state authorities put more emphasis on pollution-reducing measures, such as cars that run more economically, unleaded gasoline and catalytic converters, and even cars with electric motors.

Although mass media campaigns bombard us with information about the dangers of smoking, many people continue to smoke. Because national governments generally believe that a smoke-free society is unfeasible, measures such as no-smoking areas were designated in public buildings. Tobacco companies have introduced low-nicotine and low-tar cigarettes, and health insurance companies offer reduced rates for nonsmokers and higher tariffs for smokers.

Although some strive for an alcohol-free society, most Westerners believe that moderate alcohol consumption is harmless and even pleasant. Alcohol consumption is considered to be more dangerous in certain settings, which has resulted in national laws against drunk driving and companies implementing programs against alcohol at work.

These examples illustrate that harm reduction is mainstream thinking in Western societies. Logically, one would expect similar reactions to problems related to illicit drugs. However, the discourse on this issue is far less rational and commonly interspersed with moral persuasions. Moreover, the fact that illegal substances are involved makes it more difficult to develop comprehensive harm reduction initiatives. Nevertheless, those who plead for harm reduction measures in the field of illicit drugs may well run the risk of being labeled as unethical or irresponsible. Despite the fact that harm reduction policies can be implemented within the legal framework, advocates often are automatically labeled as "legalizers."

In this chapter, we present some examples of harm reduction strategies that have evolved in the Netherlands. It is not our intention to be advocates of the official drug policy of our country, nor to present the Dutch experience as an example to the world (Kaplan, Haanraadts, van Vliet, & Grund, 1994). We put the harm reduction measures in the framework of Dutch drug policy and try to explain them from a more general historical and cultural background.[1]

FORMAL SOCIAL CONTROL OF LICIT AND ILLICIT DRUGS

Many of the prohibited substances we now call "drugs" were freely obtainable well into the 20th century. Cannabis, cocaine, and opiates such as morphine and heroin are the best known examples. They were commonly obtained through a doctor or chemist by prescription or over the counter. During the 20th century, the legal supply of drugs has been gradually superseded by an illicit supply. New, mostly synthetic drugs have regularly appeared on the market, being added in due course to the list of forbidden drugs. In the Netherlands, drugs came under the jurisdiction of the penal system at an early stage as a result of international agreements. International penal drug control today is based largely on the Single Convention adopted in New York in 1961, which was to form the basis for all subsequent international agreements on illicit psychoactive substances (Chatterjee, 1991). Designed to replace and make previous agreements uniform, it was one of the first international agreements to be worldwide in scope.

The fundamental premise of the Single Convention is that drug use poses a danger to society as a whole and to the health of the individual user. The ideological basis is the *abstinence paradigm*, which holds that individuals are incapable of regulating their use of certain psychoactive substances in a manner that is acceptable to society and not hazardous to their health. The experimental user of drugs will, as it were, unavoidably end up a dope fiend. The prime goal of the

Single Convention was to eradicate those drugs it defined as illicit. A full range of formal methods of control are specified that may serve the attainment of full abstinence. Emphasis is clearly on measures in the sphere of criminal law, to be laid down in legislation by each participating nation.

Today, more than 35 years after the adoption of the Single Convention, the emphasis in most countries is on criminalization, yet the forbidden substances are still being used. Drug use has expanded over large geographical areas, and a variety of illicit drugs are on the market. In Western Europe since the 1960s, cannabis has developed from a relatively unknown substance to the most widely used illegal drug. Consumption of heroin spread in the 1970s, cocaine in the 1980s, and ecstasy (MDMA) and other synthetic drugs in the 1990s. This shows that criminalizing drugs has not led to total abstinence, the foremost goal of the Single Convention. (This is not to say, however, that criminalization has no effect whatsoever on drug use trends.)

Criminalization of drugs is a form of social control (Cohen, 1985). Like Cachet (1990), we define social control as the ways in which people, directly or indirectly, consciously or less consciously, attempt to influence one another's behavior, employing sanctions and drawing on values, norms, and goals shared within their group or community. There is a key distinction between informal and formal social control. Informal social control refers to direct, mutual influencing and manipulation among individuals, with no powers involved that derive from their duties as representatives of agencies of legal or sociomedical control. Under formal social control, the influencing occurs through agencies specialized in social control. Whereas informal social control is exercised from below or within, formal social control is chiefly regulation from above. Of the many types of formal social control, those of greatest interest to criminologists are legal control institutions such as the police, and the criminal justice and prison systems.

When American researcher Schur (1965) coined the term *criminalization* in 1965, he spoke of the "criminalization of deviance" as having a double stigmatization—an action held to be deviant is labeled additionally as criminal and has fundamental and irreversible consequences for the identity of the actor. According to Dutch criminologist Lissenberg (1992), the notion of criminalization refers "not only to the introduction or alteration of penalties, but also to actions of police and public prosecutors as they start proceedings which can lead to the imposition of punishment and the labeling of individuals as criminals" (p. 47). When speaking of criminalization, we must observe a distinction between *statutory* (also known as de jure or primary) criminalization and *actual* (also called de facto or secondary) criminalization. Statutory criminalization is the act of making certain behaviors punishable by including them in a criminal code. Increased statutory criminalization occurs when the proscribed behavior is redefined from a minor to a major offense, or when the penalties laid down for it in laws or official directives are increased. Actual criminalization refers to the substantive enforcement of the penal regulations applying to given behaviors. These two forms of criminalization are distinguished here to stress that written rules are not necessarily enforced rules. A similar distinction may be made for decriminalization. Statutory decriminalization is the easing of existing legal restrictions on proscribed behaviors, such as reducing them from major to minor offenses or lowering the maximum punishments they carry. Actual decriminalization is the slackening or cessation of enforcement of existing criminal regulations. Legalization is the opposite of statutory criminalization; it is the removal of existing criminal regulations. If a behavior is legalized, it is no longer subject to punishment. Legalization is the ultimate form of statutory decriminalization, but it is not the last step in the process.

Criminalization, decriminalization, and legalization are not the only forms of formal social control. Formal social control is also exercised by other disciplines and institutions, such as schools, health care systems, and other state apparatuses. In the realm of illicit drugs, these are typically drug clinics and counseling centers, with administration of control in the hands of the therapeutic and medical community. This type of regulation is referred to as sociomedical, as opposed to legal, control.

THE NETHERLANDS AND ITS DRUG POLICY

The Netherlands is a small country in Western Europe and one of the first members of the European Union. Although the vast majority of the population is ethnic white, an increasing proportion are ethnic minorities. This is particularly true in urban areas like the capital city, Amsterdam (720,000 inhabitants). As in most other European countries, alcohol and tobacco are the most widely used licit drugs in the Netherlands. Cannabis (hashish and marijuana) is the most widely used illicit drug, whereas heroin has been the illicit drug most strongly associated with problematic use and addiction for more than two decades. The figures from an extensive household survey in Amsterdam are illustrative (Table 6.1). The prevalence rates for illicit drugs in Amsterdam are about twice as high as the whole country (Langemeijeer, 1997). Not only is the use of licit drugs far more widespread than illicit drugs, current continuation (the proportion of ever-users having used a particular drug during the past month) is also much lower in the case of illicit drugs. This difference can, at least to some extent, be explained by stricter rules of informal social control (Cohen, 1990).

The predominant types of formal social control currently being applied to alcohol, tobacco, cannabis, and heroin in the Netherlands are summarized schematically in Table 6.2. The plus and minus signs show a rough ranking of the importance placed on each drug within three types of formal control—sociomedical control, penal control, and availability.

TABLE 6.1   Licit and Illicit Drug Use in Amsterdam Among 12 Years and Older, 1994 (in percentages)

Drug	Ever Used (Lifetime prevalence)	Recent Use (Last year prevalence)	Current Use (Last month prevalence)	Current Continuation
Alcohol	85.8	76.9	69.1	81
Tobacco	66.4	45.1	40.7	61
Cannabis	29.1	10.5	6.7	23
Other illicit drugs	10.6	2.9	1.2	12
Cocaine	6.8	1.7	0.7	11
Amphetamines	4.7	0.5	0.3	6
Hallucinogens	4.4	0.5	0.1	3
Ecstasy	3.1	1.4	0.6	20
Heroin	1.3	0.3	0.1	5

SOURCE: Sandwijk et al. (1995).

TABLE 6.2   Formal Control and Availability of Four Drugs in the Netherlands

	Alcohol	Tobacco	Cannabis	Heroin
Sociomedical control	++	+	—	+++
Penal control	+	—	++	+++
Availability	(+)++	++	+	—

The sociomedical control of alcohol consists, first of all, of general public education via the mass media. One specific theme in such campaigns is the prevention of drunk driving (also subject to statutory and actual criminalization). Another control mechanism is in- and outpatient treatment for alcoholics. In the general health care sector, we find many alcohol-related disorders being treated, such as cirrhosis of the liver (which is also responsible for a higher mortality rate). For tobacco, the main emphasis lies in mass media campaigns. In addition, many smoking-related, especially bronchial, ailments are treated in the general health care sector (which likewise cause increased mortality). Sociomedical control of cannabis consists mainly of drug education aimed particularly at secondary school youth. Actual in- or outpatient treatment for cannabis use is rare. For heroin, sociomedical control is in the form of ambulatory or residential treatment of users, harm reduction programs, and youth drug education. Methadone provision, through general practitioners and specialized institutions, occupies a key place in the sociomedical control of heroin use. Finally, the general health care sector is confronted with a higher than average number of drug-related accidents, illnesses (such as AIDS), and deaths.

The relationship between the four substances is somewhat different when it comes to penal control. Control of alcohol is limited to criminalizing certain kinds of behavior by users, especially drunk driving. Tobacco use is not subjected to any specific statutory criminalization. Penal control of cannabis in the Netherlands concentrates on the criminalization of dealers, with emphasis on large-scale and international cannabis trade. The most extensive application of penal control pertains to heroin and cocaine. Criminalization is in force at all levels, from international trafficking to street dealing, but for users, and addicts in particular, it focuses mainly on drug-related crimes such as theft and burglary.

Alcohol and tobacco are the most widely available of the four drugs. Soft alcoholic beverages—beer and wine—are sold in supermarkets, other retail shops, and in eating and drinking establishments. The sale of hard alcoholic drinks (e.g., gin and whiskey) is confined to specially licensed shops, pubs, and restaurants, which also sell beer and wine. Other than specialized tobacco shops, one can buy tobacco at the supermarket (usually at the checkout counter), in bars and restaurants (usually from machines), and in many other commercial establishments. The illegal but tolerated sale of cannabis in small quantities is concentrated almost entirely in so-called coffee shops (Jansen, 1989), which are concentrated in the large cities. To purchase heroin, one must have recourse to the underground market, although it can occasionally be bought on city streets from small-scale dealers.

TWO-TRACK POLICY

Drug policy in the Netherlands officially aims to strike the best balance between reduction of supply by statutory intervention and reduction of both demand and health hazards through a public health approach. This effort is revealed in two central premises of drug policy today. First, there is profound skepticism as to the efficacy of repressive measures, which is coupled with a strong reliance on prevention and other public health strategies. Second, there is the belief that the markets for soft and hard drugs should be kept separate. This has resulted in decriminalizing hashish and marijuana and tolerating small-scale vending of cannabis in coffee shops. These guiding principles have inspired key concepts like harm reduction and key interventions such as low-threshold methadone and needle exchange programs. In its concentration on sociomedical control and its de-emphasis on legal control, Dutch drug policy has come to be viewed as a maverick force outside the mainstream of international drug control. This course of action is founded in historical events.

The first Dutch drug law dates from the early 20th century (the Opium Act of 1919). That statute was aimed primarily at controlling trade in products derived from the poppy, such as opium, morphine, and heroin, as well as those derived from the coca leaf, particularly cocaine. The Act was not really prompted by any drug problem existing in the Netherlands at the time, because the substances placed under its jurisdiction in 1919 were hardly a source of social problems. As in many other Western countries, alcohol posed a far more serious problem (Gerritsen, 1993). In the first decades after the Act took effect, instances of enforcement were few. Nothing much changed after hashish—but not Indian hemp (marijuana) because it was still grown for agricultural and industrial purposes—was brought under the law by the 1928 revision (de Kort & Korf, 1992). Until the 1950s, active enforcement of the Opium Act mainly affected a handful of Chinese immigrants in Rotterdam and Amsterdam, who had brought the custom of opium smoking with them from their homeland. Even then, the emphasis was on smugglers and dealers, whereas the users themselves were largely left in peace (van Heek, 1936).

If there was so little evidence of a domestic drug problem, then why did the Netherlands take steps to regulate drug trade and consumption by criminal law? Deciding factors were the widespread use of opium in the Dutch East Indies, a former Dutch colony now known as Indonesia, and the role of the Netherlands in the world trade in opium, coca, and their derivatives. The latter interests especially made the Netherlands a key participant in the creation of the first international drug agreements, such as those of Shanghai (1909) and The Hague (1911 and subsequent years) (Chatterjee, 1991). Although the Netherlands was not particularly keen on such agreements, U.S. diplomatic pressure resulted in Dutch cooperation (de Kort & Korf, 1992; Musto, 1987). Thus, with little enthusiasm, the 1919 Dutch Opium Act came into being, and judging from contemporary crime statistics, enforcement of the law was equally lacking in enthusiasm. The banned substances were not being consumed on any great scale, but some drugs, especially the opium-based ones, were rather easy to acquire by prescription. There is little evidence of any active investigation or prosecution of offenses against the Opium Act. In practice, the Opium Act was more a statute for medicine control than a penal law (De Kort, 1995). Obligations were incurred under international agreements and would likewise play a major or even decisive role in later revisions (such as 1928 and 1976) of the Opium Act.[2]

After World War II, the Netherlands enforced the Opium Act more actively. Increasing the punitive measures of drug control can be interpreted as recognizing the American approach. This change could be due to a more positive attitude toward the United States, which, together with Canada and Britain, had been the foremost liberator from Nazism. In the aftermath of World War II, U.S.-Dutch relations were strongly influenced by such factors as the extensive economic aid that the Netherlands was receiving under the Marshall Plan and the founding of the North Atlantic Treaty Organization (NATO) (Loeber, 1992). Nylon stockings, hamburgers, Coca-Cola, frozen foods, and all kinds of other American consumer goods swept the Dutch market. The United States also took over the leading role that Germany and France had previously filled in scientific endeavors, and opportunities opened for Dutch researchers to study in the United States. American music, heard via the jukebox and other advanced equipment, was exceedingly popular in the postwar Netherlands. American movies were shown in cinemas and later on television (Roholl, 1992).

One sign of the shift in attitude toward "the American way" was the establishment of a special Amsterdam police unit for drug control. This was prompted by growing postwar concern about smuggling drugs out of leftover German stockpiles, as well as the stream of American soldiers stationed in Germany who were traveling to Amsterdam to buy marijuana. The Opium Act was amended in 1953 to make punishable the possession and sale of marijuana (de Hullu & Tillema, 1989). Nevertheless, enforcement of the Opium Act remained sporadic until the end of the 1950s.

The postwar change of direction accelerated with the onset of the 1960s. The Single Convention (1961) obliged the Dutch government to revise national legislation to conform to the new provisions, and this was completed in 1976.[3] The need for revision was not strongly felt by the government, which believed that the Convention "afforded national legislatures the prerogative to enact only those penal measures it sees fit" (de Hullu & Tillema, 1989, p. 39). Increasing cannabis use and the spread of heroin were more pressing reasons for the 1976 Opium Act revision, although during the course of the 1960s, authorities began to enforce existing laws more vigorously (de Kort & Korf, 1992).

The 1976 revision introduced a dual listing of substances. Schedule I contained the drugs that presented unacceptable risks, which are all illegal drugs except hemp (cannabis) products. The former substances are generally referred to as hard drugs. Schedule II was for the hemp products hashish and marijuana, popularly called soft drugs. Maximum penalties for hard drug trafficking, especially for import and export, were raised. Changes to the Opium Act since 1976 derived largely from obligations that the Netherlands had undertaken by signing and ratifying new international agreements.[4]

So far, we have emphasized the legal control of illicit drugs as the central pillar of the Single Convention. However, the agreement leaves room for other forms of social control, such as education and medical control. Education control refers to providing information intended to prevent drug use. Medical control concerns the treatment of individuals already taking illicit drugs, including the option of medically dispensing the drugs themselves or a substitute. Dutch drug policy, especially since 1976, is a combination of legal and sociomedical control. Legal control is expressed in intensified criminalization of drug trade (supply) paralleled by a decriminalization of drug users (demand). The increased criminalization is effected by more severe legislation applying to drug trafficking, coupled with more rigid enforcement—the focus being on hard drugs. Decriminalization, on the other hand, mainly affects the demand of the illicit drug market. In the revised Opium Act of 1976, this was brought about chiefly by lowering statutory penalties for possession of cannabis for personal use in amounts up to 30 grams (approximately 1 ounce). In practice, decriminalization has taken the form of toleration of retail cannabis trade in coffee shops under certain conditions. Where drug users are concerned, Dutch policy emphasizes sociomedical control in the form of prevention, treatment, and care. In the Netherlands, these are concentrated on users of hard drugs, in which the provision of methadone and needles to heroin users plays a crucial role.

CRIMINALIZATION AND DECRIMINALIZATION OF CANNABIS

The influence of decriminalization on trends in drug use is among the key topics in the international debate on the ramifications of legal control of illicit drugs. This discourse is dominated by two rival models: prohibitionism and antiprohibitionism. Prototypically,[5] prohibitionists stress the intrinsic harm that drugs do, and they believe that sanctions will make people refrain from using them. If existing sanctions fail to eliminate or at least curtail consumption, they should be toughened. It is feared that reducing penalties or, worse, full legalization will bring on normative erosion, widen the availability of drugs, and thereby stimulate people's willingness to use drugs like cannabis. Although antiprohibitionists agree that drugs can be intrinsically harmful, they believe that the prohibitionist approach will not succeed in keeping people from using drugs. They argue that sanctions strengthen the appeal of drug use, actual criminalization leads to secondary deviance, and repressive interventions are counterproductive. Notwithstanding their conflicting conclusions, both models presume that a direct and causal relationship exists between legal sanctions and prevalence of use. Whereas prohibitionists assume that decriminalization will bring about an increase in drug use, antiprohibitionists believe that it will cause consumption to decrease.

The Netherlands is not the only European country to make a statutory distinction between cannabis and other illicit drugs. Cannabis has been statutorily decriminalized in other countries, such as Spain.[6] Statutory decriminalization was enacted in the Netherlands in 1976 on the users' level only. The 1953 criminalizing statute gave the Dutch authorities the possibility of criminalizing the sale and possession of cannabis. Initially, this happened, although it really only started in the 1960s. This actual criminalization escalated sharply at first, affecting mainly users and petty dealers. But a distinct downturn soon followed in the first half of the 1970s, and actual decriminalization of users was already well under way before statutory decriminalization occurred in 1976. The conviction grew among Dutch authorities that cannabis use was less dangerous than it had first appeared. That, in turn, led to growing misgivings about criminalizing cannabis users, a skepticism that also extended to other punishable behaviors, such as homosexuality and abortion. The doubts flourished after police and judicial authorities realized that many arrestees did not fit their idea of criminals, being youngsters from the middle and upper classes. Actual criminalization of cannabis was putting "your own children" on trial. Whereas cannabis use had at first been labeled alien or criminal, it now took on the more neutral connotation of "different" (Leuw, 1972). The feeling grew that rather than ostracizing youth from society by criminalizing what seemed fairly harmless behavior, it was the government's task to create conditions for involving them in mainstream culture. The American sociologist Himmelstein (1983) has called this process the "embourgeoisement" of cannabis. In the Netherlands, it eventually resulted in statutory decriminalization. Viewing it a bit cynically, we might say that the spread of heroin use in the first half of the 1970s came at a convenient time for the Dutch parliament. The authorities regarded heroin as a far more ominous threat than cannabis, and they could not, in good faith, lump them together.

FROM UNDERGROUND MARKET TO COFFEE SHOPS

Because of the criminalization of cannabis in the 1960s and early 1970s, consumers had to rely on an underground market. In a subsequent period up until the early 1980s, the sale of cannabis was increasingly concentrated in youth centers with the so-called house dealers. Even before statutory decriminalization in 1976, some cities had already cautiously begun tolerating house dealers. After 1976, there were two successive developments in the actual decriminalization of the cannabis retail trade. In the late 1970s, the toleration of house dealers gained official policy status. Then, in the first half of the 1980s, came the rise of the coffee-shop phenomenon and a sharp increase in the number of such coffee shops. In the process, the cannabis retail market began to look more and more like a free market, albeit an illegal one. In light of these developments, it becomes clear that the relationship between cannabis decriminalization and trends in use cannot be adequately measured by merely pinpointing the differences pre- and post-1976.

Toward the end of the 1960s—the era of underground dealing—cannabis use spread rapidly among the Dutch youth. A similar development happened in other European countries (e.g., Germany). The antiprohibitionists' argument is lent further credence by this fact, and the fact that heroin use began to spread in both countries during the same period. They argued that criminalizing cannabis gave rise to secondary deviance, such as withdrawing into a drug-using subculture or moving on to harder drugs. The emergence of heroin use among cannabis users is evidence of this. Still, the question remains why cannabis use had not begun its spread earlier, because statutory criminalization dated from much earlier.

Taking the broader social context into account, we see that a series of other developments were under way in the late 1960s and early 1970s that changed Dutch society. One such development was the increase in the use of legal drugs. Alcohol and tobacco use were flourishing among adolescents and young adults. Unlike its peers from previous eras, this younger generation distinguished itself in many other ways and formed a much more distinct youth culture that mounted a strong challenge to existing authority structures. The counterculture of this "protest generation" was accommodated in government-subsidized youth centers. Perhaps the key difference between this and previous generations was the advent and spread of cannabis use as an integral part of an expanding youth culture with its own rapidly commercializing consumer market. In a time of "give peace a chance" and "make love not war," hashish and marijuana were peace and love drugs par excellence. Such developments were by no means confined to the Netherlands; they also occurred in Germany and other Western countries. Although this culture proclaimed itself an alternative to Western consumer society, the differences were not so great in reality.

The development of cannabis use in the course of the 1970s, the house dealers stage, does not lend clear-cut empirical support to either prohibitionism or antiprohibitionism. Cannabis use did not increase further, and in all probability, it was slowly receding. This trend followed antiprohibitionist predictions. The problem, though, is that in Germany, where cannabis users continued to be dependent on the underground market, the consumption of cannabis evolved in more or less the same way as it did in the Netherlands with its house dealers.

Along with the multiplying numbers of coffee shops in the 1980s, cannabis use among adolescents and young adults grew again, particularly in Amsterdam and other cities (Korf, 1988; Kuipers, Mensink, & de Zwart, 1993; Plomp, Kuipers, & van Oers, 1990; Reuband, 1992). This supports the views of prohibitionists, but it does not prove the antiprohibitionists entirely wrong. One of the fundamental assumptions of the former is that beginning users will almost inevitably turn into habitual users, or even hard-drug addicts, with all of the problems that this entails. This is the essence of the abstinence paradigm. This prediction fails to hold in the Netherlands. The predominant pattern of cannabis use, even today, is experimental and recreational. Compared to tobacco and alcohol users, users of cannabis are far more likely to give up cannabis eventually, and to do so at a much earlier age. Current users smoke cannabis far less frequently than alcohol users drink and tobacco users smoke (Sandwijk, Cohen, Musterd, & Langemeijer, 1995).

When comparing the Netherlands and Germany (which has more restrictive laws), similarities in cannabis use prevail (Korf, 1995; Reuband, 1992, 1995).

As far as use is concerned, the two countries show marked parallels. In patterns of consumption, similarities also predominate. Characteristic for both countries is that experimental and recreational use prevails, not habitual or daily use. Therefore, neither statutory nor actual criminalization of cannabis forms an essential condition for moderation. On this point, one of the key assumptions underlying the Single Convention of 1961—that in the absence of criminalization, habitual use will prevail—must be relegated to the realm of fables.

The longitudinal development of cannabis use in the Netherlands since the 1960s points to the conclusion that the effects of decriminalizing cannabis heavily depend on the consequences that such a measure has for the availability of the drug. During the house dealer stage, availability resembled that under a licensing system. Although no formal licenses existed, the policy of toleration meant that cannabis could be bought only at a limited number of places. In the coffeeshop phase, where availability is more like it would be in a free market, consumption has increased. However, a similar development can be observed in other countries without coffee shops (Harrison, 1997). In practice, the coffeeshop system is still a far cry from a free market system. In the latter, hashish and marijuana would be available in places like the supermarket, just as beer and tobacco are. It is hard to predict how much cannabis use would increase under such a system, and what it would be like if fully legalized. Would more people start using cannabis? At present, the number of current and former cannabis users trails far behind that of alcohol and tobacco. Would cannabis users continue using it longer? Would they go on using cannabis for most of their lives, as do alcohol users? Or will daily use become the norm, as it now is among tobacco users? These are questions that need further investigation. Even more relevant questions are the following: Why has cannabis use among youth in recent years also increased in European countries that did not decriminalize? Why is cannabis use in the United States, where criminalization is the main strategy of formal control, still higher than in the Netherlands?

SEPARATION OF MARKETS

It is unfortunate that no trustworthy estimates are available of the number of heroin users in the Netherlands during the underground market and house dealer stages of cannabis. Although population and school surveys at the time indicated that no more than a tiny segment of the populace was using or had ever used heroin, such studies allow no reliable conclusions on *trends* in the number of heroin users. Statistics on the quantities of heroin confiscated or the numbers of fatal overdoses are often seized upon as indicators of the scale of heroin use. However, such figures are not reliable parameters for estimating the size of user populations.

Two things are adequately documented with respect to the development of Dutch heroin use in the 1970s. First, heroin use started to spread during the stage of the underground cannabis market. Most of the users were white and included "heroin tourists," mostly from Germany. The large majority were intravenous users (injectors). Second, a rapid upsurge in heroin use was recorded among young Surinamese men around 1975, the year in which Surinam became independent of the Netherlands. In the years both preceding and following independence, half of the Surinam population immigrated to the Netherlands, settling, for the most part, in Amsterdam and other cities. Young Surinamese men came to play a major part in the street trade in heroin, and many of them became users themselves. However, they did not inject the heroin; rather, they smoked the vapor of heroin heated on aluminum foil (*chinezen,* or "chasing the dragon") (Grund, 1993).

Not until the mid-1980s, during the cannabis coffeeshop stage, can reasonably trustworthy estimates be given of the number of heroin users. Nationwide estimates for recent years are between 20,000 and 25,000, or between one and two tenths of 1% of the country's population. In Amsterdam, the local heroin-using population has stayed fairly stable since the mid-1980s at around 4,000-5,000 per year. Contrary to prohibitionist fears, the decriminalizing of cannabis has not caused any boost in the number of heroin users, at least not during the coffee-shop stage.

A comparison of how heroin use has developed in the Netherlands and in Germany since the mid-1980s makes it plausible that the coffee-shop system has instead been an *impediment* to beginning heroin use. The Dutch heroin-using population is rapidly aging, suggesting that there are few new users. The average age of Amsterdam methadone provision clients increases by almost one every year, and the number of young heroin addicts using services like methadone provision has shrunk over the years to a handful. In stark contrast, Germany harbors an increasing number of new, young heroin users. Such developments are in line with the expectations of antiprohibitionists.

Coffee shops are only one possible explanation for these diverging trends. Even so, it seems reasonable to assume that they have helped to stabilize drug use in the Netherlands. Cannabis street trade has practically vanished since the coffee-shop phenomenon. Heroin dealing in coffee shops has been rare and prompts swift police action to close the coffee shop.

This evidence supports the hypothesis that decriminalization of cannabis has helped create and maintain a separation of the cannabis and heroin markets with a consequent stabilization of heroin use in the Netherlands. True to prohibitionist claims, statutory and actual decriminalization appear to have contributed to some growth in cannabis use in the long run. On the other hand, partly as a result of the coffee-shop system, the Netherlands has a far lower share of new, young heroin users than do countries like Germany. Decriminalization has also brought other benefits, among them considerable savings in government spending on penal control.

HEROIN USERS IN DUTCH SOCIETY

The first constituent part of sociomedical control is prevention, which is largely in the hands of agencies subsidized by the government. This form of control is composed of primary prevention strategies, such as drug education at school, as well as secondary prevention, which is intended for individuals and groups that are already experimenting with drugs. The aim of secondary prevention is to avert heavier or more hazardous drug use. Still, other forms of prevention (tertiary prevention) focus on frequent users of drugs. These aim to confine and minimize the risks attached to frequent drug use. This type of prevention, also called harm reduction, is offered primarily to heroin users. One example is AIDS prevention through "safe use" education and needle exchange facilities for intravenous users.

The second prong of sociomedical control is treatment. Besides inpatient treatment oriented to complete abstinence, there is outpatient treatment centering around methadone. Outpatient treatment is not explicitly concerned with abstinence. In practice, both types concentrate almost solely on heroin users in Dutch society.

After a hesitant entrée in the 1960s and a slow diffusion throughout the 1970s, methadone was reintroduced in the 1980s as the cornerstone of formal sociomedical control of heroin users in the Netherlands (Buisman, 1982; van de Wijngaart & Verbraeck, 1991). The foremost goal of methadone provision is to positively influence health, or at least diminish the risks involved in heroin use (harm reduction). A second goal of methadone provision, albeit less explicitly formulated by the Dutch authorities, is a reduction in crime committed by heroin users.

Men appear to be the majority of heroin users in the Netherlands. Ethnic minority users are also overrepresented in relation to the general Dutch population. That applies only to males, however, for the representation of women is weakest among ethnic minorities. Heroin users generally come from the underprivileged sections of the populace. Most have a low level of education and little or no experience in the legal labor market, and only a small minority have steady jobs. This is in marked contrast to cannabis users, who have a higher than average level of education and are working or studying in large numbers. Another difference is that ethnic minorities are proportionally underrepresented among cannabis users (Korf, 1995).

About one third of today's heroin users in the Netherlands are injectors. (In Germany and many other European countries, the overwhelming majority are intravenous users.) The heroin users of today can perhaps be called polyusers, in that besides heroin, they use a wide variety of other legal and illegal drugs (e.g., cocaine, alcohol, cannabis), either one after the other or in combination.

HARM REDUCTION: AMSTERDAM'S RESPONSE TO THE AIDS EPIDEMIC AMONG HEROIN ADDICTS

Almost 75,000 intravenous drug users (IDUs) cumulatively through 1997 have been diagnosed with AIDS in Europe, which is more than one third of all reported cases (about 200,000) (WHO, 1997). The majority of injecting drug users with AIDS are reported in Spain (about 29,000), Italy (24,000), and France (11,000). The northern European countries have considerably lower numbers of IDUs with AIDS. Per million inhabitants, the number of drug injectors with AIDS in Spain is about 20 times higher than in the Netherlands. This can be explained by several factors: (a) a relatively low number of IDUs in the Netherlands; (b) a high percentage of Dutch IDUs in touch with drug-helping agencies at the time HIV was introduced; (c) extensive AIDS prevention campaigns in the Netherlands in the latter part of the 1980s; (d) less group consumption of drugs in the Netherlands than in Spain, which reduces the prevalence of needle sharing.

Primary drug prevention is effective in keeping the vast majority of young people from becoming addicted, and treatment is effective in helping a considerable number of addicts to lead a drug-free life. But for a specific group, these interventions do not work. Although many drug addicts have undergone various forms of drug-free treatment, they still use drugs in a harmful way. When this was realized, the concept of "harm reduction" was developed in the Netherlands. This is defined as "when a drug user is not (yet) willing or capable of stopping drug use, he/she should be assisted in reducing the harm caused to himself and others" (Buning & van Brussel, 1995, p. 92). This definition accepts that drug users may go through various phases in their drug career, from a positive drug-free period to a very destructive and harmful phase of heavy use. Instead of turning away from active drug users, the users are offered various forms of care to prevent them from dying of an overdose; from getting infected with AIDS, hepatitis, and/or tuberculosis; and from being involved in drug-related crime.

Amsterdam has a relatively high unemployment rate, especially among ethnic minority groups. However, there is a good social security system, and almost everyone has health insurance. Recall that the number of hard-drug addicts is estimated to be 4,000 to 5,000 per year, of whom about one third belong to ethnic minorities (Surinam, Dutch Antilles, Morocco, and Turkey). About 40% of hard-drug users inject, and 60% "chase the dragon." Among the injectors, about 30% are HIV-positive (Haastrecht, 1997).

The drug-helping system is well developed and ranges from harm reduction interventions (outreach, low-threshold methadone, needle exchange, drop-in centers, etc.) to drug-free therapeutic treatment and resocialization. Medical doctors, nurses, and social workers are the main professions working in the drug-helping agencies. The two main drug intervention institutes in Amsterdam are the Municipal Health Service (GG&GD) and the Jellinek Center. In addition, a number of smaller institutions are active in the drug field (e.g. Street-cornerwork, The Rainbow Foundation, Mainline, and AMOC/Deutscher Hilfsverein), and they practice mainly outreach work. Furthermore, 200 general practitioners are involved in the prescription of methadone.

The Amsterdam approach toward heroin addicts is primarily public health oriented. HIV and AIDS have contributed to this. AIDS prevention among heroin addicts is practiced from a broad perspective. The first goal is to make contact with as many addicts as possible. This is done through outreach work; through a special project for addicted prostitutes; and by visiting addicts in police stations (and giving them methadone if necessary), hospitals, the needle exchange schemes, and low-threshold methadone programs.

The Amsterdam harm reduction approach toward heroin addicts in general, and AIDS prevention more specifically, has three main components: outreach work, needle exchange, and provision of methadone. Various organizations are actively involved in outreach work. They provide concrete assistance to drug users in their own environment and distribute magazines (*Dr. Use Good, Mainline*) and other documentation on safe use and safe sex. AIDS prevention and the care for drug users with AIDS are an integral part of their work (i.e., a "buddy project" for addicted AIDS patients).

The first *needle exchange* was initiated in 1984 by the Amsterdam Interest Group of Drug Users (MDHG), which is a self-help organization. Currently, about 1 million needles and syringes are exchanged yearly at 11 different locations in the city, with the largest needle exchange run by the Rainbow Foundation. In the afternoon, they exchange needles and syringes in a building in the red-light district, whereas at night, they operate from a small van. Needles and syringes are also exchanged in methadone programs.

Methadone programs play a major role in attracting heroin addicts to treatment, stabilizing their lives, and giving them perspective to start a rehabilitation process. Although it is relatively easy for heroin addicts to enter a methadone program (they participate mostly in maintenance programs), they have to agree to their names being entered in the central methadone registration to prevent double prescriptions. There are various options: methadone-by-bus at one of the outpatient centers, from their own general practitioner, or at the structured methadone program of the Jellinek Center (which includes a detoxification program). In addition, arrested heroin addicts get methadone in the police station, as well as in the hospital.

METHADONE AND HEALTH:
SAFETY NET AND SNARE

What are the connections between methadone provision and the health of heroin users? Although the state of health of Dutch heroin users is poorer than that of their peers, methadone provision functions as a safety net for physical and other problems that heroin users can suffer. The most important demonstrable contribution that methadone makes to health is that people who take it reduce their consumption of illicit drugs. In this way, methadone acts as a temporary or permanent replacement for the drug dealer. If one lacks money for heroin, one can fall back on methadone. The impact of provision is swift: Soon after enrollment in a program, illicit drug use drops substantially, and people who leave a program are likely to start doing more illicit drugs. Also, the *longer* one stays in a program, the less money one spends on drugs, and the less heroin and other illicit drugs one is likely to take.

Although we can interpret the latter finding as a success for methadone provision, an alternative explanation might be that it is a function of "maturing out," which is a process whereby users slowly wind down their drug career as they grow older. The question remains whether some clients would diminish their intake of heroin and other drugs anyway, even without methadone provision.

Besides being a safety net, methadone provision can also be a snare, which may make the drug career last longer than it might have in the absence of methadone. Methadone can serve as a crutch to prevent someone from suffering too much from withdrawal sickness. To continue using heroin without the aid of methadone, users would be more active in prostitution or crime, for example. Many users appear to desire stability in their lives, and methadone is an effective means to achieve this. Thanks to it, withdrawal symptoms can be kept to a minimum. But because of its addictive nature and toilsome detoxification process, methadone is a controversial drug, even among its users. The fact that many heroin users persist in taking methadone to keep from getting sick has the added consequence that most of them will not give up drugs easily. Besides its pharmacological properties, other factors are doubtless at work, such as their ambivalent attitude toward their own drug use. Thus, methadone becomes a metaphorical scapegoat for the fact that they cannot, or will not, stop using drugs. In a certain sense, Dutch drug policy also has a legitimizing influence on drug use: No one is telling heroin users that they must come off drugs.

HIV AND AIDS

Within the drug population, HIV infection occurs mostly through sharing contaminated injecting gear. Rapid spread of HIV occurred during the early 1980s, with HIV prevalence among IDUs stabilizing at about 30% in Amsterdam and between 0% and 12% in other parts of the country in the 1990s (Haastrecht, 1997). A large share of HIV-positive heroin users in the Netherlands live in Amsterdam, probably because the city hosts a comparatively high percentage of heroin users. The population of intravenous heroin users also contains a relatively high number of people with HIV and AIDS. There are several possible reasons for this: (a) Amsterdam is an international city with many foreign injecting "heroin tourists," some of whom possibly brought the virus with them; (b) male IDUs who were active in prostitution could have been infected during sex with homosexual men, another population which has a high infection rate; (c) a relatively large share of heroin tourists today are seropositive, especially German women working in street prostitution; (d) the care for AIDS patients was initially concentrated in Amsterdam, and as a consequence, many AIDS patients from outside the city were registered and treated; and (e) although AIDS prevention efforts in Amsterdam started at an early stage, some IDUs had already been infected.

Obviously, methadone itself is not an HIV vaccine, but it can help reduce infection risks indirectly. Because both legal provision and the black market serve to stabilize heroin use, heroin users are less likely to panic and resort to unsafe practices. Again, we witness the role of methadone provision as a safety net. More specifically, the Dutch methadone provision programs have developed into central locations for needle exchange where drug users can turn in their used syringes for new ones.

Empirical proof of either methadone provision or needle exchange in reducing the chances of HIV infection is not easy. Although research has shown that the whole package of AIDS prevention measures has probably somewhat reduced heroin users' infection risk, the separate effects of measures like methadone provision or needle exchange are more difficult to isolate (van Ameijden, 1994; van Ameijden, Watters, van den Hoek, & Coutinho, 1995). Here, we are faced with the same problem discussed earlier about measuring the influence of methadone provision on general states of health. Comparing infection rates of methadone clients to those of nonclients overlooks the fact that methadone provision also reaches nonclients through its spillover onto the black market. The same can be said for needle exchange, where drug users who get clean syringes through the methadone programs or other drug care services put some of them on the black market, either for free or in exchange for money, goods, or services. A dichotomous classification of clients versus nonclients, or exchangers versus nonexchangers, does too little justice to the real situation. Hence, it does not permit us to judge the effectiveness of methadone provision or needle exchange in reducing the odds of HIV infection within the entire IUD population. Longitudinal epidemiological research in Amsterdam shows a substantial decrease in the cumulative incidence of HIV infection among IDUs (Haastrecht, 1997). Although a residual of HIV risk behavior remains, and new infections of HIV occur, it is very likely that interventions such as needle exchange have contributed to the reduction of the spread of HIV.

OUTREACH TO DRUG USERS

The task of outreach workers is fourfold: (a) reaching the unreachable, (b) assisting the survivors, (c) extending service utilization, and (d) using an early warning system. Outreach projects play an important role in *reaching the unreachable* by contacting drug users who are not in touch with the existing facilities, ranging from young recreational drug users to hard-core addicts. *Assisting the survivors* refers to activities that help drug users avoid major health risks (such as HIV infection or overdose), create conditions to avoid further marginalization, and assist drug users with AIDS. Examples are crisis intervention, counseling and advice, handing out condoms, providing or exchanging clean needles and syringes, referrals to treatment facilities, and monitoring the use of AIDS medication. *Extending service utilization* is the consequence of outreach workers acting as a link between active drug users and drug-helping agencies. Information about other agencies is given, and drug users are encouraged to contact them. An *early warning system* is practiced by signaling what is going on in the drug scene, such as new trends in drug use, new groups of drug users, and/or lack of facilities. Through field observations, outreach projects are able to provide their organization and policymakers with information about patterns of drug use, prevalence of drug use, AIDS-related risk behavior, and new trends in drug use.

Outreach work in the Netherlands, as in other parts of Europe, is practiced in various ways, among various groups of drug users, and with various aims. Some projects make use of volunteers. The advantage of using volunteers is that many drug users can be contacted with a relatively low budget. The disadvantage is that the training and support of volunteers takes up a lot of the paid workers' time. A number of outreach projects include ex-drug users and/or ex-prostitutes, sometimes as paid staff, sometimes as volunteers. The major advantage of using former drug users and/or prostitutes is the easy access to the drug scene. Projects that have negative experiences with ex-users indicate that they run a major risk of relapsing into drug use or are incapable of holding a nonjudgmental attitude toward the drug-involved clients. Also, drug users often do not accept another drug user in the role of expert. Some outreach projects make use of a drop-in center, where clients come for practical assistance or just a cup of tea. Although useful, the existence of a drop-in center may lead to neglecting actual street work if the center is open too many hours a day.

Most outreach projects do both "detached work" and "street work." Detached work refers to outreach work that is done in other agencies, such as prisons, police stations, and hospitals. Street work refers to outreach work done in the drug scene itself. In many countries, mobile units (vans and buses) are used to provide services to drug users. As the first in Europe in the late 1970s, the Netherlands started to provide methadone through mobile clinics (methadone buses). In 1986, health workers in London and Liverpool began exchanging needles and syringes using mobile units (vans). Today, vans are also used to contact drug-addicted street prostitutes.

Outreach teams encounter many problems, ranging from short-term funding, working in isolation, lack of referral possibilities, problems with the police and neighborhood organizations, and staff turnover. One of the major problems encountered by outreach projects is funding. In many European countries, governments encourage AIDS prevention among drug users by making extra funds available. However, this is often short-term. The experience from most outreach teams is that they need at least a year to become acquainted with the drug scene, build up a network of clients, and develop rapport with their agencies. Therefore, short-term funding will undoubtedly have negative effects on the output of the project. Second, if an outreach project is too small and not part of a larger organization, the workers may feel isolated and lack support in carrying out their work. Third, some outreach projects encounter problems when referring clients because of a lack of agencies in their area. They are faced with a limited number of clients who need all of their attention, leaving no time to get a broader scope of the drug problem in their area. Additionally, outreach workers sometimes have to deal with agencies that are reluctant to provide services to drug users, such as pharmacists who refuse to sell clean needles to drug users, or agencies that feel that drug users do not fit the profile of their clientele. Often, outreach projects also have difficulties in relating to the police, although this is far less often the case in the Netherlands than, for example, in France (Boekhout van Solinge, 1996). The police have an independent responsibility toward public order issues, which sometimes results in actions that are counterproductive to outreach work. Furthermore, many outreach teams who want to operate a drop-in center are faced with neighborhood resistance to accepting a facility in their community. The neighborhood anticipates problems caused by drug users and dealers who hang out around the center. Because these problems are real, it is important to develop good liaisons with the neighborhood and make concrete arrangements concerning opening hours, house rules, and so on. Finally, outreach teams sometimes face problems of staff turnover. They have built up their network of clients and are not able to transfer their knowledge to new workers. Another problem related to staff turnover is the lack of career possibilities for outreach workers.

NEW DRUGS

Since the mid-1980s, many new drugs have been introduced in, and spread throughout, Europe. The use of crack cocaine is still mainly restricted to the same groups that use heroin, although it has also been observed among other groups of users. However, in terms of number of users, synthetic drugs like Ecstasy (MDMA, often spelled "XTC") and similar substances are far more important. The Dutch government was not very keen on criminalizing another drug, but international pressure led to the inclusion of MDMA into the Opium Act in 1988 (other substances, such as MDEA, followed in more recent years). In practice, actual criminalization of the XTC market mainly refers to producers and upper-level traffickers. The Dutch policy reflects the priority that the government officially puts on public health in general, but also quite objectively concentrates on the practice of the Dutch XTC policy at user level. A "key principle in Dutch prevention policy is that users and potential users should be informed about the risks of drug use and the possibilities to reduce these in a realistic and credible way" (Factsheet, 1999, p. 6). Youth, parents, and intermediaries are the most important target groups of general prevention campaigns. Specific measures are taken with regard to specific groups at risk at "raves"[7] and other settings where large groups of youth meet and where the use of XTC and similar substances is common. According to the national guidelines, communities are requested to give permission to organizers of raves only if they take care of

> the availability of fresh and free water, experienced First Aid nurses, sufficient air conditioning and "cool down" facilities. Also they have to guarantee an easy entrance and exit of visitors, to prevent that weapons and drugs are brought in, and to arrange a rescue route for police, firemen and ambulance. (Factsheet, 1999, p. 6)

Throughout the country, the Adviesburo Drugs (a private foundation based in Amsterdam) practices its Safe House Campaign at raves. A team of professionals and peers provides information about the effects and risks of XTC and other "dance drugs," hands out condoms, and talks about safe sex. Moreover, within the framework of the national Drug Information and Monitoring System (DIMS), consumers can have their drugs tested on the spot. A growing number of the official local or regional drug services offer consumers testing of XTC pills for their quality (content, dosage). The aim of this facility is to reduce risks to users and prevent them from taking high dosages of substances more dangerous than they expected. If the content of a certain kind of pill appears be very dangerous to the user, information is spread quickly at settings where users meet, and sometimes in daily newspapers as well. In a nutshell, this illustrates the Dutch harm reduction approach: "It's better that you don't do drugs at all. But if you take drugs, keep it safe."

HARM REDUCTION IN THE NETHERLANDS

The Netherlands has a respectable history of harm reduction projects among drug users. The first low-threshold methadone program in Amsterdam was set up in 1979 (the methadone bus). Many workers felt embarrassed having to explain the program to experts from abroad by saying that urine checks were not done, and the goal of the program was not to strive for drug-free lives. The same happened in 1984, when the Amsterdam experts had to explain the needle exchange scheme to visiting scholars from abroad. It took some time to be open about the goals of these programs, which included helping drug users who are not yet capable of stopping, or preventing them from harming themselves and their environment.

From the Dutch experience, five aspects are concluded to be prerequisites for a fruitful implementation of harm reduction: (a) realism, (b) pragmatism, (c) building of bridges, (d) knowledge of facts and figures, and (e) optimism. First of all, one should be willing to avoid moralism and be *realistic*. If it is not possible to completely prevent drug use in prison, how can one even think of preventing drug use in an open society? Although some drug addicts benefit from treatment, there is always a considerable group of addicts that does not enter treatment, fails to go through the program, or relapses after successful treatment. Improving the quality of programs might help to some extent, but this takes a long-term commitment to research. (Apart from this, which society would be willing to pay the enormous costs if all drug addicts chose, or were forced, to undergo inpatient, drug-free treatment?) Drug abuse is a chronic, relapsing condition with many false starts before recovery is achieved. From a public health perspective, it appears more effective to take an active approach to prevent further damage through harm reduction interventions.

The second prerequisite for the successful implementation of harm reduction interventions is *pragmatism*. Pragmatism means accepting a whole range of treatment and care options, with harm reduction measures being an integral part of the whole approach.

The third aspect refers to the attitude of the workers in the drug field. Harm reduction workers should be capable of *building bridges* with other institutions and facilities, as well as the community as a whole. Consequently, workers should be willing to stay on speaking terms with opponents.

The fourth point is *knowing facts and figures.* Workers in the harm reduction field should have basic statistical knowledge of the project, such as the number of people using the project, their average age, their risk-taking behavior, and project outcome data. Simple research models are available to obtain these data quickly.

The final point is about *optimism.* A growing body of practical experience and research on the behavior of drug users in light of the AIDS epidemic has demonstrated that many drug users are capable of making at least small changes in their behavior to decrease the risk of becoming infected with HIV. This creates a new image of drug users, which conflicts with traditional social constructs. No longer can drug users simply be stigmatized as self-destructive, mentally disturbed individuals. Just like anyone else, most drug users want to survive and make the best of life, even if using drugs.

NOTES

1. For a more general overview of Dutch drug policy, see Leuw and Haen Marshall (1994) and the white paper of the Dutch government, *Drugs Policy in the Netherlands: Continuity and Change* (1996).

2. For a review of the most important adaptations of the law, see Krabbe (1989).

3. Some alterations had been made in the interim. LSD had been placed under the Opium Act in 1966 and amphetamines in 1972 (*Staatscourant,* 1972). All new substances have been put on Schedule I. Alterations to the law have also been made in recent years to better combat large-scale drug trafficking.

4. Some examples of these obligations are as follows: the 1972 Protocol amending the Convention, to which the Netherlands did not accede until 1988 because it potentially limited the leeway that nations had to apply their own interpretations of the international agreements; the 1971 Vienna Convention on Psychotropic Substances, to which the Netherlands (after long hesitation) acceded in 1992 so as not to become a weak link in international efforts against the trade in psychotropic substances; and the 1988 Vienna Convention against Illegal Traffic in Narcotic Drugs and Psychotropic Substances, which is aimed at, among other things, money laundering and trade in precursors (chemicals essential to the production of illicit drugs) and that the Netherlands ratified in 1992, again owing to international political considerations (Engelsman, 1992).

5. For the sake of clarity, let us stress that we have been sketching prototypical, polar models of the current thought on drug policy. We have done so to highlight their differences. In reality, one can encounter representatives of both poles as well as people arguing from a full range of intermediate standpoints. One might speak of a thought continuum ranging from staunchly prohibitionist, via middle-of-the-road positions, to radically antiprohibitionist.

6. For an overview of the strong variation in current legislation on cannabis in Europe, see Korf (1995).

7. Raves are generally called "house parties," after "house music." For an extensive study, see van de Wijngaart et al. (1997).

REFERENCES

Boekhout van Solinge, T. (1996). *Heroine, cocaine en crack in Frankrijk: Handel, gebruik en beleid.* Amsterdam: Cedro.

Buisman, W. R. (1982). *Methadonverstrekking in Nederland.* Bilthoven: FZA.

Buning, E., & van Brussel, G. H. A. (1995). The effects of harm reduction in Amsterdam. *European Addiction Research, 1*(3), 92-98.

Cachet, A. (1990). *Politie en sociale controle.* Arnhem: Gouda Quint.

Chatterjee, S. K. (1991). *Legal aspects of international drug control.* The Hague: Nijhoff.

Cohen, P. D. A. (1990). *Drugs as a social construct.* Utrecht: Elinkwijk.

Cohen, S. (1985). *Visions of social control.* Cambridge, MA: Polity.

de Hullu, J., & Tillema, A. J. P. (Eds.). (1989). De verdragsverplichtingen en de wetgevingsgeschiedenis. In H. G. M. Krabbe (Ed.), *De Opiumwet: Een strafrechtelijk commentaar* (pp. 15-63). Alphen aan den Rijn: Samson Tjeenk Willink.

de Kort, M. (1995). *Tussen patiënt en delinquent: Geschiedenis van het Nederlandse drugsbeleid.* Hilversum: Verloren.

de Kort, M., & Korf, D. J. (1992). The development of drug trade and drug control in the Netherlands: A historical perspective. *Crime, Law and Social Change, 17,* 123-144.

Engelsman, E. L. (1992). Preventie en internationaal drugbeleid. In W. R. Buisman & J. C. van der Stel (Eds.), *Drugspreventie: Achtergronden, praktijk en toekomst* (pp. 211-228). Houten: Bohn Stafleu Van Loghum.

Factsheet. (1999). *Factsheet 3: Harddrugsbeleid: XTC.* Utrecht: Trimbos Institute.

Gerritsen, J. W. (1993). *De politieke economie van de roes: De ontwikkeling van reguleringsregimes voor alcohol en opiaten.* Amsterdam: Amsterdam University Press.

Grund, J. P. C. (1993). *Drug use as a social ritual: Functionality, symbolism and determinants of self-regulation.* Rotterdam: IVO.

Haastrecht, H. J. A. (1997). HIV infection and drug use in the Netherlands: The course of the epidemic. *Journal of Drug Issues, 27*(1), 57-72.

Harrison, L. (1997). More cannabis in Europe? Perspectives from the USA. In D. Korf & H. Riper (Eds.), *Illicit drugs in Europe* (pp. 16-25). Amsterdam: Siswo.

Himmelstein, J. L. (1983). *The strange career of marihuana: Politics and ideology of drug control in America.* Westport, CT: Greenwood.

Jansen, A. C. M. (1989). *Cannabis in Amsterdam: A geography of hashish and marijuana.* Muiderberg: Dick Coutinho.

Kaplan, C. D., Haanraadts, D. J., van Vliet, H. J., & Grund, J. P. (1994). Is Dutch drug policy an example to the world? In E. Leuw & I. Haen Marshall (Eds.), *Between prohibition and legalization: The Dutch experiment in drug policy* (pp. 311-335). Amsterdam/New York: Kugler.

Korf, D. J. (1988). Twintig jaar softdrug-gebruik in Nederland: Een terugblik vanuit prevalentiestudies. *Tijdschrift voor Alcohol, Drugs en Andere Psychotrope Stoffen, 14,* 81-89.

Korf, D. J. (1995). *Dutch treat: Formal control and illicit drug use in the Netherlands.* Amsterdam: Thesis.

Krabbe, H. G. M. (Ed.). (1989). *De Opiumwet: Een strafrechtelijk commentaar.* Alphen aan den Rijn: Samson Tjeenk Willink.

Kuipers, S. B. M., Mensink, C., & de Zwart, W. M. (1993). *Jeugd en riskant gedrag: Roken, drinken, druggebruik en gokken onder scholieren vanaf tien jaar.* Utrecht: NIAD.

Langemeijer, M. (1997). Prevalence of drug use: A comparison between three Dutch cities. In D. Korf & H. Riper (Eds.), *Illicit drugs in Europe* (pp. 33-42). Amsterdam: Siswo.

Leuw, E. (1972). Het gebruik van cannabis onder leerlingen van voortgezet onderwijs: een poging tot interpretatie. *Ned Tijdschr Criminol, 14,* 214-255.

Leuw, E., & Haen Marshall, I. (Eds.). (1994). *Between prohibition and legalization: The Dutch experiment in drug policy.* Amsterdam/New York: Kugler.

Lissenberg, E. (1992). (De)criminaliseren. In C. Bouw, H. van de Bunt, & H. Franke (Ed.), *Kernbegrippen in de criminologie* (pp. 45-48). Arnhem: Gouda Quint.

Loeber, H. (Ed.). (1992). *Dutch-American relations 1945-1969: A partnership, illusions and facts.* Assen: Van Gorcum.

Musto, D. F. (1987). *The American disease. Origins of narcotic control.* New York: Oxford University Press.

Plomp, H. N., Kuipers, H., & van Oers, M. L. (1990). *Roken, alcohol- en drugsgebruik onder scholieren vanaf 10 jaar.* Amsterdam: VU-University Press.

Reuband, K.-H. (1992). *Drogenpolitik und Drogenkonsum: Deutschland und die Niederlande im Vergleich.* Opladen: Leske+Budrich.

Reuband, K.-H. (1995). Drug use and drug policy in Western Europe: Epidemiological findings in a comparative perspective. *European Addiction Research, 1*(1-2), 32-41.

Roholl, M. (1992). Uncle Sam: An example for all? In H. Loeber (Ed.), *Dutch-American relations 1945-1969: A partnership, illusions and facts* (pp. 105-152). Assen: Van Gorcum.

Sandwijk, J. P., Cohen, P. D. A., Musterd, S., & Langemeijer, M. P. S. (1995). *Licit and illicit drug use in Amsterdam II.* Amsterdam: University of Amsterdam, Institute of Social Geography.

Schur, E. M. (1965). *Crimes without victims.* Englewood Cliffs, NJ: Prentice Hall.

Staatscourant. (1972). No. 116. The Hague.

van Ameijden, E. J. C. (1994). *Evaluation of AIDS-prevention measures among drug users: The Amsterdam experience.* Wageningen: Posen & Looijen.

van Ameijden, E. J. C., Watters, J. K., van den Hoek, J. A. R., & Coutinho, R. (1995). Interventions among injecting drug users: Do they work? *AIDS, 9*(Suppl. A), 75-84.

van de Wijngaart, G., Braam, R., de Bruin, D., Fris, M., Maalsté, N., & Verbraeck, H. (1997). *Ecstasy in het uitgaanscircuit.* Utrecht: Centrum voor Verslavingsonderzoek.

van de Wijngaart, G., & Verbraeck, H. (1991). *Methadon in de jaren negentig.* Utrecht: Centrum voor Verslavingsonderzoek.

van Heek, F. (1936). *Chineesche immigranten in Nederland.* Amsterdam: Emmering.

White paper. (1996). *Drugs policy in the Netherlands: Continuity and change.* The Hague: Sdu.

WHO. (1997). *HIV/AIDS surveillance in Europe. Quarterly Report no. 53.* Saint-Maurice, France: WHO-EC Collaborating Centre on AIDS.

7

The Harm Reduction Movement in Brazil: Issues and Experiences

Hilary L. Surratt
Paulo R. Telles

In Brazil, harm reduction is a relatively new phenomenon. Thus, little has been documented about the scope, experience, or effectiveness of harm reduction strategies. What is clear, however, is that the concept in the Brazilian context is far more narrowly focused than in other parts of the world, and it has emerged specifically in response to the HIV/AIDS epidemic among injection drug users.

HIV/AIDS PREVENTION STRATEGIES IN BRAZIL

Brazil ranks second in the world in the number of reported cases of AIDS, with 116,389 cases identified as of August 1997 (Brazilian Ministry of Health, 1997a). Although men who have sex with men have represented the largest exposure category since the beginning of the epidemic in Brazil, the role of injection drug users has changed dramatically since the first cases were reported

AUTHORS' NOTE: This research was supported by National Institute on Drug Abuse Grant No. U01 DA08510.

some 15 years ago. From 1982 to 1986, for example, injection drug users accounted for only 6.4% of all identified cases. By 1997, however, this proportion had risen to almost 21% (Brazilian Ministry of Health, 1997a).

Although injection drug use is a primary vector of HIV transmission in Brazil, there are few published studies describing the epidemiology of HIV infection in chronic drug-using populations. Although some small-scale studies have been conducted, the general focus has been on in-treatment populations, often to the exclusion of street-based users. A pioneering effort in this regard began in 1991 in the port city of Santos, a community of some 450,000 inhabitants approximately 50 miles southeast of São Paulo. The goals of the project were to estimate the prevalence of HIV among injection drug users and to collect information that might be helpful in the development of focused intervention efforts (Alexandrino, 1991; World Health Organization, 1993). Sixty-two percent of the drug injectors studied tested positive for antibodies to HIV (Barbosa de Carvalho et al., 1996). A few studies have been conducted in Rio de Janeiro, documenting high rates of HIV risk behaviors among both injectors and noninjectors and suggesting the prevalence of infection to be somewhere between 15% and 34% (Inciardi et al., 1996; Telles, Bastos et al., 1997).

On the whole, because injection drug users in Brazil lack political power, live in social isolation, and are discriminated against—even by noninjecting drug users—they are seldomly found in traditional substance abuse treatment settings or health services programs, and they are reluctant to participate in research, demonstration, or public health projects. This paucity of attention to injectors and noninjecting drug users in Brazil demonstrates that, until recently, they were not targeted by HIV prevention initiatives, and it reflects the widespread social marginalization of the entire drug-using population.

On the whole, Brazilian health officials were slow to implement *any* programs for AIDS prevention. Scarce resources were frequently reserved for vaccination programs and for efforts to combat such tropical diseases as malaria, Chagas' disease (a parasitic infection transmitted by insects), and schistosomiasis (a parasitic disease transmitted through blood flukes), which together affect the health of millions of Brazilians (Brazilian Ministry of Health, 1997b; Flowers, 1988). In fact, during the mid-1980s, the Brazilian National Secretary of Health declared that AIDS prevention research would not be a priority, for as long as it was restricted to "minority" groups. The Secretary of Health justified this decision with the argument that Brazil had other, more serious, endemic diseases that resulted from the abject poverty of much of the general population (Lima, Bastos, Telles, & Ward, 1992). Reacting to the stigmatization of "minority group" labeling, the gay community mobilized to form advocacy groups, and as a result, during the late 1980s and early 1990s, most prevention programs were organized by and directed toward men who have sex with men.

For the general public in Brazil, government-sponsored education and information campaigns first appeared during the second half of the 1980s (Parker, 1992). In early 1987, for example, the government launched a series of television announcements that provided AIDS prevention information for a national audience. These were short-lived, however, because of federal budget cuts and pressure from the Catholic Church (Flowers, 1988). Most of the campaigns were designed for a relatively general audience and presented basic information on AIDS risk behaviors. On the other hand, to a large extent, explicit and controversial messages or promotions targeting specific groups have been absent (Parker, 1992). In addition, initial reports in the Brazilian press widely publicized rumors that people with AIDS were deliberately spreading the disease through sexual binges or purposely injecting fellow addicts with contaminated syringes (Flowers, 1988). As a result, during the early years of the epidemic, little accurate knowledge about HIV reached the public.

Going further, there has been considerable debate in Brazil about the most appropriate and effective mechanisms for developing and targeting materials for diverse audiences. Moreover, groups ranging from gay liberation organizations to conservative sectors of the Catholic Church managed to exert considerable influence on the development of government-sponsored educational campaigns. And finally, many of the obstacles that limited the federal government's ability to design and implement AIDS prevention initiatives have also affected state and local efforts. When combined with the severe limitations of most state and municipal financial resources, it is not surprising that little in the way of government-sponsored AIDS education and health promotion has emerged in most parts of Brazil (Parker, 1992).

By contrast, nongovernmental organizations (NGOs) have played an important role in AIDS education and prevention in Brazil. In late 1985, for example, an association known as *Grupo de Apoio para a Prevençao da AIDS* (Support Group for the Prevention of AIDS) was founded in São Paulo and became the first volunteer organization in Brazil concerned exclusively with AIDS-related issues. Better known as GAPA, its members were initially composed of health care workers involved in the treatment of AIDS patients, as well as activists who had been involved previously in gay rights groups. GAPA was the first NGO to become involved in AIDS health promotion, and it focused primarily on the instruction of safe sexual practices (Parker, 1992).

Shortly after the formation of GAPA, intellectuals and activists in Rio de Janeiro formed *Associaçao Brasileira Interdisciplinar de AIDS* (ABIA), the Brazilian Interdisciplinary AIDS Association, which developed into a well-respected professional organization and has played an important role as a critic of government policy on AIDS and a principal designer of health promotion materials. ABIA has been credited with the development of highly focused health promotion materials targeted to diverse populations within Brazil and with supplying many of these items to AIDS service organizations. Less vulnerable to criticism than government-produced materials, the AIDS education media developed by ABIA have been among the most direct and explicit available anywhere in Brazil (Parker, 1992). Some of ABIA's particularly important campaigns have targeted street children, construction workers, sailors, and gay-identified men. Male, female, and transvestite prostitutes have also been the focus of several campaigns, including an AIDS prevention initiative linked with the Institute for Religious Studies in Rio de Janeiro. Others at significant risk for HIV infection, however, especially injection drug users, have been largely overlooked by these efforts. Despite statistical evidence of alarming HIV seroprevalence rates among drug injectors, by the end of the first decade of the epidemic, there was still no official policy or programs directed to this particular group (Lima et al., 1992). Even by late 1996, respected Brazilian drug researchers were still lamenting the lack of political attention paid to the public health problems associated with drug abuse in Brazil (Laranjeira & Pinsky, 1996).

SYRINGE EXCHANGE

It was not until 1992 that a harm reduction approach for injection drug users was first discussed by the Brazilian National Program on STD/AIDS. The dialogue revolved around syringe exchange, and with the exception of one pioneering exchange program in Santos—initiated in 1989 but quickly closed under pressure from the Federal Narcotics Council (Alexandrino, 1991)—this discussion represented the first government initiative to systematically address the negative consequences of drug use among Brazilians.

The lack of harm reduction strategies for injection drug users in Brazil can be traced to the rigid drug legislation currently in force. Although Brazilian statutes permit the purchase and possession of syringes/needles, current drug laws are tough and anachronistic, which makes such prevention strategies as syringe/needle exchange programs difficult to implement (Barbosa de Carvalho et al., 1996). Brazil's initial antidrug law, passed in 1971, was essentially punitive in nature: It penalized both users and dealers, and it ordered hospital treatment for those with chemical dependency. The 1976 law (Brazilian Ministry of Health, 1991), still in effect, revised and expanded the original statute, as follows:

Article 12: Importing or exporting, shipping, preparing, producing, manufacturing, acquiring, selling, offering for sale, supplying even freely, storing, transporting, carrying with you, keeping, prescribing, administering or delivering in any manner, narcotic substances or those which create physical or psychological dependence, without authorization or accordance with legal regulations:

Penalty: Confinement, from three to fifteen years, and payment of 50 to 360 days-fine.[1]

Article 16: Acquiring, keeping, or carrying, for your own personal use, narcotic substances or those which create physical or psychological dependence, without authorization or accordance with legal regulations:

Penalty: Confinement, from six months to two years, and payment of 20 to 50 days-fine.

According to a number of legal scholars, this language does not necessarily define drug use per se as a crime, but rather, as in the United States, the statutes prohibit possession, manufacture, sale, and distribution (Brazilian Ministry of Health, 1991). However, the ambiguity of the legal language serves to exacerbate the debate, and, as such, many scholars and legislators argue for the creation of a legal document that explicitly decriminalizes drug use or dependency per se for the purpose of differentiating users from producers, traffickers, and dealers in the eyes of the law. Going further, in the absence of specific paraphernalia restrictions in antidrug laws, the main barrier to the implementation of needle/syringe exchange programs is the language in Paragraph 2 of Article 12, which classifies "instigating, inducing, and/or assisting" the use of drugs as criminal acts, each carrying 3- to 15-year prison sentences. Because city councils and local governments must comply with federal regulations in this area, HIV/AIDS prevention programs for injection drug users have been impeded by the threat of legal action.

More recently, there has been discussion of harm reduction strategies at the national level sparked by those seeking to reform Brazilian drug laws. Central to these reforms is the legal status of needle/syringe exchange programs, which are key features of harm reduction in Brazil. Among the issues raised in this regard was the recommendation of the 1993 Conference of Ibero-American Health Ministers that experimental interventions (needle/syringe exchange, bleach distribution) be developed to address the grave public health issue of HIV/AIDS. Building on this endorsement of harm reduction strategies, the Brazilian Federal Narcotics Council approved a six-site pilot needle/syringe exchange program proposed by the Ministry of Health in 1994 ("Incidência," 1994). Citing the need to make drug use as safe as possible for both individuals and society, the council sanctioned the operation of exchange programs in six Brazilian cities having high HIV incidence and relatively large communities of injection drug users: São Paulo, Belo Horizonte, Santos, Salvador, Rio de Janeiro, and Campo Grande. In part, these cities were also selected because they possessed a relatively well-developed structure for administering the programs, and the council insisted on tight control by their respective municipal health centers. In fact, the council specified that the following guidelines be observed: The project must be highly localized and directed to a specific clientele; there must be oversight, control, and evaluation of the project at every level; and the experimental nature of the project should be emphasized. Importantly, the council also mandated that at least 50% of each project's operating budget be applied to drug use prevention efforts (Federal Narcotics Council, 1994).

Organizations at the state level with an interest in HIV/AIDS prevention strategies were quick to act on the favorable decision of the Federal Narcotics Council. Citing a study of 13 cities conducted by the World Health Organization (which included Rio de Janeiro and Santos, Brazil), the São Paulo State Council on AIDS Issues declared harm reduction strategies to be the most effective in controlling the spread of HIV/AIDS among injection drug users (State Council on AIDS Issues, 1994). Going further, in 1995, the STD/AIDS Division of the São Paulo State Secretary of Health openly declared its position on harm reduction and delineated appropriate goals and strategies of this approach:

> The harm reduction approach [should] be the primary strategy for the state public health network when working with injection drug users. Although a broader range of actions is necessary when dealing with the issue of drugs, such as the prevention of use and treatment for substance abusers, the harm reduction strategy without a doubt presents the greatest possibility for short-term impact. The harm reduction strategy asserts that if the rehabilitation of injection drug users demands a great investment and may not be effective in the short-term, it is necessary to adopt methods low in both material and human costs which can quickly produce an impact on HIV prevention in this group. This strategy includes disinfecting injection equipment with bleach, and needle/syringe exchange by injecting drug users. The availability of sterile needles/syringes for injection drug users would diminish the risk not only of HIV infection, but other blood borne infections such as hepatitis, Chagas disease, etc. (State Secretary of Health STD/AIDS Division, 1995, p. 4)

Although support for needle/syringe exchange was evident, the Secretary of Health clearly asserted that these programs must be linked with broader prevention strategies, such as substance abuse counseling and treatment, in order to achieve the primary goals of harm reduction: prevention of needle/syringe sharing, reduction in the rate of HIV infection among injection drug users, changes in the route of drug administration from injection to noninjection, overall reduction in the use of drugs, and elimination of the use of drugs (State Secretary of Health STD/AIDS Division, 1995). Within this context, the Secretary of Health recommended that services offered to injection drug users in any context should always include counseling on STD/HIV transmission, needle/syringe cleaning, and condom use. It was further suggested that health service providers that serve large numbers of injection drug users be evaluated for the feasibility of initiating needle/syringe exchange programs as well as bleach and condom distribution initiatives.

In spite of the broad-based support for needle exchange efforts demonstrated by both federal and state agencies, the implementation of such projects has been slow and difficult. The Brazilian Ministry of Health piloted two needle/syringe exchange programs in Santos and Salvador in 1995. In Salvador, at the Federal University of Bahia, a small prevention program, including needle/syringe exchange, has been operating since March 1995. It provides services to injection drug users, which were practically nonexistent before this, and provides disposable injection equipment, condoms, HIV prevention information, and referrals for medical and social services. Little information is available regarding the effectiveness of the program in Salvador, but the fact that it has operated continuously for more than 2 years speaks to its success. Going further, a recent report by the investigators indicated that more than 5,000 syringes had been exchanged at the four sites since distribution began.

The needle exchange program in Santos was not as fortunate. Shortly after its initiation, it was closed as a result of police action. The Narcotics Police of Santos seized all of the materials used by the Institute for AIDS Research and Study (Iepas) for this HIV prevention project, including 371 eyeglass cases (where the kits containing disposable injection equipment are stored), 500 alcohol swabs for disinfecting the skin, 500 bottles of bleach for disinfecting needles/syringes, and 600 condoms ("Apreendido," 1995). The project was later moved to the neighboring area of São Vicente because of the more relaxed political climate, and syringe distribution was reinitiated. More recently, the Ministry of Health and the Federal Narcotics Council of the Ministry of Justice gave joint approval for seven needle/syringe exchange programs to be funded by international institutions ("Seringas," 1996).

Before this decision, needle/syringe exchange programs had *never* existed in Rio de Janeiro. Although Rio de Janeiro has the second largest number of reported AIDS cases in Brazil, it had reported fewer than 900 cases among injection drug users through March 1997, ranking it far below other cities in cases among this population (Brazilian Ministry of Health, 1997a; State Secretary of Health, 1997). Perhaps as a result of this trend, few studies of this population have been conducted. Those that have dealt with injection drug users in Rio de Janeiro have typically been small-scale epidemiologic or seroprevalence studies that did not provide any intervention component (see Telles et al., 1994). However, one harm reduction project is under way in Rio de Janeiro and has succeeded in accessing 65 injection drug users in its first few months of operation (Telles, Cruz et al., 1997). However, because of the legal issues surrounding needle/syringe exchange, and communications from the federal police denouncing such activities, the distribution of needles/syringes was postponed (Telles, 1997).

THE PROVIVA PROJECT

Working within this political and legal climate, it was possible to operate one of the largest harm reduction projects for drug users in all of Brazil, because needle/syringe exchange was not within the scope of work. Recognizing the critical need to slow the spread of HIV/AIDS among drug users in Brazil, in 1993, the U.S. National Institute on Drug Abuse (NIDA) funded a research demonstration prevention/intervention initiative targeting segments of the Rio de Janeiro population at high risk for HIV/AIDS acquisition and transmission. Known as PROVIVA (*Projeto Venha Informar-se sobre o Virus da AIDS*), the project is part of the NIDA Cooperative Agreement for AIDS Community-Based Outreach/Intervention Research, which includes 23 sites across the United States, Puerto Rico, and Brazil (see Figure 7.1).

The general purposes of the PROVIVA project were to develop, implement, and evaluate a community-based HIV/AIDS prevention/intervention program for cocaine injectors and snorters, as well as male transvestite sex workers. Clients were recruited by indigenous outreach workers through "targeted sampling" (Watters & Biernacki, 1989) and "chain referral" (Inciardi, 1986) strategies in specific geographic locales where drug use rates are high. Outreach was a proactive process in which workers engage potential clients in a screening process and a preliminary discussion of AIDS prevention. Hygiene kits were distributed that contained condoms, needle-cleaning equipment, AIDS prevention literature (including how to use a condom and how to clean injection equipment), and referral information for sexually transmitted disease (STD) testing and drug abuse treatment.

Eligible clients were given an appointment for intake at a project site/ assessment center. Intake included informed consent, drug testing, and administration of a standardized risk behavior assessment interview instrument. Pretest HIV prevention counseling was provided, covering such topics as HIV disease, transmission routes, risky behaviors, risks associated with crack or cocaine use, rehearsal of condom use, stopping unsafe sex practices, communication with partners, cleaning and disinfection of injection equipment, rehearsal of needle and syringe cleaning, disposal of hazardous waste material, stopping unsafe drug use, benefits of drug treatment, HIV testing, literature and referrals, and distribution of the hygiene kit.

HIV testing was provided to all clients on a voluntary basis, and posttest counseling and HIV test results were available 1 to 3 weeks after testing. An effort was made to reassess all participants at a follow-up session 3 to 5 months

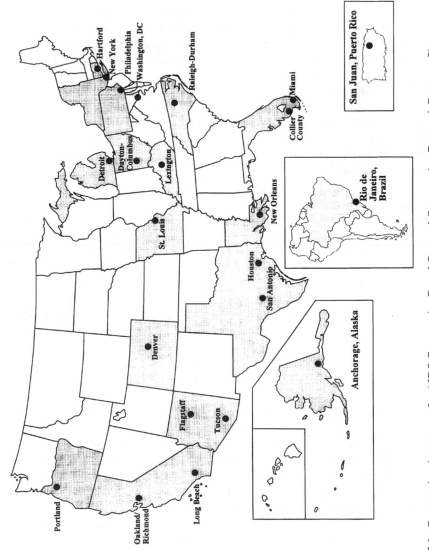

Figure 7.1. Cooperative Agreement for AIDS Community-Based Outreach/Intervention Research Program Sites

later using a standardized risk behavior follow-up assessment interview instrument, followed by HIV retesting and counseling.

The vast majority of PROVIVA's clients were recruited from Rio de Janeiro's red-light prostitution districts and *favelas. Favela* in Brazilian Portuguese means "slum." Yet it is a particular type of slum that takes its name from the hill near Rio de Janeiro where the first one appeared. The favelas began to emerge on the hillsides of Rio de Janeiro at the end of the 19th century and spread rapidly after 1930 as shelters for newly arriving migrants (Burns, 1980). Fleeing regions hit hard by drought and unemployment, rural Brazilians thronged to *cidade maravilhosa,* the "marvelous city" of Rio de Janeiro, lured by its illusionary riches. There has been a steady stream ever since, and at the close of the 1980s, it was estimated that some 1,500 *favelados* were arriving each day (Archambault, 1989). In Rio de Janeiro alone, the favelas have been estimated by Brazil's Municipal Planning Institute to number 545 and house more than 1 million people (Loveman, 1991).

By the end of June 1997, more than 1,500 cocaine users had been recruited into the intervention. Only 9.5% of these were cocaine injectors, whereas the balance were snorters. Despite a recruitment strategy that targeted injectors, outreach contacts with drug injector networks were limited, and therefore, recruitment success with this population was low. As indicated in Table 7.1, most of both the snorters and injectors were under age 35, with median ages of 29 and 30 years, respectively. The overwhelming majority of those recruited were men, which was a reflection of the gender differences in cocaine use in Rio de Janeiro combined with the greater visibility of male cocaine users on the streets and in the favelas. Both the snorters and injectors were evenly distributed across the three predominant race/ethnic groups in Rio de Janeiro (black, white, and multiracial), and most had limited educational attainment.

Anecdotal reports suggest that the drugs of choice in Rio de Janeiro are limited to alcohol, marijuana, and cocaine, and this is clearly affirmed by the data. As illustrated in Table 7.2, all had histories of cocaine use (as expected, because the project was targeting cocaine users), and almost all had used both alcohol and marijuana. The median ages of the first use of all of these drugs for both injectors and snorters were in the mid-teenage years, and most were also current users (any use in the 30 days prior to interview) of these drugs. Interestingly, however, very few had ever been in drug abuse treatment—a reflection of the general lack of drug treatment slots throughout Rio de Janeiro.

Data were collected on HIV risk behaviors and serostatus, and overall, 8.0% of the cocaine snorters and 15.9% of the cocaine injectors recruited as of June 1997 tested positive for HIV-1. The risk factor that best predicted infection among both the male and female snorters was a prior history of injecting drugs. Among the men, other significant associations were found between serostatus and length of cocaine use history, a history of exchanging sex for money, and the

TABLE 7.1:   Selected Demographic Characteristics of 1,544 Cocaine Users in Rio de Janeiro, Brazil (in percentages)

	Snorters *(N = 1,398)*	*Injectors* *(N = 146)*
Age		
18-24	29.3	26.7
25-34	42.1	41.8
35+	28.6	31.5
Median	29.0	30.0
Gender		
Male	76.2	90.4
Female	23.8	9.6
Race/ethnicity		
Black	33.6	39.0
White	27.0	47.9
Multiracial	39.4	13.1
Education		
8 years or less	83.6	65.1
9 years or more	16.4	34.9

TABLE 7.2:   Drug Use Characteristics of 1,544 Cocaine Users in Rio de Janeiro, Brazil

	Snorters *(N = 1,398)*	*Injectors* *(N = 146)*
Percentage ever used		
Alcohol	98.0	97.3
Marijuana	84.0	92.5
Cocaine	100.0	100.0
Median age at first use		
Alcohol	15.0	15.0
Marijuana	16.0	15.0
Cocaine	17.0	16.0
Median days using (past 30 days)		
Alcohol	12.0	15.0
Marijuana	3.0	7.0
Cocaine	15.0	20.0
Median years of cocaine use	11.0	14.0

TABLE 7.3:   Changes in Drug Use and Sexual Behavior Among 750 Cocaine
Snorters in Rio de Janeiro

	Baseline	Follow-up	Diff. (p value)
Cocaine use in past 30 days			
Mean # occasions	23.28	16.43	−6.85 (p < .000)
Unprotected vaginal sex in past 30 days (males)[a]			
Mean # occasions	18.08	15.60	−2.48 (p < .056)
Unprotected vaginal sex in past 30 days (females)[a]			
Mean # occasions	21.27	13.24	−8.03 (p < .022)

a. Includes only respondents who were sexually active (vaginal sex) at baseline and follow-up.

number of male sexual partners. Length of injection history was the only factor related to HIV infection for the current drug injectors.

Preliminary follow-up data on the first 750 clients who returned to PROVIVA for reassessment suggested that the intervention was effective at reducing risk for HIV. Because 3-month follow-up data were available on fewer than 30 drug injectors, this analysis focused exclusively on the snorter sample. As illustrated in Table 7.3, significantly fewer occasions of cocaine use were reported at the 3-month interview.

Specifically, cocaine use fell from 23.28 to 16.43 times ($p < .000$) in the previous 30 days. Additionally, 75 clients (10.0%) had abstained from any cocaine use in the 30 days prior to reassessment. Importantly, Tables 7.4 and 7.5 indicate that the follow-up sample was very similar to the baseline snorter sample on a variety of demographic and drug use measures, suggesting that positive outcomes were not attributable to between-group differences resulting from attrition.

DISCUSSION

In the United States, harm reduction is considered to encompass such activities as HIV/AIDS interventions, drug treatment, drug substitution therapy (maintenance on drug of choice from legal source), safer and more responsible drug use, reductions in penalties for drug-related crimes, changes in paraphernalia laws, and decriminalization/legalization of controlled substances. On the other hand, in Brazil, harm reduction has a very narrow definition that typically includes

TABLE 7.4: Baseline Demographic Characteristics of 750 Cocaine Snorters With 3-Month Follow-Up in Rio de Janeiro (in percentages)

Age	
18-24	26.0
25-34	43.2
35+	30.8
Median	30.0
Gender	
Male	77.7
Female	22.3
Race/ethnicity	
Black	31.9
White	24.9
Multiracial	43.2
Education	
8 years or less	84.3
9 years or more	15.7

TABLE 7.5: Baseline Drug Use Characteristics of 750 Cocaine Snorters With 3-Month Follow-Up in Rio de Janeiro

Percentage ever used	
Alcohol	97.6
Marijuana	84.0
Cocaine	100.0
Median age at first use	
Alcohol	15.0
Marijuana	16.0
Cocaine	17.0
Median days using (past 30 days)	
Alcohol	12.0
Marijuana	3.0
Cocaine	16.0
Median years of cocaine use	11.0

needle/syringe exchange, bleach disinfection, substitution of noninjection drug use for injection use, traditional drug treatment, and general HIV/AIDS prevention education.

Other aspects of harm reduction that have extreme visibility in different parts of the world receive little attention in Brazil. Efforts to modify the existing drug statutes have encountered virtually unlimited resistance from authorities and experts in the field. Sparked by Rio de Janeiro Governor Marcello Alencar's declaration to "smoke one and see how it is," the decriminalization of marijuana was among the suggested proposals to be debated by the Congress in February of 1996 ("Deputado," 1996). The legislation brought by a congressman from Minas Gerais proposed that the existing laws be modified to distinguish between drug users and traffickers, and to differentiate between hard and soft drugs. Brazilian criminalist Arthur Lavigne was among those who criticized this proposal:

> This new law will not punish the man who buys drugs because he is a user, but will give a penalty of at least 10 years in prison to those who sell drugs, who may do so out of absolute [financial] necessity; well, you should send everyone to jail or no one ("Deputado," 1996, p. 1).

Rio Mayor Cesar Maia also supported drug prohibition and said of the proposal, "I'm absolutely opposed to legalization, even of 'soft' drugs." According to the mayor, legalizing drug use was an experience that didn't work in any of the countries that tried it. "The results were catastrophic; today, no one talks about drug legalization anymore" ("Deputado," 1996a, p. 1). Perhaps not surprisingly, the proposed changes to existing drug legislation have not been enacted.

Other *legal* dimensions of the harm reduction movement are somewhat irrelevant in the Brazilian context. Paraphernalia laws are nonexistent, and needles/syringes generally are not used as evidence of law violations. Indeed, syringes/needles can be purchased in pharmacies without a prescription and at relatively low prices. However, anecdotal reports in focus groups with injection drug users suggest that people who "look like drug users" or fit a popular stereotype of a drug user may have problems purchasing injection equipment in pharmacies or may be asked to pay "special" prices. Injectors also indicated that it is difficult to obtain needles after regular business hours, because only "emergency" drug stores are open on nights and weekends, and they are generally located at great distances from low-income neighborhoods. As such, the issue of sterile injection paraphernalia for injectors in Brazil revolves not around legality or availability, but accessibility.

In the absence of paraphernalia restrictions, needle/syringe exchange programs have been hampered by the legislation that classifies "instigating, inducing, and/or assisting [in]" the use of drugs as criminal acts. In a recent effort to modify this statute, which is frequently interpreted by authorities to encompass needle/syringe exchange, a bill was introduced to the Congress that would add the following language to the existing law—"with the exception of actions undertaken by the public health authority" (Silva, 1997). While this bill is under study, the State of São Paulo took things one step further in September 1997 by passing a new law authorizing the State Secretary of Health to exchange syringes for drug users (Diário Oficial, 1997). São Paulo is the first state to have such a law, but it plans to begin implementation of the new statute slowly in order to avoid public resistance (Segatto, 1997). In fact, according to Pedro Chequer, the Coordinator of the National AIDS Prevention Program, several agencies have *discreetly* implemented syringe exchange in the hope of avoiding opposition, but he placed the number of programs at fewer than 10 nationally (Segatto, 1997).

Accessibility to other harm reduction strategies is also a problem in Brazil. Drug abuse treatment is frequently restricted to a few religious institutions without the resources to meet the demand, and to private clinics, which are expensive and therefore not accessible to the majority of injection drug users (Barbosa de Carvalho et al., 1996). In fact, it was not until December 1996 that the first public drug treatment clinic was opened in São Paulo state, which is the most economically progressive region of Brazil (Tomaleza, 1996). Going further, condom distribution programs directed to drug users are uncommon, especially when compared to those operating for male and female sex workers, the gay community, and sex partners of HIV-infected people. Consequently, rates of condom use among this population are extremely low, with one study reporting that 90.2% and 91.3% of drug-using men and women, respectively, did not use condoms all or most of the time (Inciardi et al., 1996).

In 1996-1997, an effort to introduce the female condom to drug-using men and women at high risk for HIV acquisition was initiated in Rio de Janeiro, in conjunction with the other harm reduction activities delivered by the PROVIVA project. The program offered intensive educational sessions to familiarize clients with the device and provided free starter packs to all participants. Interviews suggested that drug-using men and women found the female condom to be an acceptable method of HIV risk reduction (see Surratt et al., 1998). This is especially promising, given the fact that Brazilian cultural norms support the notions of male dominance and control in sexual situations. Given Brazil's economic turmoil, high rates of indigency and other social problems, conflicts between state and federal jurisdictions, and the opposition of the Catholic Church to broad-based condom distribution, the future of the female condom remains uncertain, as does the future of other neophyte harm reduction initiatives.

NOTE

1. Because Brazilian currency tends to change and/or lose value rapidly, income is frequently calculated in terms of the number of minimum salaries earned, rather than a fixed monetary value. Within this context, 50 to 360 days-fine refers to the wages that would be earned in this time period instead of specifying a particular monetary amount.

REFERENCES

Alexandrino, M. (1991, March 10). AIDS: Santos iniciará estudo com viciados. *O Globo*, p. 46.

Apreendido material anti-AIDS em Santos. (1995, December 18). *O Estado de São Paulo* [On-line]. Available: www.estado.com.br.

Archambault, C. (1989, April). Rio's shaky shantytowns. *IRDC Reports*, pp. 18-19.

Barbosa de Carvalho, H., Mesquita, F., Massad, E., Carvalho Bueno, R., Turienzo Lopes, G., Ruiz, M. A., & Nascimento Burattini, M. (1996). HIV and infections of similar transmission patterns in a drug injectors community of Santos, Brazil. *Journal of Acquired Immune Deficiency Syndromes and Human Retrovirology, 12*, 84-92.

Brazilian Ministry of Health. (1991). *Normas e procedimentos na abordagem do abuso de drogas*. Brasília: Secretaria Nacionalde Assistência à Saúde.

Brazilian Ministry of Health. (1997a, June-August). *Boletim Epidemiológico de AIDS, 10*(3).

Brazilian Ministry of Health. (1997b, November). *Indicadores: Morbidade* [On-line]. Available: www.aids.gov.br.

Burns, E. B. (1980). *A history of Brazil*. New York: Columbia University Press.

Deputado quer mudar lei sobre drogas. (1996, January 23). *O Estado de São Paulo* [On-line]. Available: www.estado.com.br.

Diário Oficial. (1997, September 17). *Assessoria técnico-legislativa* (Vol. 107). São Paulo: Official Press of the State of São Paulo.

Federal Narcotics Council. (1994, August 1). *Ata da 4ª reunião ordinária*. Unpublished minutes.

Flowers, N. M. (1988). The spread of AIDS in rural Brazil. In R. Kulstad (Ed.), *AIDS 1988*. Washington, DC: American Association for the Advancement of Science.

Inciardi, J. A. (1986). *The war on drugs: Heroin, cocaine, crime, and public policy*. Palo Alto, CA: Mayfield.

Inciardi, J. A., Surratt, H. L., Telles, P. R., McCoy, C. B., McCoy, H. V., & Weatherby, N. L. (1996, July). *Risks for HIV-1 infection and seropositivity rates among cocaine users in Rio de Janeiro, Brazil*. Paper presented at the XI International Conference on AIDS, Vancouver, BC, Canada.

Incidência da AIDS é maior entre viciados. (1994, August 2). *Jornal do Brasil*, p. 7.

Laranjeira, R., & Pinsky, I. (1996, September 16). O crack e a prefeitura. *O Estado de São Paulo* [On-line]. Available: www.estado.com.br.

Lima, E. S., Bastos, F. I., Telles, P. R., & Ward, T. P. (1992). Injecting drug users and the spread of HIV in Brazil. *AIDS & Public Policy Journal, 7,* 170-174.

Loveman, B. (1991, July). Latin America faces Public Enemy No. 1. *Institute of the Americas Hemisfile, 2,* 6-8.

Parker, R. G. (1992). AIDS education and health promotion in Brazil: Lessons from the past and prospects for the future. In J. Sepulveda, H. Fineberg, & J. Mann (Eds.), *AIDS: Prevention through education—A world view.* Oxford, UK: Oxford University Press.

Segatto, C. (1997, September 19). SP distribuirá seringas a consumidores de drogas. *O Estado de São Paulo.* Available: www.estado.com.br.

Seringas serao distribuídas para conter AIDS. (1996, June 24). *O Estado de São Paulo* [On-line]. Available: www.estado.com.br.

Silva, S. C. (1997, March 19). Governo quer distribuir seringa a viciados. *O Estado de São Paulo* [On-line]. Available: www.estado.com.br.

State Council on AIDS Issues. (1994, December 8). Projeto de prevençao ao abuso de drogas, DST e AIDS no Ministério da Saúde. *News Brief,* pp. 1-10.

State Secretary of Health STD/AIDS Division. (1997, January/February/March). *Boletim epidemiológico sobre AIDS.*

State Secretary of Health STD/AIDS Division. (1995, May). *Recomendaçoes Gerais aos profissionais de Saúde da rede pública estadual para a prevençao da infecçao pelo HIV entre usuários de drogas injetáveis.* Unpublished position paper.

Surratt, H. L., Wechsberg, W. M., Cottler, L., Leukefeld, C. G., Klein, H., & Desmond, D. (1998). Acceptability of the female condom among women at risk for HIV infection. *American Behavioral Scientist, 41,* 1157-1170.

Telles, P. R. (1997, June). *Projeto reduçao de danos entre usuários de drogas injetáveis no Rio de Janeiro: Relatório de evoluçao.* Unpublished report.

Telles, P. R., Bastos, F. I., Guydish, J., Inciardi, J. A., Surratt, H. L., Pearl, M., & Hearst, N. (1997). Risk behavior and HIV seroprevalence among injecting drug users in Rio de Janeiro, Brazil. *AIDS, 11*(Suppl. 1), S35-S42.

Telles, P. R., Cruz, M., Bastos, W., Jr., Sampaio, C., Mazzuia, R., & Guanabara, L. (1997, March). *Managing HIV diffusion among injecting drug users in Rio de Janeiro, Brazil.* Paper presented at the International Conference on Drug-Related Harm, São Paulo, Brazil.

Telles, P. R., Bastos, F. I., Mesquita, F., Stall, R., Hearst, N., & Bueno, R. (1994, August). *Assessing risk behaviors and HIV seroprevalence among IDUs in two major ports of South America.* Paper presented at the X International Conference on AIDS, Yokohama, Japan.

Tomaleza, J. (1996, December 26). Sorocaba terá clínica pública para recuperaçao de viciados. *O Estado de São Paulo* [On-line]. Available: www.estado.com.br.

Watters, J. K., & Biernacki, P. (1989). Targeted sampling: Options for the study of hidden populations. *Social Problems, 36,* 416-430.

World Health Organization. (1993). An international comparative study of HIV prevalence and risk behavior among drug injectors in 13 cities. *Bulletin on Narcotics, 45,* 19-46.

8

The Harm Minimization Option for Cannabis: History and Prospects in Canadian Drug Policy

Patricia G. Erickson

Psychoactive drugs are subject to many avenues of formal social control over their availability and uses. These governmental controls range from the least restrictive, free-market commerce of solvents and caffeine products to the total criminal prohibition of the narcotics. The illicit drug category includes cocaine, heroin, cannabis, and other drugs that have widely varying pharmacological properties. Some are stimulants, whereas others are depressants or hallucinogens. All prohibited drugs are potentially subject to incarceratory criminal sanctions for their possession or distribution. In between these two extremes lie different regulatory approaches to pharmaceuticals, alcohol, and tobacco.

Regulatory schemes generally take two forms (Glaser, 1974). The first is the professional control over the prescribing of drugs for medical purposes, with some overlay of governmental monitoring. The second form consists of the re-

AUTHOR'S NOTE: An earlier version of this chapter was presented at the ASC annual meeting session: Public Health Based Alternatives to the War on Drugs, October 26-30, 1993. Any views expressed in this chapter are those of the author and not of the Addiction Research Foundation, Toronto, or the University of Toronto.

strictions and surveillance imposed by government over the production, marketing, and sale of widely used drugs, an approach best exemplified by alcohol in Western societies (Single, Giesbrecht, & Eakins, 1991). Recently, tobacco has become more regulated in some countries, such as Canada. Very few drugs with mood-modifying properties are legalized in the sense of being available to the public at large without some form of regulatory control.

There is inevitably some overlap between the dominant models of regulation and prohibition. For example, the combination of alcohol with another risky activity such as driving can lead to a criminal charge. Also, prescription drugs such as steroids may serve an illicit market and carry criminal penalties for unauthorized distribution. The provision of tobacco products to minors may invoke noncriminal penalties in local jurisdictions, whereas major cigarette-smuggling activities can be subject to investigation and criminal prosecution very similar to illicit drug enforcement.

Along the spectrum of formal control, a public health perspective is most closely aligned to the application of regulatory law (Ashton & Seymour, 1988). Here, regulation is designed to serve the interests of public health and safety by reducing the risks associated with health-threatening behaviors. This is the predominant mode of control over most potentially harmful psychoactive substances. By establishing standards for the potency, purity, and availability of the substances, harm is prevented or minimized while permitting the "qualified" consumer (i.e., by age, residence, or other criterion) some freedom of choice over his or her drug consumption.

Although grounded in the public health perspective, harm minimization has taken specific expression in the substance use field over the past 20 years (Erickson, Riley, Cheung, & O'Hare, 1997; Heather, Wodak, Nadelmann, & O'Hare, 1993). Some consensus has developed regarding the characteristics of the harm reduction or harm minimization approach (the terms are used interchangeably). These include the disaggregation of the various consequences of substance use and the development of strategies to address specific problem behaviors. Immediate dangers to health and well-being are the priority, rather than vague, symbolic concerns about "messages to society." The approach of harm minimization is inclusionary rather than exclusionary, preferring to treat drug users as members of society rather than outcasts. It is more pragmatic than ideological, seeking methods with demonstrated ability to reduce the harms of drug use to both users and their communities.

An *aggressive* criminalization policy, with punishment as its primary objective, may run counter to public health policy and, specifically, the aims of the harm minimization approach. It took the AIDS epidemic among injection drug users (IDUs) to fully bring home the legacy of some 80 years of drug prohibition (O'Hare, Newcombe, Matthews, Buning, & Drucker, 1992). Although it had been known for decades that the degraded health status and high mortality of

IDUs could not be explained by the actions of the opiate narcotics themselves (Erickson, 1992a), rising deaths from AIDS and the ready transmission of HIV from shared injection equipment finally provoked a shift in policy in some countries, including the UK, Germany, and Australia. A focus on public health objectives, exemplified by needle and syringe exchange programs, took precedence over criminal justice intervention. Despite its implementation within the framework of prohibition, this strategy has been evaluated as an effective measure in limiting the spread of HIV/AIDS (Des Jarlais & Friedman, 1993; Stimson & Lart, 1991).

Another candidate for harm minimization is cannabis, but more than the drug use practices themselves, the emphasis has been placed on reducing the adverse consequences of criminalization to the individual and society. Severe sentences and persistent enforcement efforts continue to be meted out to users and sellers of cannabis in many countries, including the United States and Canada (Erickson, 1992b). Here, the harm that is the focus of attention is that inflicted by the threat and application of criminal sanctions. Proponents of cannabis law reform have argued that the harms resulting from the policy are out of proportion to any actual harm associated with use of the drug and, in any event, have been shown to be an ineffective deterrent of the behavior (Morgan, Riley, & Chesher, 1993). Criminal justice costs of this policy are also a substantial economic cost to society (Single, Robson, Xie, & Rehm, 1996).

It would appear that cannabis provides a suitable case study for the possibility of a shift from the criminal justice to the harm minimization paradigm. Many commentators in the field who have serious and legitimate reservations about the impact of overall drug legalization or regulation on public health make an exception for cannabis (e.g., Goode, 1993; Jacobs, 1990; Kaplan, 1988; Kleiman, 1992). Although cannabis use is not without health risks, cumulative evidence about its low addictive property, relatively infrequent consumption by the large majority of users, and few adverse health and behavioral effects at low levels of use have continued to support the "soft" drug label bestowed in the late 1960s (Goldstein, 1989; Negrete, 1988; WHO, 1998). In the late 1980s, Canada appeared to be embarking on such an experiment in harm reduction for cannabis.

THE CANADIAN SETTING

Canada's first antidrug law, largely directed against opium smoking by Chinese laborers, was initiated in 1908 and followed by increasingly harsher and more comprehensive provisions against the opiates, cocaine, and cannabis for several decades. During this period of reciprocal influence, the two countries were partners in fighting the drug trade and leaders in the global prohibition movement. Like the United States, Canada has relied primarily on a criminal justice response, invoking severe penalties, to control illicit drug use and distribution. At the time of the upsurge of cannabis use in the mid-1960s, imprisonment was possible for all possession offenses, and the harshest maximum penalty allowable in Canadian law, life imprisonment, was available for trafficking and importing. Canada went through the same process of examination of its response to drugs as did the United States, creating the Le Dain Commission. Like the Shafer Commission, this body recommended decriminalization of cannabis use, but its proposals were not enacted. Although the prevalence of illicit drug use has been generally lower in Canada than in the United States, both countries have experienced similar trends in the rise during the 1970s and the fall throughout the 1980s, and then the recent upswing in the early 1990s. Indeed, as far as tough laws and generous support of antidrug activities, there was little to distinguish the two countries until the mid-1980s, when the United States intensified its drug war, and Canada appeared to be distancing itself somewhat by adopting a new National Drug Strategy that seemed to have more in common with directions in Australia and part of western Europe (Erickson, 1992b).

Thus, Canada provides a suitable venue for a case study about a potential shift to harm reduction. Several cultural and structural conditions appear conducive to a more health-directed approach. These conditions, reviewed elsewhere by Cheung and Erickson (1997), include broad social policies—multiculturalism, universal access to health care, extensive social services—along with methadone programs and widespread needle and syringe exchange programs for the "more serious" drug problem. Canadians also have appeared less prone to drug hysteria than their southern neighbors and have been divided in their support for the existing cannabis law in past surveys, with a majority favoring no or reduced, nonjail penalties for possession (Erickson & Cheung, 1992; Jensen & Gerber, 1993).

In addition, the extensive analyses of cannabis policy conducted by Canadian scholars and Royal Commissions have consistently pointed in the direction of penalty reduction and less widespread application of criminal law (Le Dain, 1972; Solomon, Single, & Erickson, 1988). This social and cultural context would seem to provide the more tolerant milieu required for a less punitive stance toward illicit drug users. Moreover, such a shift seems more likely for cannabis users, with their sheer numbers and social proximity to mainstream society, than for opiate or cocaine users. Thus, cannabis is a kind of test case for the receptivity to the approach of harm reduction.

Despite being a perennial candidate for reform, the cannabis law, or, more specifically, the Narcotic Control Act (NCA), where cannabis has resided, has remained fundamentally unchanged since 1969 (Erickson, 1980). Historically, the Le Dain Commission majority had recommended removal of the simple possession offense in 1972. The only legislative action for the next 20 years was Bill S-19, which proposed to move cannabis into its own section of the Food and

Drugs Act (FDA) (Canada's other major drug statute) and lessen penalties. S-19 was introduced in 1974 and died in Parliament in 1976. A period of inactivity followed until 1992. Even the most recent legal initiative, the Controlled Drugs and Substances Act, which was finally proclaimed in May 1997, retains the same maximum cannabis penalties as the former NCA: six months' imprisonment for possession and life imprisonment for trafficking and importing (Fischer, Erickson, & Smart, 1996).

Besides actual reform of the drug law, harm reduction could be achieved by its selective nonenforcement, a practice adopted in the Netherlands (Leuw & Marshall, 1994). If the number of arrests of users is drastically curtailed, so, too, will be at least some of the adverse consequences of the criminalization policy (Erickson, 1980). This was not the initial response, however, to the upsurge of cannabis use in the 1970s. Canada's annual cannabis conviction rate of well over 200 per 100,000 population in 1981 was one of the highest in the world at that time (Erickson & Cheung, 1992).

Although arrests and convictions declined somewhat in the 1980s, by the end of the decade, the vigor of cannabis enforcement was renewed (Erickson, 1992b). This emphasis was perhaps even abetted by Canada's "new" National Drug Strategy, launched in 1987, which officially emphasized demand reduction over supply reduction but infused police drug squads with additional resources (Fischer, 1994). Despite steady declines in the proportion of cannabis users in student and adult populations surveyed throughout the 1980s, by the end of the decade, cannabis offenses still accounted for two thirds of all drug offenses registered (Erickson & Cheung, 1992). Maximum penalties "on the books" remained harsh, and although lengthy sentences were rarely imposed in practice, most cannabis trafficking offenders continued to be incarcerated for periods up to 2 years. The summary option was most often used for cannabis possession, with discharges (i.e., registering of a finding of guilt but not a conviction) or small fines the usual outcomes. Although the penalties were considerably less than the allowable maximum of $1,000 and 6 months' imprisonment, jail was still imposed on a small minority.

Nevertheless, the renewal of Canada's drug strategy (CDS) in 1992 explicitly pronounced harm reduction as its goal. Were the winds of change stirring? They were, but not in the expected direction. The Conservative government of Prime Minister Mulroney tabled, in June 1992, a new Bill, C-85, the Psychoactive Substances Control Act, and proceeded with second reading and legislative committee hearings 1 year later. After this bill died in 1993 when an election was called, and the Conservatives lost office, in 1994, the new Liberal government introduced virtually identical legislation, Bill C-7, with a new name, the Controlled Drugs and Substances Act. The content of Bills C-85 and C-7 and the transcripts of the hearings on them, in relation to cannabis and harm reduction, are the basis for the remaining discussion in this chapter. The focus will be on the new sections and penalties, the empirical basis for the deliberations, and the stated rationale for the bills.

NEW LAW OR OLD?

When Bill C-85 was first introduced, the accompanying press releases touted it as a "housekeeping" piece of legislation, necessary to consolidate the existing drug laws, the NCA and FDA, and to "modernize" them. A closer examination revealed some startling changes to the cannabis provisions. First, the maximum penalties for a summary first offense of simple possession were doubled, to 12 months' imprisonment and a fine of $2,000, while retaining the indictable option of 7 years. Even though, as stated above, maximum sentences were seldom imposed in the past, the apparent message to the judiciary was, "Get tougher with cannabis users."

The only specific comment relating to this penalty-increasing provision in the C-85 hearings was provided by representatives of the Canadian Police Association (representing rank-and-file police officers). These witnesses raised the possibility that simple possession, "of course confined to something like cannabis," be dealt with by "violation ticket regulations"; in other words, the person would not have to go through the court process. This suggestion was made by the police spokesperson for future consideration (i.e., "for something perhaps down the road") and offered "in the sense of saving of dollars potentially" (*Minutes, Legislative Committee on Bill C-85,* May 26, 1993 [Hereafter referred to as "*Minutes*"]).

Bill C-85 also provided a hybrid offense for trafficking in cannabis products weighing 10 kilograms (22 lbs.) or less. Similar to the simple possession offense, the prosecutor would have the discretion of proceeding either summarily or by indictment. If prosecuted summarily, the maximum penalty would be reduced to 2 years' imprisonment and a fine of $15,000, whereas the indictable option would carry a maximum of 14 years. Amounts exceeding 10 kg would automatically proceed by indictment with the life penalty still in force. When one of the committee members queried the intent of this new provision, the reply was unequivocal from the Department of Justice witness:

> The purpose behind creating a hybrid trafficking offense for cannabis was really not geared towards attacking the leaders of drug trafficking groups but rather to deal with the difficulty of court delays. [This would] thereby reduce or eliminate access to jury trials and to preliminary hearings, thereby cutting down considerably on court delays. (*Minutes,* May 13, 1993)

The witness elaborated further, indicating that the current practice for people found with relatively small amounts of cannabis, but enough to consider a trafficking charge, was to take the path of least resistance and charge them with simple possession only: "Rather than face lengthy court cases, they [prosecutors] will choose to go with a possession offense. Now . . . what is likely to happen is that small cases of trafficking will get prosecuted as trafficking cases" (*Minutes,* May 13, 1993).

Thus, the reduction aimed at here was clearly in the procedural rights of the accused, a further step in keeping with what has been described as one of the hallmarks in the evolution of Canada's narcotic laws (Giffen, Endicott, & Lambert, 1991). Those who benefit are the criminal justice officials, police, and prosecutors, who can process trafficking cases more efficiently and achieve a greater number of convictions at a lower cost by avoiding jury trials. This is also in keeping with the trend displayed in the last half of the 1980s for the Royal Canadian Mounted Police (RCMP) to investigate cannabis traffickers for progressively smaller amounts (Erickson, 1992b). The net result would be to increase the number of convictions in the more serious trafficking category while appearing to show less concern with prosecuting users for possession, but the individuals involved—the actual cases—would be the same.

FACTS OR FICTION?

When a legislative committee of the federal government is examining a new drug law for the first time in 20 years, it is not unreasonable to ask what sort of background or factual basis is provided to members for their review of the topic. At the onset of the C-85 committee's deliberations in 1993, one member noted: "I notice we have some bills we have to look over to know what we're talking about [NCA, FDA]. . . . I'm sure we'll have to know a wee bit about it before we make some sense out of this" (*Minutes,* May 11, 1993). Considerable debate ensued between government and opposition members of the committee over the chairman's revelation that they had only 2 weeks to hear witnesses, make recommendations, and report back to Parliament at the beginning of June. Nevertheless, the closure deadline of June 3 stood.

When little time and effort is allocated to providing objective assessment, perceptions of reality may suffice. At the first presentation by external (i.e., nongovernment bureaucracy) witnesses, one committee member asked: "Am I wrong that the UN has said that Canada is the number one illegal drug-misusing country on the face of the earth?" (*Minutes,* May 25, 1993). When the witness, from the Canadian Medical Association, was unable to shed light on this allegation, the member continued:

Most of us think it's the United States or Colombia or someplace, but I gather that the UN has said that Canada is actually the country with the greatest *amount* [emphasis added] of illegal drug use, at least among the industrialized democracies.

The transcripts of the hearings indicated that the committee was never provided any clarification on this question, nor any trend data or detailed evidence from surveys or other sources about the actual extent and nature of illicit drug use in Canada. The reference was undoubtedly to an earlier, prominent news story in one of Canada's leading national papers (*Globe and Mail,* April 17, 1992, pp. A1-A2). This story reported statistics reflecting the nation's high recorded drug (mainly cannabis) *offense* rate (i.e., a measure of police activity, not the prevalence of drug use and problems) (Erickson & Cheung, 1992, p. 257). Nevertheless, the apparent basis on which the committee proceeded was this assumption about Canada's number-one global ranking in illicit drug abuse.

The committee was not totally without interest in quantitative evidence, as this later interchange shows. The topic was the 10 kg provision for the new cannabis trafficking category:

> *Member:* "In order to try to visualize what's 10 kg, how much are we talking about? How big a package are we talking about?"
>
> *Witness (Dept. of Justice):* "Well, that's a little hard to say. . . . If it is marijuana, it would be a very small bale of hay."
>
> *Member:* "A bale of hay?"
>
> *Witness:* "A small bale of hay."
>
> *Chairman:* "I come from [the province of] Alberta, and there are two sizes. Small ones are about yeah big." [hand gesture]
>
> *Other Witness (Health and Welfare):* "Not the round ones."
>
> *Witness:* "They are more the Ontario version of a bale of hay." (*Minutes,* May 13, 1993)

At another point in this particular session of the hearings, a committee member asked for the number of trafficking charges and convictions for cannabis, and also for figures detailing the financial cost of enforcement. The federal government witnesses indicated that they were unable to provide any such detailed information for Canada (*Minutes,* May 13, 1993).

WAS A HARM REDUCTION APPROACH TO CANNABIS EVER CONSIDERED?

The final aspect of the hearings on Bill C-85 to be considered here is the expressed rationale for the new piece of legislation. What can we learn from the hearings about the likelihood that a new approach of harm minimization could have been implemented at this time for Canada's drug policy, or for cannabis in particular?

Fischer (1994) has shown how the activities engendered by CDS, including Bill C-85, were not consonant with its expressed philosophy of harm reduction. Early in the hearings, the opposition health critic pursued this point with government witnesses:

> *Member:* "What figures do you have in terms of estimates, with which the magnitude of substance abuse in the country could be reduced following the passage of this new legislation?"
>
> *Witness:* "I'm afraid I don't have any estimates of that nature."
>
> *Member:* "If there is no real estimate, why was it not looked at so that we can give Canadians a feel as to what this tougher deal would do to help reduce substance abuse?" (*Minutes*, May 13, 1993)

Later, another opposition member queried why the illegality of cannabis was kept in the new bill. The response indicated that any change in the status of cannabis was never an issue:

> *Witness:* "Because the bill mainly consolidates, modernizes, and enhances the current drug legislation . . . so by consolidating, we're not asked to change anything." (*Minutes*, May 13, 1993)

The members also pursued various points about the effects of decriminalization in Alaska, models of treatment of drug problems in Great Britain, and the health risks of marijuana, none of which the government witnesses were prepared to address. The discussion then became more political:

> *Member:* "Two candidates for the leadership of the Conservative party, and perhaps the [next] Prime Minister of this country, have said they've smoked marijuana." (*Minutes*, May 13, 1993)

This issue, which had surfaced in the then current (1993) leadership campaign, provoked further questioning about the possible damage to these candidates' health from smoking marijuana. Also raised was whether they could be retroactively prosecuted for committing this offense. The government witness appeared rather unprepared for these questions and provided vague answers about the statute of limitations (i.e., 6 months for summary, no limit for indictable, either of which could cover possession).[1]

A final interchange between the C-85 committee and government witnesses reaffirmed that it was business as usual as far as the predominant framework of criminalization for national drug policy:

Member: "Perhaps soft drugs are not at the same level as hard drugs.... We just give warrants to the police and say: out you go, seize, search, investigate.... I think we are using a pretty big stick to kill a pretty small animal.... We want to solve a major social problem, and we say that the government has to assume its responsibilities, but is it really assuming them?"

Witness: "The bill was not intended as a reform but more as a merger. We were amalgamating two acts."

Although the government officials presented themselves as having no choice, neither did they provide a convincing rationale for continuing the current policy. They were unprepared, or saw no necessity, to defend the effectiveness of the existing or proposed legislation and could not deal with health-directed questioning.

It is hard to dispute Fischer's (1994) conclusion, based on the C-85 hearings, that CDS simply added a new layer onto the core of long-standing prohibition policy. Harm minimization for cannabis, even in the modest sense of penalty reduction, was never seriously considered. The well-entrenched, vested interests of the narcotics law enforcement bureaucracy continued to dominate (Giffen et al., 1991).

C-85 died on the order paper of Parliament when an election was called in the summer of 1993. The momentum of the Bill was stalled by the propulsion of the marijuana issue into the middle of the Conservative party leadership campaign, as well as the attention that then became focused on the inadequacies of C-85 (ARF, 1993a). Considerable media attention ensued and provided evidence of the extensive nature of the cumulative criminalization effort directed at more than half a million cannabis users with criminal records for this offense; unlike the self-admitted political candidates with a history of using marijuana, they had not escaped prosecution. Public and expert opinion did not seem as indifferent as was perhaps expected when the Bill was prepared, and it was allowed to disappear quietly.

RISING FROM THE ASHES

This dormancy did not last for long, however, because the new Liberal government was quick to reintroduce the identical twin of C-85, Bill C-7 (the Controlled Drugs and Substances Act). This move surprised drug researchers and programmers across the country. The Liberals, as the initiators of the Le Dain Commission, were associated more with progressive approaches toward drug policy reform than was the previous Conservative administration. At least initially, there was guarded optimism among addiction professionals and reform advocates that this might be an opportunity to follow through with the notion of harm reduction, at least in the form of penalty reduction, for cannabis offenses.

Because the predecessor, Bill C-85, had already been assessed as seriously flawed when the Liberals were in opposition, by their own members, this might open the door for substantial revisions to C-7's provisions while replacing the much criticized Narcotic Control Act.

The Standing Committee on Health of the House of Commons held hearings from 1994 to 1995 (henceforth referred to as *Minutes,* 1994). This time it was the Liberal members who emphasized, "This Bill . . . it's really tidying up some of the loose ends we've had hanging around" (Fry, *Minutes,* May 10, 1994). When a number of nongovernment witnesses raised concerns about the lack of integration of Canada's official harm reduction policy with the Bill's continued emphasis on harsh penalties, even for cannabis, a familiar view of the committee as somehow powerless to make fundamental policy changes was resurrected: "It's almost like a housekeeping bill . . . this is not a policy bill, so it shouldn't be confused with drug policy" (Fry, *Minutes,* May 10, 1994). Several witnesses specifically attacked the doubling of the penalties for cannabis possession and argued for decriminalization. One typical example is this: "Bill C-7 is a remarkable bill, one that ignores the last 30 years of case law and social change in relation to illegal drugs and one that makes a mockery of the notion of public health" (Boyd, *Minutes,* May 24, 1994).

The committee was more preoccupied with what was now a 3 kg cutoff point for a hybrid (i.e., either summary or indictable) trafficking cannabis offense. Amounts greater than 3 kg would be subject to indictable proceedings, with the option of a jury trial, and a maximum sentence of life imprisonment. Questions from several committee members to justice officials indicated a persistent difficulty in understanding that the purpose of this change was to make it *easier* to prosecute traffickers (of smaller amounts), and *not* to allow this amount for personal use, as in this example: "Three kg represents a very substantial period of time of use for an individual . . . the cannabis would deteriorate before you could possibly use it all" (Szabo, *Minutes,* May 24, 1994). Despite reiteration by Justice officials, the committee chair still thought the threshold should be 1 kg, completely missing the point that the lower the amount, the fewer the people who could be charged with trafficking under this section; the higher the amount, the more who could be charged and thus dealt with expeditiously by judge alone, cutting preparation and court time, and ultimately producing more trafficking convictions.

The most explicit, anti-harm reduction testimony came from police chief representatives on the topic of the exercise of police discretion in *not* charging persons with cannabis possession. The argument has often been made in Canada that because "no one gets charged anymore, anyway" with marijuana possession, it is not necessary to change the law. (The RCMP spokesmen had actually made this point to the committee earlier with regard to their drug enforcement priorities.) However, the case for selective nonenforcement, which could be viewed as a viable harm reduction measure (cf. the Netherlands) while the law remained on the books, received no support from the police chiefs: "Across Canada . . . possession charges of even marijuana are taken regularly. . . . That is where the bulk of charges are laid" (Chief Burke, *Minutes,* May 24, 1994). And again, when committee members pursued this point: "[You ask] in policing in Canada is there discretion with respect to marijuana? No, there is not in policing. If they find it, they make an arrest. They charge." (Chief King, *Minutes,* May 24, 1994). When the matter of penalty reduction was raised, the police chiefs rejected it: "For someone to say let's start issuing traffic tickets tomorrow for marijuana, which is one of our gateway drugs, which allows us to target up [get a lead to a trafficker], I really believe it is way too soon" (Chief King, *Minutes,* May 24, 1994). An orientation to reducing the impact of criminalization on cannabis users might have prompted the committee to take action to limit the aggressive enforcement practices through legal change, but no such proposals were discussed.

After lengthy committee deliberations, which extended until final passage in the House of Commons on October 30, 1995, the Bill survived virtually intact. It went on to approval in the Senate and was given royal assent in 1996; the government then conducted an after-the-fact drug policy review with a view toward implementation. The only changes to the final version of the Controlled Drugs and Substances Act that affect cannabis are its separation from the opiates and cocaine, and placement in separate schedules. There is a summary-only offense of possession of less than 30 g of marijuana and 1 g of hashish, carrying a maximum sentence of 6 months' imprisonment and/or a $1,000 fine, just as the former NCA provided. For larger amounts, the possession offense remains summary or indictable, at the prosecutor's discretion, with a maximum sentence of 5 years less a day (i.e., precludes a jury trial). Because imprisonment, much less the maximum penalties for cannabis possession, is almost never given in practice, with the usual outcome being a discharge or small fine, these "new" provisions simply come closer to reflecting the current sentencing practices (Erickson & Cheung, 1992).

CONCLUSION

This chapter has reviewed recent cannabis policy in Canada and examined the evidence for a shift from criminal justice-oriented approaches to the public health-directed policy of harm minimization. The contradictions between the official statement of CDS and its actual implementation, particularly the example provided by the provisions and testimony for Bills C-85 and C-7, lead to the conclusion that such a shift has not occurred and is highly unlikely to unfold in the near future. If even modest reform is not possible for cannabis, then the prospects of this country embracing an even more encompassing policy for the reduction of drug-related harm are slim indeed.

Perhaps this should not be surprising, given the inertia of traditional criminal justice institutions, which have long held sway over the drug problem in Canada (Erickson, 1992b; Giffen et al., 1991). Other barriers that persist in Canada and elsewhere are the strength of neotemperance ideology, the irrationality in the public discourse on drugs, and the strength of American influence on national drug policies around the globe (Alexander, 1990; Christie, 1993; Scheerer, 1978). It remains to be seen whether Canada, which has received world renown for fostering innovative approaches in prevention and health promotion, and which has liberalized most of its policies toward other victimless crimes, will continue to see itself as an American outpost in the war on drugs.

NOTE

1. Indeed, a retiring Member of Parliament from the opposition New Democratic Party had just introduced a private member's bill to legalize marijuana, on the grounds that it would protect the two leadership candidates from prosecution, as well as permit President Clinton, another admitted marijuana "trier," to enter Canada. This bill proceeded no further (ARF, 1993b).

REFERENCES

Alexander, B. K. (1990). *Peaceful measures: Canada's way out of the "war on drugs."* Toronto: University of Toronto Press.

ARF. (1993a). Bill C-85 "retrogressive" ARF says. *The Journal, 22*(4), 1.

ARF. (1993b). Canadian MP would legalize sale and cultivation of marijuana. Fulton bill unlikely to pass, experts say. *The Journal, 22*(4), 3.

Ashton, J., & Seymour, H. (1988). *The new public health.* Bristol, PA: Open University Press.

Cheung, Y. W., & Erickson, P. G. (1997). Crack use in Canada: A distant American cousin. In C. Reinarman & H. G. Levine (Eds.), *Crack in context: Demon drugs and social justice.* Berkeley: University of California Press.

Christie, N. (1993). *Crime control as industry.* London: Routledge.

Des Jarlais, D. C., & Friedman, S. R. (1993). AIDS, injecting drug use and harm reduction. In N. Heather, A. Wodak, E. Nadelmann, & P. O'Hare (Eds.), *Psychoactive drugs and harm reduction: From faith to science.* London: Whurr.

Erickson, P. G. (1980). *Cannabis criminals: The social effects of punishment on drug users.* Toronto: ARF.

Erickson, P. G. (1992a). The law in addictions: Principles, practicalities and prospects. In P. G. Erickson & H. Kalant (Eds.), *Windows on science.* Toronto: Addiction Research Foundation.

Erickson, P. G. (1992b). Recent trends in Canadian drug policy: The decline and resurgence of prohibitionism. *Daedalus, 121,* 239-267.

Erickson, P. G., & Cheung, Y. W. (1992). Drug crime and legal control: Lessons from the Canadian experience. *Contemporary Drug Problems, 19,* 247-277.

Erickson, P. G., Riley, D., Cheung, Y. W., & O'Hare, P. (Eds.). (1997). *Harm reduction: A new direction for drug policies and programs.* Toronto: University of Toronto Press.

Fischer, B. (1994). Maps and moves. *International Journal of Drug Policy, 5,* 70-81.

Fischer, B., Erickson, P. G., & Smart, R. G. (1996). The new Canadian drug law: One step forward, two steps backward. *International Journal of Drug Policy, 7,* 172-179.

Giffen, P. J., Endicott, S., & Lambert, S. (1991). *Panic and indifference: The politics of Canada's drug laws.* Ottawa: Canadian Centre on Substance Abuse.

Glaser, D. (1974). Interlocking dualities in drug use, drug control and crime. In J. A. Inciardi & C. D. Chambers (Eds.), *Drugs and the criminal justice system.* Beverly Hills, CA: Sage.

Goldstein, A. (1989). Introduction. In A. Goldstein (Ed.), *Molecular and cellular aspects of the drug addictions.* New York: Springer-Verlag.

Goode, E. (1993). *Drugs in American society* (4th ed.). Toronto: McGraw-Hill.

Heather, N., Wodak, A., Nadelmann, E., & O'Hare, P. (Eds.). (1993). *Psychoactive drugs and harm reduction: From faith to science.* London: Whurr.

Jacobs, J. B. (1990). Imagining drug legalization. *Public Interest, 101,* 28-42.

Jensen, E. L., & Gerber, J. (1993). State efforts to construct a social problem: The 1986 war on drugs in Canada. *Canadian Journal of Sociology, 18,* 453-462.

Kaplan, J. (1988). Taking drugs seriously. *Public Interest, 92,* 32-50.

Kleiman, M. A. R. (1992). *Against excess.* New York: Basic Books.

Le Dain Commission. (1972). *Cannabis.* Ottawa: Information Canada.

Leuw, E., & Marshall, I. H. (1994). *Between prohibition and legalization: The Dutch experiment in drug policy.* New York: Kugler.

Minutes, Legislative Committee on Bill C-85. House of Commons. (1993, May 11, 13, 25, 26).

Minutes, Standing Committee on Health. House of Commons. (1994, April 28, May 2, 3, 10, 24, 25, 31, June 1, 14).

Morgan, J. P., Riley, D., & Chesher, G. B. (1993). Cannabis: Legal reform, medicinal use and harm reduction. In N. Heather, A. Wodak, E. Nadelmann, & P. O'Hare (Eds.), *Psychoactive drugs and harm reduction: From faith to science.* London: Whurr.

Negrete, J. C. (1988). What happened to the cannabis debate? *British Journal of Addiction, 83,* 354-372.

O'Hare, P., Newcombe, R., Matthews, A., Buning, C., & Drucker, E. (Eds.). (1992). *The reduction of drug-related harm.* New York: Routledge.

Scheerer, S. (1978). The new Dutch and German drug laws: Social and political conditions for criminalization and decriminalization. *Law and Society Review, 12,* 585-606.

Single, E., Giesbrecht, N., & Eakins, B. (1991). The alcohol policy debate in Ontario in the postwar era. In E. Single, P. Morgan, & J. de Lint (Eds.), *Alcohol, society and the state* (Vol. 2). Toronto: Addiction Research Foundation.

Single, E., Robson, L., Xie, X., & Rehm, J. (1996). *The costs of substance abuse in Canada.* Ottawa: Canadian Centre on Substance Abuse.

Solomon, R. R., Single, E., & Erickson, P. G. (1988). Legal considerations in Canadian cannabis policy. In J. C. Blackwell & P. G. Erickson (Eds.), *Illicit drugs in Canada: A risky business.* Toronto: Nelson Canada.

Stimson, G. V., & Lart, R. (1991). HIV, drugs, and public health in England: New words, old tunes. *International Journal of the Addictions, 26,* 1263-1277.

WHO. (1998). *Cannabis: A health perspective and research agenda.* Geneva: Author.

9

Harm Reduction in Australia: Politics, Policy, and Public Opinion

Toni Makkai

The drug of choice in Australian society is alcohol, and although the temperance movement was active in Australia, alcohol was never prohibited (Makkai, 1993b, 1994). Prior to federation in 1901, opium and cocaine were as widely available as alcohol and tobacco, although they were usually consumed in patent medicines. At the turn of the century, racist concerns primarily about the Chinese resulted in the various states introducing legislation to ban opium use. At this time, the medical profession was also seeking to enhance its professional status by restricting the availability of patent medicines via prescription (Manderson, 1993). They were successful in their bid to control prescribing, and a general policy of drug maintenance under the control of general practitioners continued until the early 1950s. Concurrently, international outcry over the high levels of heroin use resulted in the federal government banning the importation of heroin, and Australian states banned the manufacture of heroin within their jurisdictions. Prohibition of a range of substances had been successfully imple-

AUTHOR'S NOTE: My thanks to Peter Grabosky, Lana Harrison, and Ian McAllister for comments on an earlier draft. As always, Margrit Davies responded on queries via the Internet with frightening efficiency. Opinions expressed herein are those of the author and not necessarily those of the Australian Institute of Criminology.

mented with little public discussion or debate; Australians had little interest in drug policy until the 1960s.

The 1960s and 1970s bore witness to increasingly draconian legislation enacted to deter illicit drug use. For all intents and purposes, the criminal justice system had little effect on the availability and use of illicit drugs. By the early 1980s, AIDS had arrived on the scene, civil liberties were being increasingly eroded, the profits from organized crime were growing exponentially, and public officials were being corrupted by the large sums of money involved in the drug trade (Wodak, 1992). The election of the Labor federal government in 1983 created the opportunity for a reevaluation of drug policy. Avoiding the political minefield of the legalization/prohibition debate, the new government presented a harm minimization strategy. This approach was most clearly defined in the 1993-1997 National Drug Strategic Plan:

> Harm minimization is an approach that aims to reduce the adverse health, social and economic consequences of alcohol and other drugs by minimising or limited the harms and hazards of drug use for both the community and the individual without necessarily eliminating use. (Ministerial Council on Drug Strategy, 1993, p. 4)

This chapter focuses on selected policies that the Australian government has pursued from 1985 until 1996 to deal with drug-related problems. The chapter is divided into three sections. The first section provides an overview of the political structure that determines the direction and implementation of public policy and how this directly relates to drug policies. The second section focuses on some specific policies that the Australian government has sought to develop, and the third section focuses on the extent of public support for various policies dealing with drug use. Licit and illicit drugs are dealt with as both have been of equal importance in the development of a national drug policy in Australia.

POLITICS

Australia has a land mass almost the size of the United States, but its population is considerably smaller—17.5 million people. It is one of the most urbanized countries in the world, with 80% of the population living in large coastal cities, as most of the country is uninhabitable. Although a federal political system operates as in the United States, the nature of the political system owes more to British parliamentary practice than to the U.S. style of presidential politics. Australia has six states and two territories, each of which has its own legislature that is elected either every 3 or every 4 years; federal elections are held every 3 years.[1] At the federal level, and in all but one of the states, there is a bicameral system of government. Voting is compulsory at state and federal elections.[2] The head of state is the Queen of England, and her representative in Australia is the Governor General.[3]

Australia has one of the most stable and conservative democracies in the Western world. It is largely characterized by a two-party system, with some minor parties as well. The two major parties are the Australia Labor Party and the Liberal Party of Australia, the latter being in almost permanent coalition with the National Party of Australia. Broadly speaking, Labor is associated with more left-wing policies, whereas the Liberals are more closely associated with conservative policies. Unlike the U.S. system, there is strong party discipline, and members cannot vote against party policy despite their own views or preferences. The result is that it is rare for government legislation not to obtain a majority vote in the House.

Party discipline has been an important factor in the recent development of Australian drug policy. Unlike the United States, where populism is a significant factor in determining the stance taken by elected representatives, in Australia, representatives are bound by party discipline to adhere, at least publicly, to the party's agenda.[4] Neal Blewett, the federal health minister responsible for introducing the first national drug policy in 1985,[5] has said that party discipline in Australia was an important factor that enabled the government to pursue a policy of harm reduction (Allsop, 1995, p. 275).

A second important factor in the development of a national drug policy has been the financial arrangements between the federal and state governments. In terms of financing government activity, the federal and state governments have the right to raise taxes; however, uniform taxation legislation was introduced by the federal government in 1942. In return, the states receive a yearly grant from the federal government. These financial arrangements have provided a mechanism whereby the federal government can shape national- as well as state-level social and economic policies over which it has no direct control. Using financial inducements, the federal government has been able to encourage or even coerce state governments to spend on particular programs or to even change legislation to conform to national or international standards.

A third factor has been the important role of the state in the everyday lives of Australians. Since federation, the growth of the Australian welfare state has resulted in the decline of religious institutions in civil society and the subordination of domestic family life to the state. This has led Walters and Crook (1993) to note that "in contemporary Australia, perhaps more than in other capitalist societies, the state has the power to reproduce the status quo or to alter it" (p. 572). The Australian state intervenes in the daily lives of ordinary Australians to a greater extent than in the United States or the United Kingdom. Coupled with the inherent conservatism of Australian society, Australians are much less questioning about state-mandated activity, and they are much more likely to comply with such mandates. The most clear example of this is compulsory voting in both federal and state elections; public support for and compliance with this law is very high (McAllister, 1994, pp. 27-30).

THE ORIGINS OF HARM MINIMIZATION

Harm minimization was formally introduced in 1985 when a joint federal state meeting of health ministers agreed to a National Campaign Against Drug Abuse (NCADA). The campaign was committed to minimizing the harmful effects of licit and illicit drug use. The policy did not include a commitment to prohibition; the priority was reducing harm, even if that meant that drug use continued. How was it that a national effort was coordinated within a federal system? And why was it that health rather than legal issues dominated the campaign? Five factors explain this innovative leap in Australian drug policy. These factors were as follows:

1. The interest of the political elite in the issue

2. The political ideology of the federal government

3. State dependence on federal finances

4. The interest in containing HIV infection

5. The visible lack of inner-city ghettos largely dependent on drug-related activities and racked with drug-related violence

In 1985, Prime Minister Hawke was asked on a national television show if one of his daughters had injected heroin. His response was dramatic and emotional. In tears, he admitted that this had been an ongoing problem for his and many families. Heroin drug use crossed class and gender lines and reached into the families of the political elite. Hawke promised that the federal government would make drugs a priority area. However, he did not see drug use as a law-and-order issue.

At the same time, it was apparent that Australia faced a major HIV crisis. The minister for health, Neal Blewett, was a risk taker who was not interested in a U.S.-style "war on drugs" (Allsop, 1995, p. 275). He knew that only radical policies would arrest the spread of HIV into the heterosexual population. He also knew that a major source of transmission was the use of needles by drug addicts. AIDS and drug policy were inextricably linked, and the fear of an AIDS epidemic was so great that it allowed policymakers to suggest solutions that previously would have been unthinkable.

In April 1985, a Special Premier's Conference was convened with all of the state premiers and the prime minister to discuss the drug problem. They agreed to fund the National Campaign Against Drug Abuse (NCADA) for 3 years.

NCADA policy was to be determined by the Ministerial Council on Drug Strategy (MCDS), and Hawke was a major supporter of the campaign throughout his period as prime minister. A political elite committed to the project, as well as strong party discipline, were both critical to establishing the national drug policy.

The federal government agreed that the basis of funding NCADA programs was that the federal government would match dollar-for-dollar funding by the state and territory governments. National activities would be funded by the federal government alone (Department of Health and Human Services, 1994, p. 10). The cost-sharing arrangements were a major incentive for the states to combine and to reach compromises that would allow for the development of a uniform policy agenda across the country.

One of the first major initiatives undertaken was to distribute a report providing details on all major licit and illicit drugs to 5 million households. At the same time, a 30-second national television advertisement alerted people to its proposed distribution, and another advertisement encouraged people to read it. Information kits on all drugs were available on request. By 1988, national survey data showed that three fourths of the community had heard that there was a national campaign against drug abuse; one third had seen the booklet, and one fifth had seen the information kits.

Within NCADA, a significant element of the campaign was the media and public information component called the Drug Offensive. The Offensive disseminated drug information via the mass media and other information channels, sponsorship of a variety of community events including sport and cultural activities, and public relations activities such as antidrug rock concerts (Department of Community Services and Health, 1988). Campaigns were both broad as well as targeted at specific drugs and groups in the community. In 1986 and 1987, heroin and alcohol were the drugs targeted, and young people and Aboriginal and Torres Strait Islander people were the focus of special campaigns.

Between 1985 and 1991, a range of national guidelines was endorsed by the MCDS. These guidelines included national health policy statements on tobacco and alcohol, a national strategy on cocaine, national guidelines on methadone, and a national action plan on amphetamines (Kerr, 1991, p. 37). Regular independent evaluations identified certain groups as requiring special attention. The initial campaign identified women, Aboriginal and Torres Strait Islander people, young people, and prisoners. The first evaluation in 1988 recommended that injecting drug users and people from non-English-speaking backgrounds be included as special population groups. The 1991 evaluation suggested that older people, those living in remote locations, the unemployed, and polydrug use be given special consideration (Second Task Force on Evaluation, 1992).

Health Minister Blewett had always regarded the two major licit drugs, alcohol and tobacco, as significantly more harmful to Australians than the illicit drugs. So, even though most people in the early days of NCADA associated the campaign with reducing the harm caused by illicit drugs, he maintained a strong emphasis on alcohol and tobacco. He was well aware that enforcement agencies desire money, and he wanted to ensure that the money allocated to NCADA went to more important, long-term preventive measures (Allsop, 1995). Neal Blewett stood down in 1990.

The second evaluation of the campaign in 1991 concluded that there was a greater need for cooperation between the health and law enforcement sectors (Ministerial Council on Drug Strategy, 1992). The law enforcement agencies had opposed harm minimization because it did not automatically embrace prohibition, but now they agreed that this was the most pragmatic approach, and they were brought into the partnership. The campaign was henceforth to be called the National Drug Strategy. In terms of overall spending, 63% of NCADA funds over the previous 6 years had been spent on treatment and rehabilitation (Second Task Force on Evaluation, 1992).

The National Drug Strategy reaffirmed its commitment to harm minimization and that alcohol and tobacco were responsible for most drug-related deaths and the costs associated with drug abuse (Ministerial Council on Drug Strategy, 1992). Three key policy goals were laid out in the strategic plan:

- To minimise the level of illness, disease, injury and premature death associated with the use of alcohol, tobacco, pharmaceutical and illicit drugs.

- To minimise the level and impact of criminal drug offences and other drug-related crime, violence and antisocial behavior within the community.

- To minimise the level of personal and social disruption, loss of quality of life, loss of productivity and other economic costs associated with the inappropriate use of alcohol and other drugs. (Ministerial Council on Drug Strategy, 1993, p. 6)

The National Drug Strategy called on each of the states and territories to develop 3- to 5-year strategic plans with annual action plans that would reflect local priorities and activities within the overall national policy.

With the addition of law enforcement support, the MCDS established the National Drug Crime Prevention Fund for research specifically on "law enforcement related projects which complement the National Drug Strategic Plan" (Department of Health and Human Services, 1994, p. 107). NCADA had established two national research centers, one on the west coast and the other on the east coast (Department of Health and Human Services, 1994, p. 3). Funding for these centers was renewed under the National Drug Strategy. In addition, research grants are provided annually via the Research Into Drug Abuse Program, and the federal government conducted national surveys of drug use (similar to the U.S. National Household Surveys on Drug Abuse) in 1985, 1988, 1991, 1993, 1995, and 1998.

TABLE 9.1: Consequences of Drug Use in Australia

	Number of Deaths (1992)	*Costs (1989)[a]*	*Percentage Who Have Ever Tried (1995)*	*Percentage Who Use Regularly (1995)*
Tobacco	18,965	$6.84	67	23
Alcohol	6,574	$6.03	90	47[b]
Marijuana	0	—	31	13[c]
Opiates	492	$1.44	2	0.4
Other	25[d]	—		

SOURCES: Collins and Lapsley (1991); Makkai and McAllister (1997).
a. In billions.
b. Use 1 day a week or more.
c. Used in the past 12 months.
d. Restricted to cocaine, amphetamines, and LSD.

Neither of the two independent reviews of the campaign in 1988 and 1991 recommended a change in the fundamental commitment to harm minimization as the central principle guiding national drug policy. Over the past decade, a range of policies has been introduced at both the state and federal levels without necessarily requiring abstinence on the part of users or as a major policy goal. The years since 1985 have seen more changes in public policies toward drugs than in any comparable period of time this century. We look now at some of these policies for tobacco, alcohol, marijuana, and other illicit drugs.

TOBACCO

Reduction in exposure to tobacco smoke has been a major focus of the National Drug Strategy. Table 9.1 shows that 23% of Australians regularly use tobacco, tobacco accounts for more drug-related deaths in Australia than do any of the other drugs, and tobacco is a significant cost to Australian society. Early on, the campaign sought to quantify the costs to Australian society of drug use and commissioned two economists to undertake this work (Collins & Lapsley, 1991). This exercise was important in demonstrating that the major economic costs were the legal rather than the illegal drugs, and that the total cost of drug abuse outweighed total revenue from alcohol and drug consumption via taxation and other revenue mechanisms.

Major policy initiatives have occurred at both the state and federal levels with regard to tobacco. Smoking was banned on all domestic flights (including international flights once they entered Australian air space) in 1987, in all federal government buildings in 1988, in all print media in 1990, and in all airports in 1992. In addition, a ban on broadcasting and publication of tobacco advertisements became effective in mid-1993.[6] In 1989, the federal government banned the manufacture, importation, and selling of chewing tobacco and snuffs (McAllister, Moore, & Makkai, 1991, p. 184). State governments continued to increase taxes on tobacco products, and some states have banned outdoor advertising of cigarettes on billboards, taxis, and shop awnings. The private sector followed suit, especially with passive smoking cases looming, so that by 1995, virtually all major firms had banned smoking in the workplace.

Some states established Health Promotion Funds with a special tax on tobacco products. These funds have been used to buy out tobacco sponsorship of sporting and cultural events and fund treatment and rehabilitation centers as well as research. In 1994, the Australian Capital Territory introduced legislation to ban smoking in all public indoor areas. A major review of the health warnings on cigarette packs resulted in new health warnings in 1995. In terms of effectiveness, data show that the overall rates of smoking and smoking-related deaths in Australia have declined since the late 1970s. However, community surveys suggest that the initiation of smoking by younger women is increasing (Department of Health and Human Services, 1994).

ALCOHOL

Australians consume more alcohol per capita than do Americans (Department of Health and Human Services, 1994, p. 27; Makkai, 1994). Alcohol is embedded in cultural norms and practices; the vast majority of Australians have tried it, and around half drink alcohol at least once a week or more (see Table 9.1). The National Health Policy released by the MCDS in 1989 called for the minimization of harm, with special attention being paid to underage drinking, hazardous drinking, and drunk driving (Department of Health and Human Services, 1994). Like tobacco, the consumption of alcohol has been declining, and from 1988-1989 to 1992-1993, "per capita consumption of pure alcohol fell by 13 percent" (Department of Health and Human Services, 1994, p. 13).

In 1992, the National Health and Medical Research Council released a series of recommendations regarding responsible drinking behavior (National Health and Medical Research Council, 1992). The report argued that it was pointless to promote abstinence; reductions in harmful levels of drinking were a more realistic goal. These recommendations formed the basis for the promotion of safe drinking levels by the campaign. Over the past decade, a series of antidrinking campaigns at the national and state levels has been conducted. A major national campaign was "Alcohol and Violence Tears You Apart," which used both print and visual media. Two thirds of people in the 1993 national drug survey reported that they had seen the posters, and more than half had seen the television commercial (Makkai, 1993a). However, the evaluation showed that although the mass media campaign had raised awareness of drunkenness, violence, and alcohol, it had had less impact in getting people to think about their own drinking behavior (Makkai, 1993a).

NCADA, in conjunction with the alcohol industry in 1990-1991, produced national guidelines on responsible serving of alcohol. From the 1960s, there had been a general move to deregulate the alcohol industry and to increase opening hours and outlets selling alcohol. This trend has been reversed, with Western Australia, the Northern Territory, and the Australian Capital Territory introducing legislation to control the number of liquor licenses and outlets (Craze & Norberry, 1994). However, public drunkenness, a criminal offense, was repealed in all states because it was viewed as more harmful to jail such offenders. However, prosecutions for serving intoxicated customers were rare (Stockwell, 1994, p. 6), and Australian citizens have begun to seek recourse to the civil law, successfully winning lawsuits against licensees who permit drunken customers to remain on the premises. In 1993, the Department of Health and Human Services hosted a National Symposium on Alcohol Misuse and Violence. Eight major reports were commissioned.

The federal government has used taxation as one mechanism to affect consumers. They increased the taxes on alcohol but placed a lower tax on low-alcohol beer. Consumption data show that there has been a reduction in consumption of regular beer and an increase in the consumption of low-alcohol beer (Department of Health and Human Services, 1994, p. 15). Drunk driving has been a major problem, and the states responded as early as the 1960s. All states except Western Australia had decreased the maximum allowable blood alcohol content level to .05 by the early 1990s. Western Australia eventually complied when the federal government threatened to withdraw financial support for major road-building programs. All states now have random breath testing. Alcohol-related road deaths dropped 66% between 1982 and 1992. However, binge drinking among young people and alcohol-related antisocial behavior are still major problems (Makkai, 1993b).

MARIJUANA

In his first few weeks as Minister for Health, Neal Blewett indicated that he thought marijuana could be decriminalized. The political furor that followed taught Blewett an invaluable lesson—drug policy was as much about politics and public opinion as it was about rational scientific discourse. He backed off on the issue, realizing that the federal government could do little because it was the states that had jurisdiction over law enforcement. However, he sought to encourage and protect those states that wanted to pursue some reform on this issue (Allsop, 1995). In 1987, the South Australian government moved to make possession of small amounts of cannabis a misdemeanor. Blewett ensured that the MCDS did not publicly criticize South Australia's policy (Allsop, 1995).

During the past decade, two states undertook major reviews of the issues surrounding marijuana. The first report to appear was from the Queensland Criminal Justice Commission (1994), and cannabis was its sole focus. The second came from Victoria in 1996, and the report, *Drugs and Our Community,* focused on all illicit drugs (Premier's Drug Advisory Council, 1996). The policy recommendations from both reports were, to a large extent, a reflection of state politics. In 1985, Queensland had introduced legislation to deal with illicit drug use, which was far more severe there than in the other states. The legislation did not distinguish between cannabis and other drugs and required judges to give mandatory sentences (Manderson, 1993). An initial discussion paper (Advisory Committee on Illicit Drugs, 1993) by the Queensland Criminal Justice Commission created a storm, for it raised the issue of cannabis legalization and showed that cannabis was the second most valuable commodity produced in the state. The political and media response was to condemn the discussion paper. The final report steered well clear of such radical ideas or unpalatable findings, suggesting that cannabis remain illegal but that there be separate offenses for possession and cultivation of lesser quantities of cannabis.

Victoria introduced legislation that lessened the penalties for possession or use of small quantities of cannabis in 1983. Victoria had also taken reform on other controversial moral issues, legalizing prostitution in the 1980s. By the time the report was handed down, the premier, Jeff Kennett, had indicated that he was not opposed to cannabis reform. The most controversial recommendation that came from the report was that possession of small amounts of cannabis be legalized. In an unprecedented manner, the head of the advisory committee directly addressed the Victorian parliament. However, weeks of media speculation and debate saw the mobilizing of opponents to reform, resulting in Kennett saying that the issue would not be decided now. It would be revisited at a later date.

In addition to these developments, the then federal minister for justice requested that the MCDS collate current information on cannabis use in Australia. As a result, a National Task Force on Cannabis was convened in 1992, and four definitive research reports were commissioned (Ali & Christie, 1994). These papers have been favorably reviewed, and they covered the health and psychological consequences of cannabis use (Hall, Solowij, & Lemon, 1994); legislative options for cannabis in Australia (McDonald, Moore, Norberry, Wardlaw, & Ballenden, 1994); patterns of cannabis use in Australia (Donnelly & Hall, 1994); and public perceptions of cannabis legislation in Australia (Bowman & Sanson-Fisher, 1994). The Task Force concluded that "these findings give strong support to the concept of separating the widespread use of cannabis from the criminal sector" (Ali & Christie, 1994, p. 43). The MCDS responded by commissioning the Australian Institute of Criminology to examine "the social impact of various actual and potential legislative responses to cannabis" (McDonald & Atkinson, 1995, p. iv).

In the past decade, two states have changed their legislation on cannabis. In 1986, South Australia reformed its Controlled Substances Act so that possession of small amounts of cannabis was subject to a fine. If the fine was paid within 60 days, no record of the offense was kept. At the same time, heavier penalties for trafficking were introduced. In 1992, the Australian Capital Territory (ACT) amended its Drugs of Dependence Act with the introduction of a similar expiation scheme for both adults and juveniles. The difference between the two schemes was in terms of the amounts specified under the Acts. In South Australia, individuals could possess up to 100 gm of cannabis and 10 cannabis plants; in the ACT, the limit was 25 gm of cannabis and five cannabis plants. Recent evaluations (Christie, 1991; Donnelly, Hall, & Christie, 1995; Makkai & McAllister, 1997) of the South Australian legislation have shown that

- Consumption does not appear to have increased

- The number of drug offenders appearing in the courts had declined dramatically

- Almost one half of offenders fail to pay the fine, resulting in a conviction

- The proportion of people being issued expiation notices has increased noticeably

The net widening effect of the legislation has caused concern, and it appears that those who are least able to pay, such as the unemployed, are disproportionately less likely to pay the fine within the 60 days. A recent South Australia advisory committee has recommended that the number of plants be reduced from 10 to 4 because recent police research indicates that crime syndicates have been exploiting the legislation.

OTHER ILLICIT DRUGS

The National Drug Strategy has involved a variety of mass media campaigns directed at a range of illicit drugs. The campaign has tended to respond to changes in drug use patterns so that in the early days, heroin campaigns focused on the link between injecting drug users and HIV. In more recent times, the increase in use of amphetamines has resulted in a nationwide campaign. Of particular concern has been the increasing trend to inject amphetamines, and a national amphetamine strategy was endorsed by the MCDS. Such national campaigns involve both print and visual media, as well as developing drug education packs for schools. In 1990-1991, for example, 25% of funds allocated to prevention within the campaign's cost-share arrangements was directed toward school-based alcohol and other drug education. The National Drug Strategy recommended that drug education should be part of a comprehensive and integrated approach to health education generally. This reflected a commitment toward public health prevention rather than primary prevention.

The link between AIDS and drug policy has been of considerable importance in introducing more pragmatic approaches. Wodak (1992) has estimated that "there may be approximately forty to sixty million individual acts of injections of street drugs in Australia each year" (p. 51). Needle exchange programs were established and expanded rapidly in response to this problem. In Victoria during 1995, more than 2 million needles and syringes were distributed and just under 1 million used needles and syringes were returned (Premier's Drug Advisory Council, 1996, p. 53). Although Australia has a high incidence of AIDS, it still has a low rate of HIV infection in injecting drug users (Wodak, 1992, p. 51; Wodak, Stowe, Ross, Gold, & Miller, 1995). However, injecting drug users have very high rates of hepatitis B and C (Wodak et al., 1995).

Methadone maintenance was endorsed as an effective harm minimization strategy in the early days of the campaign. In 1985, national guidelines were endorsed, and in 1993, the federal government, in co-operation with the state and territory governments, agreed to a national policy on methadone treatment. As a result, the number of treatment slots available in methadone programs has been increasing. In 1985, there were 2,203 clients, and by 1994, there were 14,996 (Department of Health and Human Services, 1994, p. 97). All states except for the Northern Territory run ongoing methadone programs. Methadone maintenance plays a central role in the management of opioid dependence in Australia (Mattick & Hall, 1994; Ward, Mattick, & Hall, 1994). Most methadone is distributed via medical doctors, and in Victoria, 90% of people on the methadone program are under the care of a general practitioner and collect their daily dose at local pharmacies (Premier's Drug Advisory Council, 1996, p. 54).

Heroin is widely available in Australia, and seizure rates are estimated to be between 3% and 10% (Weatherburn & Lind, 1995, cited in Premier's Drug Advisory Council, 1996). At present, heroin dependence in Australia is treated via methadone maintenance, detoxification, or counseling. However, research shows that methadone programs vary in their effectiveness in terms of discontinuing treatment or reducing criminal behavior (Bammer, 1995). The consideration of heroin (diacetylmorphine) maintenance dates back to 1979, but no official inquiry or commission has recommended that it be introduced. In 1991, the ACT Select Committee on HIV, Illegal Drugs and Prostitution approached the Australian National University to consider this issue.

Careful research was then conducted over the next 4 years examining the feasibility of providing diacetylmorphine as a maintenance treatment. The final report (Bammer, 1995) recommended that two controlled pilot studies be conducted in Canberra, each lasting 6 months. If the outcomes were positive, then the trial should be expanded to three Australian cities for a further 2-year evaluation. Although heroin had been prescribed in Australia hospitals until the early 1960s, heroin has now become associated solely with drug traffickers and violence. Over the 4 years, controversy surrounded the study even though its sole purpose was to evaluate only the feasibility of such a project.

Legal scholars advised that the trial would not violate international treaties; however, it would require cooperation from both the federal government and the states. The ACT would have to enact a nonenforcement agreement, amend existing legislation, or introduce special legislation (Bammer, 1995). The diacetylmorphine would have to be either imported or manufactured domestically. Manufacture of the substance locally would probably require amendments to state legislation. If diacetylmorphine were to be imported, the federal government would have to agree to provide the necessary licenses and permission. Because the ACT is landlocked, changes may be required to legislation in surrounding states to enable the transportation of the substance.

The report was presented to the ACT government in June 1995. A task force was convened to undertake a 3-month consultation with all interested parties. In January 1996, the task force recommended that the ACT government support the first pilot study. The ACT government response was that financial assistance would be required from the federal government and that other Australian states would have to support the trial (Bammer, 1996). The last MCDS supported the heroin trial, along with a number of other innovative schemes. After a week of intense debate and moral panic fueled by some media organizations, the prime minister indicated that the heroin trial would not proceed. This was in the context of reduced funding for national health and law enforcement agencies and a rising death toll in heroin-related deaths. In 1979, there were 79; by 1996, this had increased to 620.

PUBLIC OPINION

Since 1985, the campaign has collected data on drug use and public opinion at regular intervals. From 1985 to 1995, the percentage of those associating illicit drugs with the "drug problem" declined from 91% to 75%, whereas those mentioning licit drugs increased from 9% to 25% (see Figure 9.1). The overt recognition of the importance of harm minimization strategies with regard to the licit drugs is reflected in the modification of public opinion over time.

Both federal and state governments have undertaken a series of measures to reduce the harm associated with tobacco smoking. In particular, they have led the way in banning the advertising of tobacco products and their use in federal buildings. The private sector has followed suit, and the vast majority of medium-to large-size firms no longer allow smoking inside their buildings. Aside from the family home, the remaining indoor areas where smoking remains legal are

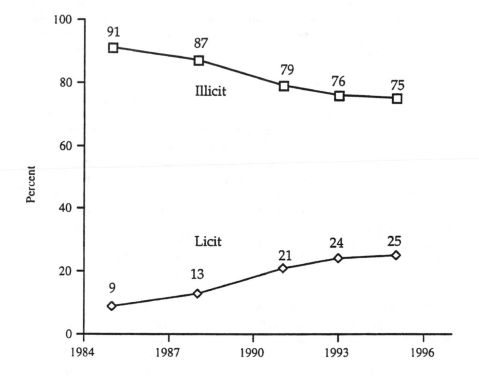

Figure 9.1. Mentions of Licit and Illicit Drugs as Part of the Drug Problem, 1985-1995[a]

SOURCE: 1985-1995 NDS surveys.

a. Estimates are for respondents aged 20 years or older.

largely restaurants, shopping centers, and pubs/clubs. Table 9.2 shows that there is strong support for banning smoking in restaurants and shopping centers, with less support for pubs/clubs.

Although people may see particular drugs as part of the drug problem, the extent to which they are prepared to regulate these drugs may vary depending on the drug concerned and the range of possible options available. The campaign has focused on the harm associated with excessive use of alcohol in the past couple of years. Table 9.3 examines the extent to which ordinary citizens would support various regulatory strategies to control alcohol use. A variety of regulatory strategies were provided, some focusing on demand and some on supply. The public is much more in favor of strategies that affect demand rather than supply. Strong public support is shown for the strict enforcement of the law against serving customers who are drunk. Between 1993 and 1995, there has been increased

TABLE 9.2: Public Opinion Toward Banning Smoking in Public Places, 1993-1995[a]

| | *Percentage Strongly Support or Support* | | |
	1993	*1995*	*Change 1993-1995*
Shopping centers	70	76	+6
Restaurants	74	73	−1
Pubs/clubs	43	44	+1
N	3,113	3,371	

SOURCE: 1993, 1995 National Drug Strategy surveys.
a. Estimates are for respondents aged 20 years or older. The question was "To what extent would you support or oppose measures such as . . . banning smoking in . . .?"

TABLE 9.3: Attitudes Toward the Availability of Alcohol, 1993 and 1995[a]

| | *Percentage Strongly Support or Support* | | |
	1993	*1995*	*Change 1993-1995*
Supply			
Increase the price of alcohol	44	33	−11
Reduce the number of outlets that sell alcohol	35	34	−1
Reduce trading hours for all pubs and clubs	29	40	+11
Ban alcohol sponsorship of sporting events	33	38	+5
Limit advertising for alcohol on TV until after 9:30 p.m.	55	76	+21
Raise the legal drinking age	39	53	+14
Demand			
Increase the number of alcohol-free public events	67	72	+5
Increase the number of alcohol-free zones/dry areas	69	73	+5
Enforce more strictly the law against serving customers who are drunk	87	92	+5
Serve only low-alcohol drinks, such as low-alcohol beer, at sporting events/venues	67	74	+7

SOURCE: 1993, 1995 National Drug Strategy surveys.
a. Estimates are for respondents aged 20 years or older. The 1993 question was "To reduce the problems associated with excessive alcohol use, such as liver damage, cancer of the oesophagus, motor vehicle accidents or violence, looking at the card, to what extent would you support or oppose the following measures?" The 1995 question was "To reduce the problems associated with excessive alcohol use, to what extent would you support or oppose . . . ?"

TABLE 9.4: Legalization in the Morgan Gallup Surveys, 1977-1996 (in percentages)[a]

"Should marijuana be legalized?"	*1977*	*1979*	*1982*	*1984*	*1987*	*1989*	*1991*	*1993*	*1995*	*1996*
Yes	24	23	27	31	25	29	29	33	33	33
No	66	67	62	63	69	63	63	58	59	58
Can't say	10	10	11	6	6	8	8	9	8	9
Total	100	100	100	100	100	100	100	100	100	100

SOURCE: Morgan Gallup Reports; Bulletin, April 23, 1996.
a. All of the surveys were national samples of adults, aged 18 years and older, conducted by personal interview.

support for all supply-and-demand strategies except for increasing the price of alcohol. The strongest increase in support is found for limiting alcohol advertising and raising the legal drinking age (currently 18 years).

There has been major debate in Australia as to whether the laws in relation to marijuana should be changed. Although two states have undertaken detailed studies of marijuana laws, and another two states have greatly reduced the penalties associated with using small amounts of marijuana, in no state or territory is the use of cannabis legal. Between 1977 and 1996, the Morgan Gallup Survey company consistently asked "Should marijuana be legalized?" Table 9.4 shows the distribution of responses over this time. In 1977, around one fourth of Australians thought that it should. Over the next 19 years, there has been a gradual increase in the proportion supporting legalization, so that by 1996, one third of the public was in favor of such a strategy.

The controlled provision of heroin to those dependent on the substance is currently under consideration as a harm minimization strategy in the Australian Capital Territory. Figure 9.2 examines the extent to which people support legalizing the personal use of heroin and increasing the penalties for sale or supply of the drug. There is clearly no support for legalizing the personal use of heroin, and there is strong support for increasing the sanctions for traffickers in the drug. However, responses to these all-or-nothing questions should be viewed carefully. Table 9.5 shows how ordinary Australians would allocate their money in dealing with the four types of drugs—alcohol, tobacco, marijuana, and heroin/cocaine.

Respondents could choose between education, treatment, and enforcement. Prevention was a legitimate long-term goal of the campaign, and key players in the National Drug Strategy viewed education and treatment as more positive strategies than law enforcement. This perspective is also reflected in public opinion. Education and treatment are the preferred strategies for dealing with the use of drugs, with the average amounts allocated to these strategies being higher than what they would allocate to enforcement. Within the total average

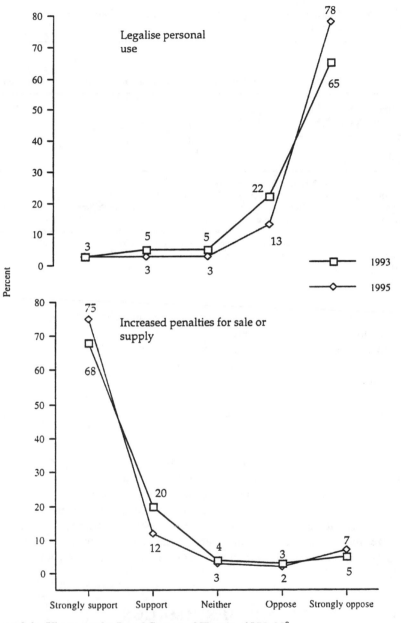

Figure 9.2: Views on the Legal Status of Heroin, 1993-95[a]

SOURCE: 1993-1995 National Drug Strategy surveys.

a. Estimates are for respondents aged 20 years or older. The questions were "To what extent would you support or oppose . . . the personal use of heroin being made legal . . . increased penalties for the sale or supply of heroin?"

TABLE 9.5: Priorities for Policies Toward Four Drugs, 1993 and 1995 (in mean dollars)[a]

	1993			1995		
	Education	Treatment	Enforcement	Education	Treatment	Enforcement
Marijuana	51	21	27	47	24	30
Heroin/cocaine	46	26	27	36	24	40
Tobacco	61	25	14	52	30	18
Alcohol	49	30	21	43	28	29

SOURCE: 1993, 1995 National Drug Strategy surveys.
a. Estimates are for those aged 18 years or older. The question wording was "For each drug, I'd like to find out how you would allocate $100 over these three areas to reduce the use of that drug. Starting with alcohol, if you were given $100 to spend on reducing alcohol use, how much would you allocate to each of these areas: education (e.g., information); treatment (e.g., counselling, therapy); law enforcement (e.g., stop illegal sale or use)." Question wording and position of the question in the questionnaire schedule greatly affect responses. For more detailed discussions of these issues, see Makkai and McAllister (1997a), Bowman and Sanson-Fisher (1994), and Hall and Nelson (1994).

amounts allocated to treatment and education, the majority is allocated to education for all of the drugs considered.

Interestingly, almost the same average amounts would be allocated to enforcement for marijuana ($30) and alcohol ($29). The data suggest that a stronger move has occurred toward enforcement as a strategy for dealing with alcohol than has been the case for marijuana. Thus, the increase in average amounts from 1993 to 1995 for alcohol was $8, compared to $3 for marijuana. Enforcement is generally not seen as a viable option for tobacco, although respondents still allocated $18 to this strategy.

Even though the public would overwhelmingly not legalize heroin, this does not automatically translate into an enforcement regime. The average amount they would allocate to enforcement for heroin and cocaine is $40 out of $100 in 1995; the remaining $60 would be allocated to education and treatment. The data do show, however, that between 1993 and 1995, people have increased the average amount they would spend on enforcement with regard to these drugs. In 1993, people allocated an average $27 on law enforcement, increasing to $40 in 1995.

THE FUTURE OF HARM MINIMIZATION

Given that public opinion on drug reform largely opposes reform and that the political will for reform came from the federal government and its bureaucracy, what is the future of the harm minimization policy in Australia given that a conservative federal government was elected in 1996?

Michael Woolridge was appointed the federal minister for health in the new conservative government. Upon taking office, he indicated that he did not see any reason why marijuana could not be decriminalized. The young Liberals had already accepted the decriminalization of marijuana as part of its policy agenda. Immediately, the new prime minister, John Howard, publicly stated that the conservative government would oppose marijuana reform. Woolridge, like one of his predecessors, Neal Blewett, learned that marijuana reform is more about politics than about rational public policy.

The conservative government was elected as a party that supports small business, family values, and small government. These ideological views are already having a dramatic effect on federal drug policy. Although the federal health bureaucracy has driven the drug agenda and debate for the past 10 years, almost immediately, the new government had closed the major section that had been running the drug strategy. The new government viewed illicit drug policy as of minor importance to their overall health strategy; it was now returning to its natural home in the states and law enforcement agencies.

The reform of heroin law remains unchanged. The heroin trial is off the political agenda at present. However, various state premiers have called for a drug summit, along with a range of organizations with interests in the drug field. The federal government continues to resist moving in this direction, although the prime minister has convened his own advisory committee to report to him with strategies for dealing with the illicit drug problem. The prime minister knows that there are votes to be lost in controversial proposals, just as the ACT legislative assembly discovered when they tried to legalize marijuana for medical purposes and the Victorian government flirted, unsuccessfully, with legalizing the possession of small amounts of marijuana.

These events suggest that further education and treatment strategies developed under a rubric of harm minimization are unlikely to be promoted by the federal government; there will be a greater emphasis on law enforcement as a strategy to minimize harm. There may also be ideological tensions between policies that emphasize particular harm minimization options and conservative policies on the family. It is certainly the case that the goal of small government will result in a withdrawal of the government from some policy areas with a general downsizing of the federal bureaucracy. Because drug reform is not high on the policy agenda, it is an obvious target for cutbacks at the federal level. Without an ideological commitment from the political elite and a strong federal bureaucracy, the creativity and innovation of Australian drug policy, with its special emphasis on nationally integrated policies and harm minimization, faced an uncertain future in 1996.

NOTES

1. The six states are Queensland, New South Wales, Victoria, Tasmania, South Australia, and Western Australia. The two territories are the Northern Territory and the Australian Capital Territory. The national capital of Australia is Canberra, and it is located in the Australian Capital Territory.

2. There are three levels of government: federal, state, and local. However, local government is not constitutionally recognized and is concerned with a limited range of matters.

3. Traditionally, the prime minister recommends to the Queen the person who should be appointed as governor general. This is largely a ceremonial position; however, the governor general can dismiss the elected head of state—the prime minister—and this occurred in 1975, causing a constitutional crisis.

4. They can, of course, seek to change or modify party policy through internal discussion, debate, and lobbying.

5. Although the federal and state governments have implemented a variety of drug policies since the turn of the century, it was not until 1985 that "a national approach to drug problems based on clearly enunciated principles with a commitment of new resources" (Wardlaw, 1992b, p. 3) was established under the MCDS. "The MCDS represents both Federal, State and Territory interests *and* has oversight of the NCADA, a national drug control program which is itself a Federal/State enterprise" (Wardlaw, 1992a, p. 150).

6. The legislation does allow for limited exemptions for sponsorship advertising.

REFERENCES

Advisory Committee on Illicit Drugs. (1993). *Cannabis and the law in Queensland: A discussion paper.* Brisbane: Author.

Ali, R., & Christie, P. (1994). *Report of the National Task Force on Cannabis.* Canberra: AGPS.

Allsop, S. (1995). Harnessing harm reduction in Australia: An interview with the Hon. Neal Blewett. *Drug and Alcohol Review, 14,* 273-282.

Bammer, G. (1995). *Feasibility research into the controlled availability of opioids.* Canberra: National Centre for Epidemiology and Population Health.

Bammer, G. (1996). When science meets policy. *International Journal of Drug Policy, 7*(1), 46-51.

Bowman, J., & Sanson-Fisher, R. (1994). *Public perceptions of cannabis legislation.* Canberra: AGPS.

Christie, P. (1991). *The effects of cannabis legislation in South Australia on levels of cannabis use.* Adelaide: Drug and Alcohol Services Council.

Collins, D., & Lapsley, H. (1991). *Estimating the economic costs of drug abuse in Australia* (NCADA Monograph Series No. 15).

Craze, L., & Norberry, J. (1994). The objectives of liquor-licensing laws in Australia. In T. Stockwell (Ed.), *An examination of the appropriateness and efficacy of liquor licensing laws across Australia* (pp. 35-56). Canberra: AGPS.

Department of Community Services and Health. (1988). *Taking the initiative 1986-87.* Report of the second year of the National Campaign Against Drug Abuse. Canberra: AGPS.

Department of Health and Human Services. (1994). *Statistics on drug abuse in Australia, 1994.* Canberra: AGPS.

Donnelly, N., & Hall, W. (1994). *Patterns of cannabis use in Australia.* Canberra: AGPS.

Donnelly, N., Hall, W., & Christie, P. (1995). The effects of partial decriminalisation on cannabis use in South Australia 1985 to 1993. *Australian Journal of Public Health, 3,* 281-287.

Hall, W., & Nelson, J. (1994). *Public perceptions of cannabis legislation in Australia.* Canberra: AGPS.

Hall, W., Solowij, N., & Lemon, J. (1994). *The health and psychological consequences of cannabis use.* Canberra: AGPS.

Kerr, S. (1991). The National Campaign Against Drug Abuse policy development and program implementation. In J. White (Ed.), *Drug problems in our society: Dimensions and perspectives* (pp. 37-42). South Australia: Drug and Alcohol Council.

Makkai, T. (1993a). *Awareness and effectiveness of the National Campaign Against Drug Abuse and the drug offensive.* Canberra: AGPS.

Makkai, T. (1993b). *Drugs, anti-social behavior and policy choices in Australian society.* Canberra: AGPS.

Makkai, T. (1994). *Patterns of use: Australia and the United States.* Canberra: AGPS.

Makkai, T., & McAllister, I. (1993). Public opinion and the legal status of marijuana in Australia. *Journal of Drug Issues, 23,* 409-427.

Makkai, T., & McAllister, I. (1997a). *Marijuana in Australia: Patterns and attitudes.* Canberra: AGPS.

Makkai, T., & McAllister, I. (1997b). *Patterns of drug use in Australia, 1985-95.* Canberra: Department of Health and Family Services.

Manderson, D. (1993). *From Mr Sin to Mr Big.* Melbourne: Oxford University Press.

Mattick, R., & Hall, W. (1994). A summary of recommendations for the management of opioid dependence: The quality assurance in the treatment of drug dependence project. *Drug and Alcohol Review, 13,* 319-326.

McAllister, I. (1994). *Political behaviour in Australia.* Melbourne: Longmans.

McAllister, I., Moore, R., & Makkai, T. (1991). *Drugs in Australian society: Patterns, attitudes and policies.* Melbourne: Longmans.

McDonald, D., & Atkinson, L. (Eds.). (1995). *Social impacts of the legislative options for cannabis in Australia phase 1 research.* Canberra: Australian Institute of Criminology.

McDonald, D., Moore, R., Norberry, J., Wardlaw, G., & Ballenden, N. (1994). *Legislative options for cannabis in Australia.* Canberra: AGPS.

Ministerial Council on Drug Strategy. (1993). *National drug strategic plan 1993-1997.* Canberra: AGPS.

National Health and Medical Research Council. (1992). *Is there a safe level of daily consumption of alcohol for men and women?* Canberra: AGPS.

Premier's Drug Advisory Council. (1996). *Drugs and our community.* Melbourne: Victorian Government.

Queensland Criminal Justice Commission. (1994). *Report on cannabis and the law in Queensland.* Brisbane: Author.

Second Task Force on Evaluation. (1992). *No quick fix: An evaluation of the National Campaign Against Drug Abuse.* Canberra: Ministerial Council on Drug Strategy.

Stockwell, T. (Ed.). (1994). *An examination of the appropriateness and efficacy of liquor licensing laws across Australia.* Canberra: AGPS.

Walters, M., & Crook, S. (1993). *Sociology one.* Melbourne: Longman Cheshire.

Ward, J., Mattick, R., & Hall, W. (1994). The effectiveness of methadone maintenance treatment: An overview. *Drug and Alcohol Review, 13,* 327-336.

Wardlaw, G. (1992a). Discussion. In M. Bull, D. McDowell, J. Norberry, H. Strang, & G. Wardlaw (Eds.), *Comparative analysis of illicit drug strategy* (pp. 145-157). Canberra: AGPS.

Wardlaw, G. (1992b). Overview of national drug control strategies. In M. Bull, D. McDowell, J. Norberry, H. Strang, & G. Wardlaw (Eds.), *Comparative analysis of illicit drug strategy* (pp. 1-37). Canberra: AGPS.

Wodak, A. (1992). Beyond the prohibition of heroin. In P. O'Hare et al. (Eds.), *The reduction of drug related harm* (pp. 49-61). London: Routledge.

Wodak, A., Stowe, A., Ross, M., Gold, J., & Miller, M. (1995). HIV risk exposure of injecting drug users in Sydney. *Drug and Alcohol Review, 14,* 213-222.

10

The Harm Reduction Roles of the American Criminal Justice System

James A. Inciardi

For the better part of the 20th century, there has been a concerted belief in what has been referred to as the "enslavement theory of addiction" (Inciardi, 1992, pp. 263-264). The theory has two premises. First, the great majority of those who use heroin, cocaine, and other illegal drugs commit crimes because they are enslaved to their drugs of choice. Second, because of the high prices maintained by drug black markets, otherwise law-abiding users are forced to commit crimes in order to support their habits.

The origins of the enslavement theory of addiction date back to 19th-century America with the early clinical writings about morphine dependence (see Terry & Pellens, 1928), but its most complete elucidation appeared during the 1960s in the work of researchers David W. Maurer and Victor H. Vogel (Maurer & Vogel, 1978, pp. 286-287). They described how potential addicts first experimented with small doses of some addicting drug, not realizing what it would do to them, or thinking that addiction would never happen to them. Maurer and Vogel went on to portray how the neophyte addicts noticed before long that the amount of the drug they had been taking failed to give them the intense pleasure they had felt in the very early stages of use. In time, they increased not only the size of their dose, but also the frequency. Over time, the addicts noticed that more and more of their wages went for drugs; that they had to buy at bootleg sources; and that they had less and less money for food, rent, and other necessities. In fact, other things became less meaningful to them, and they became heavily preoccupied with simply supporting their drug habits. Before long, it became obvious to them that they needed increasing amounts of money on a regular basis, that legitimate earnings would not provide enough, and that crime was the only alternative. Hence, the birth of new criminal addicts!

The theory, of course, is not without some logic. During the latter part of the 19th century and the early years of the 20th, the use of narcotics was fairly widespread, and both morphine and heroin were readily available through legal channels. When the Harrison Act was passed in 1914, users had to embrace the black market to obtain their drugs. Since that time, the possession of narcotics has remained a crime, and most users seem to have criminal records.

From a harm reduction perspective, it is asserted that enslavement theory has considerable merit, and that drug control legislation, drug law enforcement procedures, and penalties for drug law violations do more harm than good. Many supporters of harm reduction argue that if the criminal penalties attached to marijuana, heroin, and cocaine possession and sale were removed, several things would occur: The black market would disappear, the violence associated with drug distribution would cease, the prices of illegal drugs would decline significantly, and users would no longer have to engage in street crime in order to support their desired levels of drug intake (Trebach & Inciardi, 1993).

Within the context of these remarks, a number of points need to be examined. The first is that the Harrison Act, in and of itself, did not create the entire street subculture of addict criminals. The second point is that, for the most part, enslavement theory is a myth, because most street addicts were enmeshed in criminal lifestyles before they became involved with black-market drugs. Third, like it or not, drug laws and the criminal justice process are here to stay. Moreover, although mandatory minimum sentences for drug user/dealers are inappropriate sanctions that tend to crowd prisons that are already filled to capacity, they, too, will likely remain—at least for a while. Finally, because the criminal justice process is effective in "capturing" tens of thousands of drug-involved offenders each year, there is an important harm reduction role that it can play. Specifically, the criminal justice system is in an excellent position to provide quality substance abuse treatment to the scores of drug users that come to its attention.

DRUGS, CRIME, AND PUBLIC POLICY

It would appear that American drug policy originated from two competing models of addiction. In the *medical model,* addiction was considered to be a chronic and relapsing disease that should be addressed in the manner of other physical disorders by the medical and other healing professions. The *criminal model* viewed addiction as one more of the many antisocial behaviors manifested by the growing classes of predatory and dangerous criminals. Many commentators have viewed the Harrison Act of 1914 as the ultimate triumph of the criminal model over the medical view, and as such, that single piece of legislation served to shape the direction of drug policy for years to come and generations yet unborn (see King, 1972, 1974; Lindesmith, 1965; Trebach, 1982). Or, as Auburn University sociologist Charles E. Faupel put it:

> The long-term result of this legislation was dramatic. Narcotics use was transformed from a relatively benign vice practiced by some of society's most respectable citizens to an openly disdained activity prohibited by law, relegating the narcotics user to pariah status in most communities. (Faupel, 1991, p. 151)

Professor Faupel's statement, however, is a considerable overstatement, for history suggests a somewhat alternative story. Briefly, the Harrison Act required all people who imported, manufactured, produced, compounded, sold, dispensed, or otherwise distributed cocaine and opiate drugs to register with the Treasury Department, pay special taxes, and keep records of all transactions (see Walsh, 1981). As such, it was a revenue code designed to exercise some measure of public control over narcotics and other drugs. Certain provisions of the Harrison Act permitted physicians to prescribe, dispense, or administer narcotics to their patients for "legitimate medical purposes" and "in the course of professional practice." But how these two phrases were to be interpreted was another matter entirely.

On one hand, the medical establishment held that addiction was a disease and that addicts were patients to whom drugs could be prescribed to alleviate the distress of withdrawal. On the other hand, the Treasury Department interpreted the Harrison Act to mean that a doctor's prescription for an addict was unlawful. The U.S. Supreme Court, however, quickly laid the controversy to rest.

In *Webb v. U.S.* (249 U.S. 96 [1919]), the Court held that it was not legal for a physician to prescribe narcotic drugs to an addict-patient for the purpose of maintaining his or her use and comfort. Two years later, in *Whipple v. Martinson* (256 U.S. 41 [1921]), it was held that within the framework of governmental responsibility for the public health and welfare, the state had a legitimate interest in regulating the use of "dangerous habit-forming drugs." The following year, the decision in *United States v. Behrman* (256 U.S. 280 [1922]) not only reaffirmed this position, but also went one step further. The *Behrman* decision declared that a narcotic prescription for an addict was unlawful, even if the drugs were prescribed as part of a "cure program." The impact of these decisions combined to make it almost impossible for addicts to obtain drugs legally.

In retrospect, numerous commentators on the history of drug use in the United States have argued that the Harrison Act snatched addicts from legitimate society and forced them into the underworld (see Brown, Mazze, & Glaser,

1974, p. xiii; King, 1974, p. 22). However, this cause-and-effect interpretation tends to be a rather extreme misrepresentation of historical fact.

Without question, at the beginning of the 20th century, most users of narcotics were members of legitimate society. In fact, the majority had first encountered the effects of narcotics through their family physician or local pharmacist or grocer. Over-the-counter patent medicines and home remedies containing opium, morphine, and even heroin and cocaine had been available for years, and some even for decades (Inciardi, 1992, pp. 2-11). In other words, addiction had been medically induced during the course of treatment for some perceived ailment. Yet long before the Harrison Act had been passed, before it had even been conceived, there were indications that this population of users had begun to shrink (Morgan, 1974). Agitation had existed in both the medical and religious communities against the haphazard use of narcotics, defining much of it as a moral disease (see Terry & Pellens, 1928). For many, the sheer force of social stigma and pressure served to alter their use of drugs. Similarly, the decline of the patent medicine industry after the passage of the Pure Food and Drug Act in 1906 was believed to have substantially reduced the number of narcotics and cocaine users (Courtwright, 1982). Moreover, by 1912, most state governments had enacted legislative controls over the dispensing and sales of narcotics. Thus, in all likelihood, the size of the drug-using population had started to decline years before the Harrison Act had become the subject of Supreme Court interpretation.

Even more important, however, there are historical indications that a well-developed subculture of criminal addicts had emerged many years before the passage of the Harrison Act. By the 1880s, for example, opium dens had become relatively commonplace in New York and San Francisco, and the police literature of the era indicates that they were populated with not only "hop heads" (addicts), but also smokers who were gamblers, prostitutes, and thieves as well (Byrnes, 1886, p. 385). Importantly, the opium den, "dive," or "joint" was not only a place for smoking, but also a meeting place, a sanctuary. For members of the underworld, it was a place to gather in relative safety to enjoy a smoke (of opium, hashish, or tobacco) with friends and associates. The autobiographies of pickpockets and other professional thieves from generations ago note that by the turn of the 20th century, opium, morphine, heroin, and cocaine were in widespread use by criminals of all manner (Anonymous, 1922; Black, 1927; Hapgood, 1903; Irwin, 1909; Scott, 1916; White, 1907). And, it might also be pointed out here that the first jail-based program for the treatment of heroin addiction was established in the infamous New York Tombs (Manhattan City Prison) 2 years before the Harrison Act went into effect (Lichtenstein, 1914). At the time, it was estimated that some 5% of the city's arrestees were addicted to narcotics. Thus, although the Harrison Act *contributed* to the criminalization of addiction, subcultures of criminal addicts had been accumulating for decades before its passage.

Going further, despite the contentions of the enslavement theory, there has never been any solid empirical evidence to support it. From the 1920s through the close of the 1960s, hundreds of studies of the relationship between crime and addiction were conducted.[1] Invariably, when one analysis would support enslavement theory, the next would affirm the view that addicts were criminals first, and that their drug use was but one more manifestation of their deviant lifestyles. In retrospect, the difficulty lay in the way the studies had been conducted, with biases and deficiencies in research designs that rendered their findings to be of little value.

Research since the middle of the 1970s with active drug users in the streets of New York, Miami, Baltimore, and elsewhere has demonstrated that enslavement theory has little basis in reality (see Inciardi, 1986, pp. 115-143; Johnson et al., 1985; McBride & McCoy, 1982; Nurco, Ball, Shaffer, & Hanlon, 1985; Stephens & McBride, 1976). All of these studies of the criminal careers of heroin and other drug users have convincingly documented that although drug use tends to intensify and perpetuate criminal behavior, it usually does not initiate criminal careers. In fact, the evidence suggests that among the majority of street drug users who are involved in crime, their criminal careers were well established prior to the onset of either narcotics or cocaine use.

DRUG-INVOLVED OFFENDERS

Anyone who has spent any length of time in drug abuse treatment facilities, the court system, or the corrections industry, or has had extensive contact with street drug users in some capacity, has recognized that there is something different about most heroin and cocaine addicts. Most are not otherwise law-abiding citizens who became enslaved to drugs and were forced to commit crimes to support their habits. Those who have worked with drug-involved offenders have found repeatedly that drug abuse and criminality are but symptoms of a complex behavioral disorder that cannot be properly addressed through either decriminalizing drugs or incarcerating offenders. Dr. Douglas S. Lipton of New York's National Development and Research Institute, Inc. has conveniently listed and explained the aspects of this disorder, referring to them as crime-related "impedimenta" to social functioning. The major ones are as follows:

- *Inadequacy:* characterized by a pervasive feeling of inability to cope with needs; a generalized feeling of helplessness; the inability to plan ahead; frequent feelings of despair, negativism, and cynicism; diffuse anxiety, not seen as related to a specific cause; the perception of tasks as likely to lead to failure rather than success; and a disproportionate fear (and anticipation) of rejection

- *Immaturity:* characterized by the inability to postpone gratification; a general attitude of irresponsibility; a preoccupation with concrete and immediate objects, wishes, and needs; an orientation of the individual as "receiver" and a tendency to view others as "givers"; manipulativeness; selfishness; and petulance

- *Dependency:* characterized by difficulty in coping with unstructured or complex environments, anxiety in situations requiring independent action, feelings of guilt with respect to the above elements of dependency, and feelings of resentment toward what is believed to be the source of dependency

- *Limited social skills:* characterized by a lack of ability to articulate feelings and ideas, and a resulting inability to communicate meaningfully with others except at superficial levels; lack of ability to function in subordinate-superordinate roles (e.g., inability to take orders from a superior in a work situation); inability to "take the role of the other" (i.e., empathize with others); and inadvertent, socially disapproved behavior (e.g., use of language inappropriate to various social situations, dress inappropriate for job interviews, and failure to conform to norms of personal hygiene)

- *Limited education:* characterized by functional illiteracy or a conspicuous disproportion between the individual's level of education and his or her potential level, or both

- *Vocational maladjustment:* characterized by a lack of appropriate technical skills for employment that would be meaningful to the individual, or a conspicuous disproportion between the aptitudes of the individual and realistic opportunities, or both

- *Cognitive deficiency:* characterized by a state of mental retardation, restricted mental potentiality, or incomplete development existing from birth or early infancy, as a result of which the individual is confused and bewildered by any complexity of life, overly suggestible and easily exploited, and able to achieve a mental age within a range of only 8 to 12 years

- *Compulsive pathology:* characterized by a sense that criminal behavior is forced upon the individual against his or her will; inability to obtain any lasting satisfaction from the act committed (e.g., no apparent gain to the individual from act nor any reason for injury to another); and repetition of such acts

- *Antisocial attitudes:* consisting of a configuration of values and viewpoints that are defined by society as delinquent, criminal, and antisocial. An individual who possesses antisocial attitudes demonstrates positive affective responses toward trouble, toughness, smartness, excitement, fate, autonomy, and short-run hedonism.

- *Substance dependency:* characterized by alcoholism or drug addiction, or both, to the extent that offenders with this characteristic typically (a) have several years' experience as a street drug addict or alcoholic, (b) have many failed treatment experiences, (c) are driven to use their chosen substance regardless of consequences while on the street, (d) are preoccupied with thoughts about their substance of choice while institutionalized, and (e) intend to use the preferred substance upon discharge (Lipton, 1989)

These characteristics may appear singly or in any combination in any individual at any given time. The drug abuse treatment and psychiatric literatures have documented the presence of impedimenta among substance abusers through literally hundreds of studies.[2]

To reiterate, drug addiction is typically but one symptom of a complex of problems that cannot be addressed by legalizing drugs and making them even more available than they are now. Moreover, there is a whole literature that suggests that drug abuse is *overdetermined behavior.* That is, physical dependence is secondary to the wide range of influences that instigate and regulate drug-taking and drug-seeking behaviors. Drug abuse is a disorder of the whole person, affecting some or all areas of functioning. In the vast majority of drug offenders, there are cognitive problems: Psychological dysfunction is common; thinking may be unrealistic or disorganized; values are misshapen; and, frequently, there are deficits in educational and employment skills. As such, drug abuse is a response to a series of social and psychological disturbances. Thus, the goal of treatment should be *habilitation* rather than *rehabilitation.* Whereas rehabilitation emphasizes the return to a way of life previously known and perhaps forgotten or rejected, habilitation involves the client's initial socialization into a productive and responsible way of life (Inciardi & Scarpitti, 1992). What the large drug offender population needs is not freely available drugs, but habilitation in long-term residential treatment.

CRIMINAL JUSTICE AND HARM REDUCTION

Because drug laws and drug control will persist, and because drug-involved offenders will continue to be arrested and prosecuted, the logical strategy is to use harm reduction approaches for making a more humane use of the criminal justice system. One of the long-standing harm reduction initiatives associated with the drug control activities of the criminal justice system is the Treatment Alternatives to Street Crime (TASC) network. TASC represents an efficient and humane use of the criminal justice system, for it acts as an objective bridge between two separate institutions: justice and the drug treatment community. The justice system's legal sanctions reflect concerns for public safety and punishment, whereas treatment emphasizes therapeutic intervention as a means for altering drug-taking and drug-seeking behaviors.

Under TASC, community-based supervision is made available to drug-involved individuals who would otherwise burden the justice system with their persistent, drug-associated criminality. More specifically, TASC identifies, assesses, and refers drug-involved offenders to community treatment services as an alternative or supplement to existing justice system sanctions and procedures. In the more than 100 jurisdictions where TASC currently operates, it serves as a court diversion mechanism or a supplement to probation or parole supervision. After referral to community-based treatment, TASC monitors the client's progress and compliance, including expectations for abstinence, employment, and improved personal and social functioning. It then reports treatment results back to the referring justice system agency. Clients who violate the conditions of their justice mandate (diversion, deferred sentencing, pretrial intervention, probation, or parole); their TASC contract; or their treatment agreement are typically returned to the justice system for continued processing or sanctions (Bureau of Justice Assistance, 1988; Inciardi & McBride, 1991). Evaluation data indicate that TASC-referred clients remain in treatment longer than do non-TASC clients, and as a result, they have better posttreatment success. As such, it is important that TASC be expanded because of the harm reduction role it can play in interrupting a drug offender's criminally involved lifestyle.

In addition to TASC, perhaps the most important harm reduction initiative would be expansion of therapeutic community treatment in jails and prisons. The therapeutic community, better known as the "TC" by practitioners in the drug field, is unquestionably the most appropriate form of drug abuse treatment in correctional settings because of the many phenomena in the prison environment that make rehabilitation difficult. Not surprisingly, the availability of drugs in jails and prisons is a pervasive problem. In addition, there is the violence associated with inmate gangs, often formed along racial lines for the purposes of establishing and maintaining status, turf, and unofficial control over sectors of the penitentiary for distributing contraband and providing protection for other inmates (Bowker, 1980; Fleisher, 1989; Johnson, 1987). And finally, there is the prison subculture, a system of norms and values that tends to militate against successful treatment.

In contrast, the therapeutic community is a total treatment environment isolated from the rest of the prison population—separated from the drugs, the violence, and the norms and values that militate against treatment and rehabilitation. The primary clinical staff of the TC are often former substance abusers—recovering addicts—who themselves were rehabilitated in therapeutic communities. The treatment perspective of the TC is that drug abuse is a disorder of the whole person—that the problem is the *person* and not the drug, that addiction is a *symptom* and not the essence of the disorder. In the TC's view of recovery, the primary goal is to change the negative patterns of behavior, thinking, and feeling that predispose drug use. As such, the overall goal is a responsible, drug-free lifestyle (De Leon & Ziegenfuss, 1986; Yablonsky, 1989). Recovery through the TC process depends on positive and negative pressures to change, and this is brought about through a self-help process in which relationships of mutual responsibility to every resident in the program are built (De Leon, 1985).

In addition to individual and group counseling, the TC process has a system of explicit rewards that reinforce the value of earned achievement. As such, privileges are earned. In addition, TCs have their own specific rules and regulations that guide the behavior of residents and the management of their facilities. Their purposes are to maintain the safety and health of the community and to train and teach residents through the use of discipline. TC rules and regulations are numerous, the most conspicuous of which are total prohibitions against violence, theft, and drug use. Violation of these cardinal rules typically results in immediate expulsion from a TC.

Therapeutic communities have been in existence for decades, and their successes have been well documented (see De Leon, 1990). Yet few exist in jail and prison settings. It has been demonstrated, however, that prison-based TCs are effective in not only addressing the problems of drug dependence, but also dealing with issues of prison management. On this latter point, prison TCs have been found to be the cleanest and most trouble-free sectors of the institutions in which they are housed (Inciardi, Martin, Butzin, Hooper, & Harrison, 1997; Lipton & Wexler, 1988; Toch, 1980; Wexler & Williams, 1986).

POSTSCRIPT

What may appear surprising to many readers is the fact that harm reduction initiatives in prisons and jails have become a major interest of both the Corrections Program Office of the U.S. Department of Justice and the Office of National Drug Control Policy. Although the terms *harm reduction* and *harm minimization* are never used, treatment in corrections, work release, and other sectors of the criminal justice system has become a major mandate. Based on studies documenting the effectiveness of treatment programs designed for drug-involved offenders (Anglin et al., 1996; Inciardi et al., 1997; Lipton, 1995; Tunis, Austin, Morris, Hardyman, & Bolyard, 1996), federal funding for corrections-based treatment has been mandated to increase dramatically in the years to come ("Administration Plans," 1998; McCaffrey, 1997).

NOTES

1. For bibliographies and analyses of the literature on drugs and crime, see Austin and Lettieri (1976), and Greenberg and Adler (1974).

2. Some of the more recent studies on this topic include Ball and Ross (1991); Platt, Kaplan, and Mc Kim (1990); Blume (1989); Stoffelmayr, Benishek, and Humphreys (1989); Meek, Clark, and Solana (1989); Wallen and Weiner (1989); Wolfe and Sorensen (1989); De Leon (1989); Chatlos (1989); Gorney (1989); Clark and Zwerben (1989);

Schlenger, Kroutil, and Roland (1992); Regier et al. (1990); Weiss and Collins (1992); Bachman et al. (1992); Bauer, Yehuda, Meyer, and Giller (1992); McLellan, Luborsky, Woody, O'Brien, and Kron (1981); Turner and Tofler (1986); Hanson (1990); Goodwin, Cheeves, and Connell (1990); Winfield, George, Swartz, and Blazer (1990); Cloninger and Guze (1970); Brown and Anderson (1991); Christie et al. (1988); Washton (1989); Washton and Gold (1987); Gerstein and Harwood (1990); Onken and Blaine (1990); Spotts and Schontz (1980); Wallace (1991); Simpson and Sells (1990); and Nowinski (1990).

REFERENCES

Administration plans increased treatment and testing in prisons. *Substance Abuse Report, 29,* 1-3.

Anglin, M. D., Longshore, D., Turner, S., McBride, D. C., Inciardi, J. A., & Prendergast, M. (1996). *Studies of the functioning and effectiveness of Treatment Alternatives to Street Crime (TASC) programs.* Los Angeles: UCLA Drug Abuse Research Center.

Anonymous. (1922). *In the clutch of circumstance: My own story.* New York: D. Appleton.

Austin, G. A., & Lettieri, D. J. (1976). *Drugs and crime: The relationship of drug use and concomitant criminal behavior.* Rockville, MD: National Institute on Drug Abuse.

Bachman, S. S., Batten, H. L., Minkoff, K., Higgens, R., Manzik, N., & Mahoney, D. (1992). Predicting success in a community treatment program for substance abusers. *American Journal of Addictions, 1,* 155-167.

Ball, J. C., & Ross, A. (1991). *The effectiveness of methadone maintenance treatment.* New York: Springer-Verlag.

Bauer, L. O., Yehuda, R., Meyer, R. E., & Giller, E. (1992). Effects of a family history of alcoholism on autonomic, neuroendocrine, and subjective reactions to alcohol. *American Journal of Addictions, 1,* 168-176.

Black, J. (1927). *You can't win.* New York: Macmillan.

Blume, S. B. (1989). Dual diagnosis: Psychoactive substance abuse and personality disorders. *Journal of Psychoactive Drugs, 21,* 135-138.

Bowker, L. (1980). *Prison victimization.* New York: Elsevier.

Brown, G. R., & Anderson, B. (1991). Psychiatric morbidity in adult inpatients with childhood histories of sexual and physical abuse. *American Journal of Psychiatry, 148,* 55-61.

Brown, J. W., Mazze, R., & Glaser, D. (1974). *Narcotics knowledge and nonsense: Program disaster versus a scientific model.* Cambridge, MA: Ballinger.

Bureau of Justice Assistance. (1988). *Treatment alternatives to street crime.* Washington, DC: U.S. Department of Justice.

Byrnes, T. (1886). *Professional criminals of America.* New York: G. W. Dillingham.

Chatlos, J. C. (1989). Adolescent dual diagnosis: A 12-step transformational model. *Journal of Psychoactive Drugs, 21,* 189-202.

Christie, K. A., Burke, J. D., Regier, D. A., Rae, D. S., Boyd, J. H., & Locke, B. Z. (1988). Epidemiologic evidence for early onset of mental disorders and higher risk of drug abuse in young adults. *American Journal of Psychiatry, 145,* 971-975.

Clark, H. W., & Zwerben, J. E. (1989). Legal vulnerabilities in the treatment of chemically dependent dual diagnosis patients. *Journal of Psychoactive Drugs, 21,* 251-258.

Cloninger, R., & Guze, S. B. (1970). Psychiatric illness and female criminality: The role of sociopathy and hysteria in antisocial women. *American Journal of Psychiatry, 127,* 79-87.

Courtwright, D. T. (1982). *Dark paradise: Opiate addiction in America before 1940.* Cambridge, MA: Harvard University Press.

De Leon, G. (1985). The therapeutic community: Status and evolution. *International Journal of the Addictions, 20,* 823-844.

De Leon, G. (1989). Psychopathology and substance abuse: What is being learned in therapeutic communities. *Journal of Psychoactive Drugs, 21,* 177-188.

De Leon, G. (1990). Treatment strategies. In J. A. Inciardi (Ed.), *Handbook of drug control in the United States* (pp. 115-138). Westport, CT: Greenwood.

De Leon, G., & Ziegenfuss, J. T. (1986). *Therapeutic communities for the addictions.* Springfield, IL: Charles C Thomas.

Faupel, C. E. (1991). *Shooting dope: Career patterns of hard-core heroin users.* Gainesville: University of Florida Press.

Fleisher, M. S. (1989). *Warehousing violence.* Newbury Park, CA: Sage.

Gerstein, D. R., & Harwood, H. J. (Eds.). (1990). *Treating drug problems.* Washington, DC: National Academy Press.

Goodwin, J. M., Cheeves, K., & Connell, V. (1990). Borderline and other severe symptoms in adult survivors of incestuous abuse. *Psychiatric Annals, 20,* 22-32.

Gorney, B. (1989). Domestic violence and chemical dependency: Dual problems, dual interventions. *Journal of Psychoactive Drugs, 21,* 229-238.

Greenberg, S. W., & Adler, F. (1974). Crime and addiction: An empirical analysis of the literature, 1920-1973. *Contemporary Drug Problems, 3,* 221-270.

Hanson, R. K. (1990). The psychological impact of sexual assault on women and children: A review. *Annals of Sex Research, 3,* 187-232.

Hapgood, H. (1903). *The autobiography of a thief.* New York: Fox, Duffield.

Inciardi, J. A. (1986). *The war on drugs: Heroin, cocaine, crime, and public policy.* Palo Alto, CA: Mayfield.

Inciardi, J. A. (1992). *The war on drugs II: The continuing epic of heroin, cocaine, crack, crime, AIDS, and public policy.* Palo Alto, CA: Mayfield.

Inciardi, J. A., Martin, S. S., Butzin, C. A., Hooper, R. M., & Harrison, L. D. (1997). An effective model of prison-based treatment for drug-involved offenders. *Journal of Drug Issues, 27,* 261-278.

Inciardi, J. A., & McBride, D. C. (1991). *Treatment Alternatives to Street Crime (TASC): History, experiences, and issues.* Rockville, MD: National Institute on Drug Abuse.

Inciardi, J. A., & Scarpitti, F. R. (1992, March). *Therapeutic communities in corrections: An overview.* Paper presented at the annual meeting of the Academy of Criminal Justice Sciences, Pittsburgh.

Irwin, W. (1909). *The confessions of a con man.* New York: B. W. Huebsch.

Johnson, B. D., Goldstein, P. J., Preble, E., Schmeidler, J., Lipton, D. S., Spunt, B., & Miller, T. (1985). *Taking care of business: The economics of crime by heroin users.* Lexington, MA: Lexington Books.

Johnson, R. (1987). *Hard time: Understanding and reforming the prison.* Monterey, CA: Brooks/Cole.

King, R. (1972). *The drug hang-up: America's fifty year folly.* New York: Norton.

King, R. (1974). The American system: Legal sanctions to repress drug abuse. In J. A. Inciardi & C. D. Chambers (Eds.), *Drugs and the criminal justice system.* Beverly Hills, CA: Sage.

Lichtenstein, P. M. (1914, November 14). Narcotic addiction. *New York Medical Journal, 100,* 962-966.

Lindesmith, A. R. (1965). *The addict and the law.* Bloomington: Indiana University Press.

Lipton, D. S. (1989). *The theory of rehabilitation as applied to addict offenders.* Unpublished manuscript.

Lipton, D. S. (1995). *The effectiveness of treatment for drug abusers under criminal justice supervision.* Washington, DC: National Institute of Justice.

Lipton, D. S., & Wexler, H. K. (1988, August). Breaking the drugs-crime connection. *Corrections Today,* pp. 144, 146, 155.

Maurer, D. W., & Vogel, V. H. (1978). *Narcotics and narcotic addiction* (3rd ed.). Springfield, IL: Charles C Thomas.

McBride, D. C., & McCoy, C. B. (1982). Crime and drugs: The issues and the literature. *Journal of Drug Issues, 12,* 137-152.

McCaffrey, B. R. (1997). *The national drug control strategy.* Washington, DC: GPO.

McLellan, A. T., Luborsky, L., Woody, G. E., O'Brien, C. P., & Kron, R. (1981). Are the "addiction-related" problems of substance abusers really related. *Journal of Nervous and Mental Disease, 169,* 232-239.

Meek, P. S., Clark, H. W., & Solana, V. L. (1989). Neurocognitive impairment: An unrecognized component of dual diagnosis in substance abuse treatment. *Journal of Psychoactive Drugs, 21,* 153-160.

Morgan, H. W. (1974). *Yesterday's addicts: American society and drug abuse, 1865-1929.* Norman: University of Oklahoma Press.

Nowinski, J. (1990). *Substance abuse in adolescents and young adults: A guide to treatment.* New York: Norton.

Nurco, D. N., Ball, J. C., Shaffer, J. W., & Hanlon, T. F. (1985). The criminality of narcotic addicts. *Journal of Nervous and Mental Disease, 173,* 94-102.

Onken, L. S., & Blaine, J. D. (Eds.). (1990). *Psychotherapy and counselling in the treatment of drug abuse.* Rockville, MD: National Institute on Drug Abuse.

Platt, J. J., Kaplan, C. D., & Mc Kim, P. (Eds.). (1990). *The effectiveness of drug abuse treatment: Dutch and American perspectives.* Malabar, FL: Robert E. Krieger.

Regier, D. A., Farmer, M. E., Rae, D. S., Locke, B. Z., Keith, S. J., Judd, L. L., & Goodwin, F. K. (1990). Comorbidity of mental disorders with alcohol and other drug abuse: Results from the Epidemiologic Catchment Area (ECA) study. *Journal of the American Medical Association, 264,* 2511-2518.

Schlenger, W. E., Kroutil, L. A., & Roland, E. J. (1992, February). *Case management as a mechanism for linking drug abuse treatment and primary care: Preliminary evidence from the ADAMHA/HRSA linkage demonstration.* Paper presented at the National Institute on Drug Abuse Technical Review Meeting on Case Management, Bethesda, MD.

Scott, W. (1916). *Seventeen years in the underworld.* New York: Abingdon.

Simpson, D. D., & Sells, S. B. (Eds.). (1990). *Opioid addiction and treatment: A 12-year follow-up.* Malabar, FL: Robert E. Krieger.

Spotts, J. V., & Shontz, F. C. (1980). *Cocaine users: A representative case approach.* New York: Free Press.

Stephens, R. C., & McBride, D. C. (1976). Becoming a street addict. *Human Organization, 35,* 87-93.

Stoffelmayr, B. E., Benishek, L. A., & Humphreys, K. (1989). Substance abuse prognosis with an additional psychiatric diagnosis: Understanding the relationship. *Journal of Psychoactive Drugs, 21,* 145-152.

Terry, C. E., & Pellens, M. (1928). *The opium problem.* New York: Bureau of Social Hygiene.

Toch, H. (Ed.). (1980). *Therapeutic communities in corrections.* New York: Praeger.

Trebach, A. S. (1982). *The heroin solution.* New Haven, CT: Yale University Press.

Trebach, A. S., & Inciardi, J. A. (1993). *Legalize it? Debating American drug policy.* Washington, DC: American University Press.

Tunis, S., Austin, J., Morris, M., Hardyman, P., & Bolyard, M. (1996). *Evaluation of drug treatment in local corrections.* Washington, DC: National Institute of Justice.

Turner, T. H., & Tofler, D. S. (1986). Indicators of psychiatric disorder among women admitted to prison. *British Medical Journal, 292,* 651-653.

United States v. Behrman, 256 U.S. 280 (1922).

Wallace, B. C. (1991). *Crack cocaine: A practical treatment approach for the chemically dependent.* New York: Brunner/Mazel.

Wallen, M. C., & Weiner, H. D. (1989). Impediments to effective treatment of the dually diagnosed patient. *Journal of Psychoactive Drugs, 21,* 161-168.

Walsh, G. P. (1981). *Opium and narcotic laws.* Washington, DC: GPO.

Washton, A. W. (1989). *Cocaine addiction: Treatment, recovery, and relapse prevention.* New York: Norton.

Washton, A. W., & Gold, M. S. (Eds.). (1987). *Cocaine: A clinician's handbook.* New York: Guilford.

Webb v. U.S., 249 U.S. 96 (1919).

Weiss, R. D., & Collins, D. A. (1992). Substance abuse and psychiatric illness: The dually diagnosed patient. *American Journal on Addictions, 1,* 93-99.

Wexler, H. K., & Williams, R. (1986). The Stay 'N Out Therapeutic Community: Prison treatment for substance abusers. *Journal of Psychoactive Drugs, 18,* 221-230.

Whipple v. Martinson, 256 U.S. 41 (1921).

White, G. M. (1907). *From Boniface to bank burglar.* New York: Seaboard.

Winfield, I., George, L. K., Swartz, M., & Blazer, D. G. (1990). Sexual assault and psychiatric disorders among a community sample of women. *American Journal of Psychiatry, 147,* 335-341.

Wolfe, H. L., & Sorensen, J. L. (1989). Dual diagnosis patients in the urban psychiatric emergency room. *Journal of Psychoactive Drugs, 21,* 169-176.

Yablonsky, L. (1989). *The therapeutic community: A successful approach for treating substance abusers.* New York: Gardner.

Index

About the Contributors

Benjamin Bowser, PhD, is Professor of Sociology and Social Services at California State University, Hayward, and Associate Editor of *Age Race Relations Abstracts* (London). His areas of research include race relations, community-based studies of drug abuse and HIV/AIDS prevention, and research methods. His most recent publications include the edited *Racism and Anti-Racism in World Perspective* (1995) and *Impacts of Racism on White Americans* (2nd ed., 1996) with Raymont Hunt. His research has been reported in more than 30 journal articles, and he has received funding from NSF, FIPSE, CDC, NIDA, NIMH, The Robert Wood Johnson Foundation, the Rockefeller Foundation, and the University of California University-wide AIDS Research program.

Ernst C. Buning is a clinical psychologist who has been working in the drug field since 1977. He has done outreach work; set up the mobile methadone-by-bus project in Amsterdam; and has been involved in various research projects, among which was the evaluation of the Amsterdam needle exchange scheme. As a senior policy staff member of the Amsterdam Municipal Health Service, he has been active in defining the Amsterdam harm reduction approach to the drug problem. Currently, he is senior staff member at the Bureau International Affairs of the Amsterdam Municipal Health Service, where he is responsible for coordinating the European network of methadone providers (Eur-Methwork); informing visiting experts about the Dutch approach to the drug problem; and organizing workshops, training courses, and conferences.

Donna Chen, MD, MPH, received her MPH from the University of California at Berkeley and her MD from the University of California at San Francisco. Work on needle exchange evaluation was completed while she was a researcher with the Centers for Disease Control and Prevention Needle Exchange Evaluation Project at the Center for AIDS Prevention Studies, University of California at San Francisco. She is currently Chief Resident in Psychiatry at Columbia University, College of Physicians and Surgeons and the New York State Psychiatric Institute. After completing residency training, she will be a Clinical Prevention/Services Research Scientist with the Southeastern Rural Mental Health Research Center, University of Virginia, in addition to continuing with clinical work.

Ernest Drucker, PhD, is Director, Division of Community Health, and Professor in the Department of Epidemiology and Social Medicine at Montefiore Medical Center, Albert Einstein College of Medicine in New York, where he was founder and (from 1970-1990) Director of the Methadone Treatment Program at Montefiore. He is currently a Senior Fellow of The Lindesmith Center/Open Society Institute, and editor-in-chief of *Addiction Research,* an international peer review journal. Since 1985, he has been conducting epidemiological and policy studies of AIDS and its relationship to drug use and addiction in the United States and abroad. He was Founding Chairman of the Board (1990-1995) of Doctors of the World (USA) and is currently Chairman of the Board of Positive Health Project, an AIDS service and prevention program in the Times Square area of New York City. He has also been a Fogarty International Fellow of the World Health Organization, an AIDS Policy Fellow of AmFAR (studying international comparisons of AIDS and drug policies), and Visiting Professor (1992-1993) at The Woodrow Wilson School of International Affairs of Princeton University.

Patricia G. Erickson, PhD, is a Senior Scientist with the Addiction Research Foundation Divison, Centre for Addiction and Mental Health. She is also Adjunct Professor and member of the Graduate Faculty in the Department of Sociology at the University of Toronto, and she has just completed a 3-year term there as Director of the Collaborative Graduate Program in Alcohol, Tobacco and Other Psychoactive Substances. She received her doctorate from the University of Glasgow, Scotland. Her most recent books are *The Steel Drug: Cocaine and Crack in Perspective* (1994) and a co-edited collection, *Harm Reduction: A New Direction for Drug Policies and Programs* (1997). She is the author or co-author of more than 50 scientific books, articles, or chapters dealing with illicit drugs and drug policy, and she has been invited to speak at numerous professional and community meetings.

Lana D. Harrison, PhD, is the Associate Director and a senior scientist in the Center for Drug and Alcohol Studies at the University of Delware. She has worked on the three largest epidemiological studies of drug use in the United States: the Monitoring the Future study, the Drug Use Forecasting study, and the National Household Survey on Drug Abuse. Her research interests center on drug epidemiology, the drug-crime nexus, improving survey methodology, and comparative international research on drug use. She has numerous publications in these areas.

James A. Inciardi, PhD, is Director of the Center for Drug and Alcohol Studies at the University of Delaware; Professor in the Department of Sociology and Criminal Justice at Delaware; Adjunct Professor in the Department of Epidemiology and Public Health at the University of Miami School of Medicine; Distinguished Professor in the Núcleo de Estudos e Pesquisas em Atençao ao Uso de Drogas at the State University of Rio de Janeiro; and Guest Professor in the Department of Psychiatry at the Federal University of Rio Grande do Sul in Porto Alegre, Brazil. He received his PhD in sociology at New York University and has a background in law enforcement, corrections, drug abuse treatment, and research. He is currently involved in a number of harm reduction projects, including the development and evaluation of prison-based treatment programs for drug-involved offenders and HIV prevention/intervention research in several parts of Brazil. Moreover, he is the author of 45 books and more than 225 articles and chapters in the areas of substance abuse, criminology, criminal justice, history, folklore, public policy, AIDS, medicine, and law, and he has extensive research, clinical, field, and teaching experience in both substance abuse and criminal justice.

Katherine Irwin is a doctoral student in sociology at the University of Colorado, Boulder. Her related interests include deviance, criminology, qualitative methods, and gender.

Jim Kahn, MD, MPH, is Associate Adjunct Professor of Health Policy and Epidemiology at the Institute for Health Policy Studies, University of California, San Francisco. He has extensively studied the effectiveness and cost-effectiveness of HIV prevention in injecting drug users (IDUs), including treatment of drug dependence, needle exchange, HIV counseling and testing, extended counseling, and street outreach. He is currently participating in a team modeling the effectiveness and cost-effectiveness of individual and group interventions to prevent HIV infection in IDUs. He is also a co-investigator responsible for similar analyses in two program evaluations of HIV prevention efforts in IDUs (needle exchange in San Jose, California, and multipronged HIV prevention in Sacramento, California). In addition, he is developing a testing method to do economic evaluation of treatment on behavioral and economic effects of the withdrawal of SSI benefits from injecting drug users, which occurred on January 1, 1997.

Dirk J. Korf (MA in child psychology, PhD in criminology) is Associate Professor at the Bonger Institute of Criminology at the University of Amsterdam. Formerly, he has been an outreach worker and director of a drug service. He has done extensive research on deviance, drug use, and drug trade in particular, in the Netherlands as well as in other countries. He is Chair of the European Society of Social Drug Research (ESSD) and associate editor of the *Journal of Drug Issues* (JDI).

Sandra D. Lane, PhD, MPH, RN, is a behavioral scientist at the Onondaga County Health Department in Syracuse, New York; Project Director of the Syracuse Healthy Start Project; and Research Associate in the Department of Anthropology at Syracuse University. She received her doctorate in medical anthropology from the University of California, San Francisco and Berkeley, and her MPH in epidemiology from the University of California at Berkeley. She was the Ford Foundation Program Officer for Reproductive Health for the Middle East (1988-1992) and served as a member of the World Health Organization's Steering Committee on Operational Research (1992-1995). Her research interests include health policy, bioethics, and reproductive health. She has conducted research in rural and urban Egypt, Liberia, the United States, and Canada.

Peter Lurie, MD, MPH, is a Medical Researcher at Public Citizen's Health Research Group in Washington, D.C. After obtaining his medical degree from Albert Einstein College of Medicine, he completed residencies in family practice at the University of California, San Francisco and in preventive medicine at the University of California, Berkeley, where he also obtained an MPH. He was the principal investigator of a major study of needle exchange programs for the Centers for Disease Control and Prevention and continues to evaluate interventions for injection drugs users in the United States and Brazil. He has written on the subject of needle exchange for a number of medical journals, as well as for lay publications. He has also been involved in a number of HIV epidemiology studies in Africa, Asia, and Brazil. Through his association with Public Citizen's Health Research Group, a Ralph Nader-founded advocacy group in Washington, D.C., he conducts advocacy in occupational health, pharmaceutical policy, and research ethics.

Toni Makkai, PhD, has recently taken up an appointment at the Australian Institute of Criminology in Canberra, Australia. Prior to this, she was Senior Lecturer in sociology at the University of Salford, Manchester, England. Her publications are on public opinion, drug policy, patterns of drug use, compliance, and regulation. Her most recent publications include *Marijuana in Australia: Patterns and Attitudes* (1997) with Ian McAllister, and *Drugs in Australia: Patterns of Use and Policy Options* (in press), also with Ian McAllister.

Pat O'Hare is Founder and Executive Director of the International Harm Reduction Association, editor of the *International Journal of Drug Policy,* and Executive Director of the annual International Conference on the Reduction of Drug Related Harm (since 1990). He was Director of the Mersey Drug Training and Information Centre in Liverpool from 1988 until 1993 and Drug Policy Advisor to the Mersey Regional Health Authority in the UK, and he worked with the Regional Health Policy Unit in formulating policy. He is co-editor of three books on the reduction of drug-related harm and has written on many aspects of the phenomenon of drug use, including HIV prevention, education, and drug policy. He has been invited to speak on the subject at international conferences and seminaries in many countries, including Australia, the United States, Canada, Italy, France, Belgium, Germany, Spain, Poland, and the Netherlands.

Diane Riley, PhD, is a policy analyst with the Canadian Foundation for Drug Policy and Assistant Professor of Medicine, Faculty of Medicine, University of Toronto. She has studied the socio- and biobehavioral effects of drug use for more than 20 years, working in Australia, Canada, England, Papua New Guinea, and Sweden. She conducted treatment research at the Addiction Research Foundation and worked with community groups to establish the first bleach kit program and first syringe exchanges in Toronto. She is a founding member of the Canadian Foundation on Drug Policy and the International Harm Reduction Association, and a member of the Board of Directors of the Canadian HIV/AIDS Legal Network. Her publications are in the areas of drug treatment and policy, AIDS, harm reduction, learning theory, and psychophysiology.

Marsha Rosenbaum, PhD, is a sociologist and director of the San Francisco office of the Lindesmith Center, a drug policy institute. Since 1977, she has been the principal investigator on 10 grants funded by the National Institute on Drug Abuse and completed studies of women heroin addicts, methadone maintenance treatment and policy, MDMA (Ecstasy), cocaine, and drug use during pregnancy. She is the author of *Women on Heroin; Just Say What? An Alternative View on Solving America's Drug Problem; Pursuit of Ecstasy: The MDMA Experience* (with Jerome E. Beck); *Kids, Drugs and Drug Education: A Harm Reduction Approach; Pregnant Women on Drugs: Combating Stereotypes and Stigma* (with Sheigla Murphy); and numerous scholarly articles about drug use, addiction, women, treatment, and drug policy. As director of the San Francisco office of The Lindesmith Center, she sponsors educational seminars, publishes, speaks, and disseminates information about drug policy. She works with the San Francisco district attorney as well as the Department of Public Health on the implementation of a harm reduction approach to criminal justice and drug treatment. She serves on the boards of the Jewish Community Center of San Francisco, the Harm Reduction Coalition, Family Watch, and Humanistic Alternatives to Addiction Research and Treatment.

Hilary L. Surratt, MA, is an Associate Scientist in the Center for Drug and Alcohol Studies at the University of Delaware; Project Director of an HIV/AIDS seroprevalence and prevention study in Rio de Janeiro, Brazil; and Project Director of a female condom multisite study. Both projects are funded by the National Institute on Drug Abuse. She received her MA from the University of Florida and has numerous publications in the areas of AIDS, substance abuse, and drug policy.

Paulo R. Telles, MD, MPH, is a researcher and psychiatrist in the Núcleo de Estudos e Pesquisas em Atençao ao Uso de Drogas at the State University of Rio de Janeiro. His work includes a variety of HIV epidemiologic and prevention studies, and currently he is the director of a needle exchange program in Rio de Janeiro.